D0615498

The University, Society and Government

Copyright 1970, by the Steering Committee of the Commission

The University, Society and Government

The Report of the Commission on the Relations Between Universities and Governments

COMMISSIONERS:

René HURTUBISE

Donald C. ROWAT

THE UNIVERSITY OF OTTAWA PRESS

Ottawa, 1970

LA
417
.5
.C57

1/26/71

Preface

The profound changes that technological progress has brought to contemporary society in recent years have greatly affected the functioning of social and political institutions. The university certainly has not escaped the influence of these changes; in fact, it is often at the very heart of the problems through the actions of its own members. A privileged place, where freedom of thought and expression flourish, the university has contributed a great deal to the progress of society. At the same time, the important share of public funds devoted to institutions of higher learning leads the legislator into exercising control over the operations of these institutions. The proper balance between the need for autonomy by the universities and control over their functioning by society is not easy to determine; the numerous and diverse government-university structures erected in the various Canadian provinces bear witness to this.

The university community had been made increasingly aware of these questions in recent years by each of its essential components : professors, students and administrators. It therefore made arrangements to study this complex problem seriously. The following groups :

— Canadian Association of University Teachers (CAUT)

— Association of Universities and Colleges of Canada (AUCC)

— Canadian Union of Students (CUS)

— Union générale des étudiants du Québec (UGEQ)

agreed in the spring of 1967 to form a Steering Committee which would be responsible for delimiting the main aspects of the problem, ensuring the finances for a comprehensive study, and retaining the services of Commissioners who would undertake this study and make whatever recommendations they thought best. The members of the Steering Committee were as follows :

David Fish, AUCC, Secretary
A. B. B. Moore, AUCC
Jacques St-Pierre, CAUT, Chairman
J. Percy Smith, CAUT
Robert Tessier, UGEQ
Douglas Ward, CUS

As its first task, the Steering Committee defined the Commissioners' mandate in the following terms :

1. *To consider the distinctive role of universities in the changing Canadian society, particularly with respect to their responsibilities for the development of this role at the various levels of society : community, provincial, regional, national and international;*

2. *To determine the need, nature and extent of a) university autonomy, b) government and public control of universities;*

3. *To recommend the appropriate instruments by which relations between universities and governments can be established that do justice to their responsibilities.*

The Committee then obtained a generous grant ($150,000) from the Ford Foundation, which was very much interested in the proposed study.

The Committee was fortunate enough to retain the services of M. René Hurtubise, at that time Associate Professor in the Faculty of Law, Université de Montréal, and now Vice-Rector for Studies and Research, Montreal campus of the Université du Québec, and of Dr. Donald C. Rowat, Professor of Political Science, Carleton University.

Commissioners Hurtubise and Rowat, assisted by able supporting staff, have devoted over a year to their work. They covered the whole of Canada, met numerous personalities from the world of higher education, held public hearings and informal discussions, studied many and voluminous briefs . . . and spent much time in reflection !

The report they submit in the pages that follow, and for which they take full responsibility, contributes an important element to the collective reflection of our society regarding the role of the universities and of the mechanisms which should regulate the relations between universities and governments.

Of course, the question has not been exhausted; it would be rash to imagine that definitive solutions could be arrived at in fifteen months. The Hurtubise-Rowat Report will none the less mark an epoch. It will throw a new light upon the nature of this complex problem, and will doubtless serve as a basis for future reflections. If one judges by the numerous briefs and studies prepared, and the considerable interest aroused by the work of the Commission, the Hurtubise-Rowat Report will make a most important contribution to the solution of the problem of the relations between universities and governments.

To all those who made this report possible — to the Commissioners and their associates, to the members of the Steering Committee and to the Ford Foundation — may I be allowed to express the sincere gratitude of the Canadian society.

Jacques ST-PIERRE

Table of Contents

Part III
PROBLEMS OF FEDERALISM

APPENDIX

Introduction

In 1965 and 1966 two reports were published which were of great significance for university affairs. One was the report of the Commission on University Government in Canada and the other was the report of the Commission on Financing Higher Education in Canada. [1] The one on university government made recommendations designed to reform the internal government of universities. The process of implementing its recommendations within the various universities across Canada still continues. But it dealt only incidentally with government-university relations. The report on finance assessed the rapidly growing and future financial needs of Canadian universities. It made recommendations to governments designed to meet those needs, but it, too, dealt only incidentally with government-university relations. It concentrated on *how much* should be paid to support universities but did not explore fully *how* this help should be given, or what the pattern of relations between universities and governments should be. Yet the progressive and massive shift in the sources of university support from private to public funds had meant that a serious problem of government-university relations was arising: how could this support be given, and how could formerly private universities be turned into public institutions, without interfering unduly in their affairs ?

Moreover, the recommendation by the Commission on Financing Higher Education for greatly increased financial support from the federal government brought to a head the growing problem of federal intervention in the field of education. A change in federal-provincial financial arrangements in the fall of 1966 resulted in all general state support for universities being paid to them by the provincial governments. Thus universities can now be regarded as part of the provincial

[1] Commission sponsored by the Canadian Association of University Teachers and the Association of Universities and Colleges of Canada (Sir James Duff and Robert O. Berdahl, Commissioners), *University Government in Canada* (Toronto and Quebec, 1966); and Commission to the Association of Universities and Colleges of Canada (V. W. Bladen, Chairman), *Financing Higher Education in Canada* (Toronto and Quebec, 1965).

systems of public education, and a new relationship between universities and the provincial governments has rapidly developed. Whereas formerly most universities tented to be regarded as private institutions, greatly increased state support and public interest have turned them into public institutions. This new relationship has come about so quickly that neither universities nor governments have had time to think through its full implications.

a) THE NATURE OF THE COMMISSION

It is to the credit of the sponsors of our Commission that, despite the speed of this development, they were able to perceive it before it actually occurred. As early as 1965 some of them recognized that this problem area existed as a gap between the areas being studied by the two above-mentioned commissions. The Canadian Association of University Teachers therefore proposed to its counterpart student organizations and to the association of universities that they jointly sponsor a third commission to study this area. It was thought best that the commission should not be supported financially by either the sponsoring organizations or the federal or provincial governments, since they would all be objects of study, so to speak; to preserve its independence, the commission should not be financially dependent upon any of them. Instead, the sponsors were able to secure a grant from the Ford Foundation to finance a small commission for a fifteen-month study, and a steering committee was created with representatives from the four sponsors: the Association of Universities and Colleges of Canada (AUCC), the Canadian Association of University Teachers (CAUT), the Canadian Union of Students (CUS), and l'Union générale des étudiants du Québec (UGEQ).

The steering committee made two important decisions regarding the nature of the commission. First, it decided that, unlike the two previous university-based commissions, this commission should proceed like a governmental commission in the sense that it should publicly call for briefs and hold public hearings. The committee made this decision because it felt that, because the problems were so new and complex, one of the main objectives of the commission should be to stimulate thought and discussion not only within the university community but also among the general public. Second, the committee decided that viable conclusions about the desirable relations between universities and governments could not be arrived at without considering the role of universities in society.

We as commissioners agreed that there should be public hearings and that the role of the university in society should be included in our terms of reference. But the effect of these decisions from our point of view — especially considering the limited budget and length of the project — was to turn a difficult assignment into one that was virtually impossible. Nearly every university activity has some relation to government; and since universities are concerned with all human knowledge, their relations with society are extremely complex. However, we had the temerity to undertake the task, not with the intention of reaching definitive conclusions on the problems to be studied, but because we believe that these problems are important. It has been said that one of the most difficult aspects of solving social problems is finding out what they are. We hope that during our public hearings and in this Report we have at least helped to pose the right questions and to sort out the problems in an orderly fashion.

b) THE WORK OF THE COMMISSION

We were appointed as full-time commissioners in May 1968. At the beginning of our assignment, in order to gather ideas on the principal problems falling within the vast scope of our terms of reference, we held two seminars — one on May 17, 1968, in Montreal, and a second from July 22 to 26 under the kind auspices of the Canada Council at its Stanley House in the Gaspé Peninsula. These seminars were widely representative; they included government officials and members of interested groups in society as well as students, professors and university administrators. We should like to thank the participants for their contribution to our work.

In August, Commissioner Rowat travelled to Australia and Asia, where he gathered information on universities in that region of the world and, in October, Commissioner Hurtubise made a similar study tour of France, Western Germany, Switzerland and Yugoslavia. Members of the Commission also travelled across Canada to meet informally with executives of student and faculty associations, university administrators, provincial premiers and ministers of education, and officials of provincial university commissions and departments of education, as well as federal officials.

At an early stage in our work we were fortunate in obtaining the services of M. Michel Pelletier, graduate of the Universities of Montréal and Grenoble, as Executive Secretary, and Dr. B. B. Kymlicka, Associate Professor of Political Science at the University of Western Ontario, as Director of Research. The Commission's staff prepared a long question paper based on our terms of reference which was distributed as a "thought stimulator" to any organization expressing its intention of presenting a brief. We received a total of 93 briefs from a wide variety of university-based and other organizations, and held public hearings on them in the main cities across Canada between mid-January and mid-April 1969. A list of the briefs is contained in the Appendix to this Report.

Although our funds for research were limited, we also commissioned twenty short research studies on a variety of topics related to our terms of reference. A list of them is also contained in the Appendix, and they are being published in two volumes, along with the Commission's question paper, concurrently with this Report.

c) THE NATURE OF OUR REPORT

We do not pretend that our Report covers all of the subjects encompassed within our wide terms of reference. Considering our brief term of appointment and the short period we had within which to draft the Report — about three months after the end of our public hearings — we had to concentrate on what we considered to be the main problems. This no doubt resulted in some arbitrary selection of topics according to our own prejudices. But we take comfort from the thought that everyone has his prejudices. As our Director of Research was fond of saying, "Everyone should know his own prejudices."

We have come to know some of ours, and hope that we have managed to resist their influence to some extent.

The Report is divided into three parts, the first two of which deal with the relations between the university and society and between the university and government. Because Canada is a federation, special problems of government-university relations have been created by the division of powers between the central and provincial governments. We have therefore devoted Part III to discussing these problems and making recommendations for their solution.

In the Appendix we give information on the special bodies that have been created recently as intermediaries between the provincial governments and the universities. Since these bodies are so new and so little is known about them outside their home provinces, we have included statements on their composition and powers, and a comparative chart of basic information on them. For two of the three single-university provinces we have included the university's board of governors instead, since it takes the place of an intermediary body.

In Parts II and III of the Report we make recommendations to both universities and governments. However, many of the problems that we discuss are so complex and vary so much from one province or region to another that it is impossible to arrive at uniform global conclusions. A number of our conclusions are therefore cast in the form of suggestions or proposals rather than firm recommendations. For this reason we have not numbered our recommendations, nor have we given a separate summary of them.

There were two topics mentioned in our terms of reference which, regretfully, we were unable to deal with fully. These are the international role of universities and the relations of the university to the local community. The former has created problems regarding the responsibilities of government in this area, and also serious problems of federal-provincial relations. The second topic is important because of the need for closer links between universities and local or regional governments. We feel that special studies should be made of these topics.

Because our area of study was so vast, there were of course many other important topics and problems which, though more or less related to our terms of reference, we were unable to deal with. We present the following list of some of them, in the hope that other people will take them up for study: the ideal size and location of universities (because of the simultaneous relation of size and location to efficiency, economy, student unrest and geographic accessibility); the meaning of academic freedom for students; the role and nature of university extension work, and the problems connected with part-time study; the social and economic implications of university failures and "wastage rates"; the year-round operation of universities (because of its relation to economy and the convenience of students); [2] province-wide salary scales for professors; the unitary system of university government; the idea of including appeals against the decisions of university officials within the jurisdiction of a provincial Ombudsman. [3]

d)   ACKNOWLEDGEMENTS

Our Steering Committee has helped us with many difficult problems, and we should like in particular to thank the chairman of the Committee, Professor Jacques St-Pierre, Directeur, Centre de Calcul, Université de Montréal, for the time and energy he has devoted to helping and advising us. We should also like to thank the numerous officials of university and government organizations and of student and faculty associations who so willingly provided us with information, and the presidents of all the universities at which we held public hearings for providing space and facilities for the hearings. Our task would have been impossible without the able help of our professional and secretarial staff: Dr. Kymlicka and M. Pelletier, who worked with us as a team in all aspects of our study and contributed

[2] Only two universities in Canada operate on the three-semester system, Guelph and Simon Fraser. The system involves many financial and administrative problems, but the students at both universities seem to favour it because of its greater flexibility for them. See the brief to our Commission from the Students' Union, University of Guelph.

[3] An Ombudsman for education has been suggested by the Ontario Provincial Committee on Aims and Objectives of Education in its *Report : Living and Learning* (Toronto, 1968), 155.

much to the planning and drafting of the Report; Mrs. Audrey Forster, our secretary, who tirelessly organized our hearings; Mlle Lucille Beaudry and Miss Beth Armstrong, our research assistants; and Miss Gillian Payne, our stenographer. We should like to thank all of them for their cheerful devotion to the work of the Commission.

René HURTUBISE
Donald C. ROWAT

October 1969.

PART I

The University and Society

1. The University as a Reflection of its Era

A difficulty encountered by those who wish to understand the world in which they live lies in the facility of the human mind to deceive itself: the mind projects its concepts and categories onto reality before having fully perceived and grasped things as they exist. Words double this difficulty because they have a reality of their own, quite independent from the idea they are meant to signify or transmit. The idea or the content may vary, yet the word remains the same. Thus, our understanding of the term "university" has fallen prey to this deformation of knowledge; around the term has blossomed an abundant rhetoric, of which the main users, and probably the first victims, have been the academics themselves.

During our hearings across Canada, we found that academics, however shrewd and eminent in their specialization, are often quite complacent in holding a simplistic and false view of the role the university plays in society, and of the importance of their contribution to the progress of humanity as a whole. In a study done for our Commission, Professor H. Mayo has tackled one of their myths: the a-political character of the university, the disinterested and serene attitude of intellectuals gathered together in the supreme interest of Truth and Science.

Indeed, many academics have declared that their discipline knows no boundaries. Their horizons are limitless, international, more precisely, internationalistic. Thus, a professor in a Canadian university might pride himself on being simultaneously a chemistry teacher at the university, an advisor on scientific policy for the Canadian Defence Research Board, and a member of the board of directors of an American chemical industry. According to this principle, the horizons of the true university are boundless, for its activities benefit the whole of humanity. Universities should not be identified with any particular place.

Others hold a less simplistic view of the university. They see a hierarchy among insitutions. Certain universities, often the oldest, are said to have reached full maturity and to be the true, full-fledged universities. Other institutions are either declining or are launched on the path that leads the "emergent" ones to that perfection of achievement characteristic of the great universities. Thus a faculty member at Memorial University in Newfoundland may reason as if his institution were or should be the University of Toronto (or more likely in this case, Oxford or Cambridge). Similarly, a teacher of the humanities in the Prairies may long for his own humanistic vision of the university, which bears no relation to and has no roots in the historical development of Western Canada. Typically, professors have an ideal of a university in their heads, and want the institution in which they find themselves to conform to that ideal.

Such an aspiration, however, may be actually harmful to the institution and the society that they really want to help. It is certainly useful to use the experience of other countries and to study how other societies have solved similar problems, but we must make sure that the situation and problems are really similar. It is often disastrous to transpose into a given society an institution which has evolved within qualitatively and quantitatively different social conditions.

This frequent error has led us to devote the first two chapters to a description of the facts as we see them. Our purpose will be to situate the idea of the university in time and space. We will attempt to outline certain types of universities through history, and then to see how these relate to the Canadian scene, which itself is very different from one region to another.

There is nothing very new or original about this approach. As early as 1930, Abraham Flexner, probably preceded by others, was insisting on the historical relativity of universities:

> Every age, every country, has its unique concrete needs and purposes. For that reason there can be no uniform university type persisting through the ages, transferable from one country to another. Every age does its own creating and reshaping; so does every country. [1]

---

[1] Abraham FLEXNER, *Universities : American, English, German* (New York, 1968), 43. (First edition, 1930).

In fact, we propose to take up and apply to contemporary Canadian universities the program of analysis that Flexner outlined in the first pages of his book: to show that the university is a reflection of its era, and to analyze the characteristics of his period in order to deduce what the nature of the universities should be in 1930. Such is the difficult task we wish to assume.

It may be useful to recall that in the 'thirties societies went through a period of crisis. Flexner therefore studied universities during, if not a turning point, at least a crucial period of history. Like many others, we believe that our highly industrialized societies are undergoing a new growth crisis, if not a profound structural mutation. If such is the case, it makes our endeavour that much more analogous to Flexner's, and underlines the necessity of situating universities in an historical and sociological perspective.

A. THE HISTORICAL MODEL

If, like any other institution, the university is a product of its era, we should be able to establish a parallel between the evolution of society and the successive transformations of the university. This is what we shall now attempt to demonstrate.

To the best of our knowledge, such a parallel has never been fully developed. We therefore believe that we are blazing the trail for a study which should be pursued and hopefully taken over by historians, for we are convinced that this research could lead to a better understanding of the interplay of the social forces that underlie the evolution and transformation of social structures, particularly those of the educational system. It will suffice here to sketch a brief outline of this approach to the history of the university.

Historians generally date the appearance of institutions similar to those we call universities in the later Middle Ages, about the eleventh or twelfth centuries. For our purposes, the history of Western society since then may be divided into three great periods, each characterized by a corresponding type of social organization. According to this perspective, there would be the type of society which preceded the industrial revolution, the medieval or traditional society; the type of society which grew out of the industrial revolution, characterized by the factors of capitalist production and operating more or less according to the principles of economic and political liberalism; and, finally, the type of society still evolving and beginning to appear, especially in the United States, identifiable by the development, beyond traditional capitalist enterprise, of conglomerate enterprise.

This outline of social history allows us to situate ourselves simultaneously on two levels. One is purely chronological, which delimits the first period from the Middle Ages up to the middle of the eighteenth century in England, and later in countries where the industrial revolution took a longer time to arrive. But there is also another level, that of the "organic" age of societies, if we adopt the notion of stages of development or growth, of which W. W. Rostow — among others — has been the theoretician. From this point of view, it is possible to compare the age of various countries according to their stage of development. One can conclude, for instance, that in 1960 the United States had reached a higher degree of maturity than Great Britain, even though it had undergone its industrial revolution a century later. Both growth and process of maturation have been more rapid. Accordingly, contemporary traditional societies which have not undergone their industrial revolution have probably more in common with seventeenth or eighteenth century France or England than with their twentieth century counterparts.

These three types of societies, these three stages of development, reached at different times in different countries, should each have its corresponding historical type of university: the medieval or traditional university (depending on the situation), the liberal university, and more recently the conglomerate university or "multiversity", which has already developed in the United States.

It would be vain to try to seek to establish here, in such a bird's-eye view of the evolution of universities, a close relation between the type of society and the suggested types of university. The industrial revolution did not erupt suddenly in any country where it took place. It required a long incubation period, and developed in different ways according to the traditions and circumstances peculiar to each country. Nor have its effects been the same in each country, nor in the different eras when it took place, whether in the eighteenth, the nineteenth or the twentieth century. Authors have discerned many different "waves". According to some authors, we are now experiencing a third or fourth wave rather than a new industrial revolution.

Similarly, each type of university may have taken on a particular form depending on the country. In France, the university that was born with the French Revolution and developed with the industrial revolution, is a state university, and its structures are different from those of capitalist enterprise. [2] And in North America, where religious denominations have played such an important role in colonization and in political and social development, it is impossible to ignore the common phenomenon of the church-related university. It seems necessary to distinguish this as a separate type of university, and perhaps also a type created by the joint efforts or at least close co-operation of religious bodies and the rising business class.

It may therefore be foreseen that a deeper historical analysis would reveal a somewhat longer list than our three types of university. We submit these categories only as a preliminary outline to a much more specialized and detailed study. Meanwhile, it may be useful to recall that in tracing a parallel between the evolution of the whole society and that of particular institutions, one often finds a staggering of institutional development, since every evolving society has sectors which are lagging as opposed to those which are ahead and thriving. Thus there is likely to be a lag in the case of the educational system because important social transformations rarely act directly on it, but instead through the mediation of the rising generations of teachers and students. However great the legislative or administrative reforms, the educational system often lags behind.

[2] In this particular case, the beginnings of change in the educational system may have preceded Napoleon and probably date back to Louis XIV. As a result of the transformation of the regime in France, substituting a bourgeois state for the monarchy, the university itself was transformed. It may have become a bourgeois institution without having adopted the structure of a board of governors (or directors) similar to that of capitalist enterprise. However, this is only a hypothesis, which needs to be verified.

B.   THE MEDIEVAL OR TRADITIONAL UNIVERSITY

The first universities followed very closely the appearance of a series of new phenomena within the medieval society. The formation of cities created an urban society, parallel to and often opposing the feudal society. Within the emerging city, and probably due to it, were formed the guilds or professional corporations which were later to acquire such power and strength. These new structures allowed individuals to escape the feudal system and to be protected from the oppressive requirements and privileges of the lords, without having to seek refuge in monasteries or religious orders.

The importance of this development is that, before the rise of universities, intellectual life was concentrated in the monasteries and episcopal schools. In escaping from domination by the monastery or the religious hierarchy, intellectuals acquired a new freedom but at the same time forfeited all the protections and excessive privileges of the feudal regime. The city gave them the framework which would protect them against the unwarranted intervention of the local lords. Thus, even at that time, universities were an urban phenomenon.

It is quite probable that the kings hastened to grant them charters freeing them from feudal servitude, because these new institutions, like the cities and the guilds, undermined the powers of the lords and allowed a king to establish a firmer authority over his vassals. It is true that the religious hierarchy, particularly the Pope, retained a great influence over academic studies by means of theology, which was recognized at that time as the queen of the sciences. But medicine, by doing away with magical trappings, opened the first breach into the omnipotence of theology. Converging factors then delivered the natural sciences from theology and philosophy, to lead Western civilization to the age of enlightenment. It should not be forgotten that law, the other great discipline of the medieval university, was an indispensable instrument in the political struggle between the kings and feudal lords: without the aid of jurists, how else could the kings have secured the authority they so badly needed after the invasion by the barbarians and the fall of the Roman Empire ?

Even during that period the universities were subjected to the power struggle taking place in society, and it is not surprising that they reflected the emerging social structure which was replacing the former religious and feudal structure. Universities, as a product of cities, were created in the image of the new urban institution and social force, the professional corporation. Their charters listed the same privileges as those obtained by the trade guilds, notably enfranchisement; also, they grouped together "masters" and "students" (or apprentices) who were aspiring to the "mastership" one day. Such similarities are still found today, not only in the structural organization of certain universities, in the terms used to designate diplomas, and in the nature of certain privileges reserved to academics, but also in a host of small details such as the ceremonial surrounding the granting of degrees.

With the consolidation of the new political powers, supported by the progressive separation of the natural sciences and philosophy from theology, the evolution of the university and the knowledge that it dispensed were pushed forward. The medieval university is in a way the embryo of what we refer to as the traditional university, which reached its apex in the nineteenth century. The idea of the university so ardently defended by Cardinal Newman is the ideal description of this traditional university. But his defence was probably also the swan song of this declining type of university, for in Britain the impact of the century-old industrial revolution was beginning to be felt on the academic structures. The first colleges of the universities of London and Durham, which had been founded thirty years earlier, were challenging the monopoly of Oxford and Cambridge, and the creation of the "Red Brick" universities was imminent. Thus a new type of university was being introduced in Britain, but almost a hundred years later than the corresponding social mutation. It is interesting to note that a similar phenomenon, in somewhat different form, was taking place at the same time in France and the United States.

Today there are still examples, though greatly mutilated ones, of this traditional university. The more eminent would be Oxford and Cambridge. In Canada, one could probably find more or less faithful replicas of it. Is it not true that Quebec's "collèges classiques", now superseded by the "collèges d'enseignement général et professionnel" (CEGEP), were inheritors of the humanist tradition of the eighteenth century ? It is possible, in retrospect, to ask ourselves if they were not a manifestation of the traditional character of Quebec's French-speaking society. The industrial revolution was brought to Quebec by an English-speaking minority, and the people of Quebec submitted to this industrialization more than they willed or promoted it. From then on, two societies coexisted in Quebec: one, traditional, with "collèges classiques" and universities turning out, until recently, a majority of physicians, lawyers and priests; the other, industrial, supported by a modern university which produced engineers, chemists and administrators, along with physicians and lawyers.

Elsewhere in Canada are a number of institutions that were inspired by the traditional "Oxbridge" type of university, and which continue to be influenced by it. To mention only a few, we cite, as examples, Queen's University in Ontario, Acadia University in Nova Scotia, Mount Allison University in New Brunswick, and even a new institution, Trent University in Peterborough.

It should be understood that we are not making a value judgement in thus showing the link between the traditional university and such institutions. The reputation of these universities is unquestionable. We only wish to suggest that this historical approach raises a number of questions which could make us more aware of the origin and the nature of some of the problems experienced by certain types of institutions. For instance, does the substitution of the CEGEP for the "collège classique" not indicate a profound transformation of the Quebec society ? Are the tensions between Queen's or Trent and the surrounding community due to a discrepancy between the traditional idea of a university and the twentieth century social environment ? Are the financial difficulties felt at Trent and Mount Allison more the result of a traditional and costly form of higher education than of a simple growth in costs and the refusal of government to meet them ?

C.   THE LIBERAL UNIVERSITY

Although caused by the profound social transformations of the industrial revolution, the rising liberal university did not necessarily follow closely in the footsteps of industrialization in every country. In the case of Great Britain, a hundred years elapsed before the capitalist business class, with their newly acquired powers, were able to control the universities. If it is admitted that industrialization had completely transformed England by the middle of the eighteenth century, it took until 1870 before the first "Red Brick" universities were created.

What was the nature of these modern universities ?

> Their foundation is due to local efforts; their endowments come largely from local pockets; they are aided by grants from local municipal authorities; and their students, though to a slowly decreasing extent, are drawn from local areas. [3]

And who were the people responsible for their foundation ?

> [They were] members, for the most part, of wealthy and influential families, *engaged in business* . . . [4]

Not only was the creation of these institutions a reflection of the power of the newly rising dominant class, but they were even built in the suburbs along with the factories of the era; they had walls of brick or stone rapidly blackened by the smog, long corridors and identical classrooms.

In France, the gap was not a lengthy one between the industrial revolution and the appearance of the liberal university. One could even argue that its appearance was contemporary with the rise of industry, since the napoleonic university had been created in 1808. But, as Antoine Prost has indicated, institutions of higher education were paper institutions until 1870. [5] Perhaps the situation as it evolved in the United States undermines our hypothesis of the necessity of a gap between the advent of industrialization and the creation of the liberal university, since the first modern university to appear there (according to Flexner) was Johns Hopkins in 1876. The later

---

3   Bruce TRUSCOT, *Red Brick University* (London, 1951), 26.
4   *Ibid.* (Our italics.)
5   *L'enseignement en France : 1800-1967* (Paris, 1968).

that industrialization revolutionizes a country, the shorter seems to be the gap.

Following the social upheavals of the industrial revolution, then, higher education changed hands. Where the state took on the responsibility of creating new institutions, we must not let that mislead us. In France, for example,

> From Napoleon to Ferry the educational system was founded on a conception of society which all enlightened minds agreed upon, regardless of their political or religious divergencies. There was "l'école des notables" and "l'école du peuple": on the one hand were the lycées and collèges, foundations of the napoleonic university, where sons of the bourgeoisie and those aspiring to public office received a humanist culture which was identified with total culture; on the other hand were the schools where the rudiments of learning were dispensed . . . to the children of the lower classes . . . [6]

University structures were also changed, and were modelled on the organizational structures of capitalist private enterprise. On this point we may cite Professor Mayo's study (p. 6):

> The Board of Governors is comparable to the corporation's board of directors (except that university Boards are accountable to no one, because there are no shareholders). The President is comparable to the general manager, and is accountable only to the Board, which generally appoints him. The academic administrators (vice-presidents and deans) correspond to divisional heads of the business firm . . .

The numerous examples of state universities found not only in France but also in the United States and Canada may seem to contradict our generalization. Yet such is not the case, for most of these institutions are juridical persons quite distinct from the state (even in France, according to the new law on higher education), and have their own boards of governors. This allowed the Board of Regents of the University of California to place at the entrance of every one of its different campuses (including Berkeley) a sign indicating that this public university was the "private" property of the Board of Regents, which had power to forbid access to anyone it judged undesirable.

[6] André LATREILLE, in an article reviewing the above-mentioned book by M. Prost, Le Devoir (31, VII, 69).

The university changed not only in ownership and structure, but most of all in content. It may be that this was an objective of the new business class in gaining control over higher education. One wonders whether they might not have been aware that, by creating liberal universities, they were giving themselves the indispensable tool for ensuring their position of power in society. The new institutions would be preparing the recruits and training the better-qualified manpower needed by their enterprises. It has been argued, for instance, that this was the intent behind the creation of the Free University in Brussels. Often, however, capitalists (and capitalist enterprises) looked upon themselves as enlightened patrons or philanthropists subsidizing humanitarian and social endeavours, rather than businessmen acting in their own interests. [7]

At any rate, following the diversification and refinement of the modes of production, the university subdivided its teaching, and the traditional professions were largely supplanted by modern skills and professions: administration, accountancy, engineering, chemistry, physics, various technical skills, etc. To justify this diversification of teaching, the Americans referred to the "service" function of the university.

> Instead of a culture which is falsely encyclopedic, man-darinal and ornamental, destined to form intellectuals who are beyond (or beside) reality, industry gives the university the task of producing in great quantity professionals who are immediately useful in production, applied research and man-agement. [8]

This utilitarian conception of the university gave rise to a multiplicity of subjects in American universities, extending even to such things as judo and the art of cooking an egg. [9] With "service" as an objective, the universities got involved in farms,

---

[7] Probably many of them were not this naive. It was important for the wealthy capitalist of the late nineteenth century to exhibit his power and at the same time justify his enormous wealth in the eyes of the public by such philanthropic gestures. Today individual philanthropy has been replaced by the philanthropy of big corporations, which are equally anxious to display their power by building luxurious sky-scrapers, etc. Thus the enterprise has replaced the individual (whose importance and power varies according to the power of the enterprise). See Paul A. BARAN and Paul M. SWEEZY, *The Monopoly Capital* (New York, 1966).

[8] André GORZ, *Le socialisme difficile* (Paris, 1967), 56.

[9] FLEXNER, *op. cit.*, 55.

hotels and sawmills. Flexner thoroughly stigmatized this notion of "service", and said that American universities are composed of three sections: "They are secondary schools and colleges for boys and girls; graduate and professional schools for advanced students; service stations for the general public." [10] Professor Mayo was more charitable in his characterization of Canadian universities that have followed the American pattern: they are to the old-style university what the modern drugstore is to the old pharmacy.

Flexner violently opposed this outrageous diversification of the content of higher education, and made an attempt to define what the modern university should be like. But just as Newman was describing an ideal but outdated type of university, Flexner was still clinging to the ideal of the liberal university, while on the horizon one could already distinguish the traits of a new type of university, the multiversity or conglomerate. It is our belief that most Canadian universities could be classified as liberal universities, with the exception of the University of Toronto, which is very close to becoming what Clark Kerr refers to as the multiversity.

D.   THE MULTIVERSITY OR CONGLOMERATE

How did Flexner in 1930 describe the university? "A genuine university is an organism characterized by highness and definiteness of aim, unity of spirit and purpose." [11] And he deplored the fact that American institutions of the time were so far removed from this ideal. [12] Yet, a little over thirty years later, Clark Kerr, former president of one of these tentacular universities that Flexner had castigated, was proposing as a model the type of conglomerate that these overgrown American

---

[10]   *Ibid.*, 45.
[11]   *Ibid.*, 178.
[12]   "But it is quite obvious that the institutions which we have used for purposes of illustration — the best that we possess — are not organisms: they are merely administrative aggregations, so varied, so manifold, so complex that administration itself is reduced to budgeting, student accounting, advertising, etc. Such aggregations, even though called universities, simply do not possess scientific or educational policy, embodied in some appropriate form... They are secondary schools, vocational schools, teacher-training schools, research centres, 'uplift' agencies, businesses — these and other things simultaneously" (*ibid.*, 179).

universities had become. Paraphrasing Flexner, here is how he described what he refers to as the multiversity:

> The contemporary university is not an integrated organism. It is a pluralistic organization with many component parts, each of them capable of highness and definiteness of aim, unity of spirit and purpose, each of them (in the best of all university worlds) possessing the energy and the funds to accomplish its specific task. [13]

It may be premature yet to opt categorically for one or the other of these conceptions. But we forecast that Clark Kerr's multiversity, although undesirable in many respects, is what the great universities in our large urban centres are almost inevitably evolving toward. Modern industrial society is producing new phenomena such as the megalopolis, and this raises new questions. For example, is it only by accident that there is a heavy concentration of very large universities in the densely populated urbanized region that spreads from Windsor to Quebec city ?

One thing certain is that the structure of the multiversity markedly resembles the structure of the economic conglomerate — the consortium of enterprises that economists acknowledge is becoming a predominant form of economic organization in American society and, indirectly, in the world. The traditional capitalist enterprise was replaced by liberal capitalist enterprise, and now it appears that liberal enterprise will be overwhelmed by the economic conglomerates. [14]

---

[13]   KERR's *Introduction* to FLEXNER's *Universities*, xiv-xv.

[14]   "Nowadays, more than 70 percent of amalgamations are of the conglomerate type, concentrating together in one enterprise corporations which operate in absolutely unrelated fields. Consolidations among competitors — the horizontal type — cover about 12 per cent of the amalgamations, while back in the fifties they represented more than 30 per cent. The traditional forms of amalgamations, horizontal (when an enterprise buys out its competitors) or vertical (when the enterprise buys its suppliers or customers) remain, but the dominant form is that which takes place by diversification or conglomeration."   Richard J. BARBER, "The New Partnership, Big Government and Big Business", *New Republic* (August 13, 1966). For an excellent discussion of this new phenomenon, see Celso FURTADO, "La concentration du pouvoir économique aux Etats-Unis et ses projections en Amérique latine", *Esprit* (April, 1969). See also, "Giant Mergers are stirring up Giant Questions", *N.Y. Times* (October 6, 1968), sec. 3, p. 1:" 'The conglomerate, in every sense of the word, is a new economic frontier', says David N. Judelson, President of Gulf and Western Industries Inc. It appears now that this new kind of corporation is destined to become the bulwark of the economy of the future, even as it is bolstering the economy of today."

When a conglomerate takes over a new enterprise in a newly developed sector, often having no connection with the sectors already incorporated, it does not seek to integrate the administration of the acquired enterprise into a centralized administrative structure. Each unit remains autonomous in relation to the master enterprise, and may even at times compete with one of the enterprises of which it is a conglomerate part. Thus the basic features of the conglomerate corporation are: great autonomy of the units, an unlimited spectrum of sector activities, occasional co-ordination, a possible alliance or conspiracy of conglomerate members, and a superstructure crowning the whole but leaving each unit to act independently. All of these features admirably fit the description of the modern multiversity.

During our hearings at the University of Toronto, the dean of one of the professional faculties told us that he thought it was a waste of time for him and his faculty to participate in meetings of the University's Senate. As dean of this particular faculty he did not see why he should be concerned with the problems of the numerous other faculties and departments. Moreover, the greater part of the funds for this faculty come from sources other than the University and the province's Department of University Affairs. Thus we see that the multiversity is not one universe but several, each moving in its own direction. Indeed, some people are even proposing that the facts of the situation be acknowledged by splitting up the conglomerate and turning the professional faculties into separate universities.

CONCLUSION

Newman described the traditional university, Flexner, the liberal university, and now Clark Kerr is promoting the multiversity. Each of these three types corresponds to an era, and especially to a particular type of society. The needs of the traditional society are quite different from those of a society which is on the threshold of the post-industrial era. In Canada, while there are still regions which have hardly been touched by industrialization, there are others where the industrial and demographic concentration easily compares with the most advanced technological societies. It would seem futile and unrealistic to superimpose a multiversity on a society which had not yet gone beyond the stage of the traditional economy. It is therefore important to ask what type of society we are dealing with, before establishing a policy for the development of a particular kind of university.

2. Canadian Society and its Universities

In the first chapter we have shown the changing nature of the university throughout the ages. In the second, we shall try to place contemporary Canadian society in historical perspective — that is, to apply a spatial dimension to our temporal model.

We shall try first to determine the nature of Canadian society by finding its place in the proposed development model: pre-industrial, industrial and post-industrial. This, of course, is a global approach, mainly involving a contrast with American society, which has already reached — at least partially — the post-industrial stage, as evidenced by the existence of business conglomerates. We shall also examine to what extent Canadian society is homogeneous. This will lead us to look at it from two aspects: 1) the socio-cultural aspect, because it tends to structure society and because we recognize it as the basic factor underlying diversity of cultures; 2) the socio-economic aspect, which will lead us to ask whether Canada has well-defined regions. We shall try, finally, to determine what implications for Canadian universities flow from the stage of development of a society and from the differences between the regions within which the universities are located. In short, just as previously we have located the concept of the university in time, now we are going to try to locate it in space so far as Canada is concerned.

A. THE STAGE OF DEVELOPMENT OF CANADIAN SOCIETY

Our historical model ended with a description of the post-industrial society, as exemplified by the United States. There is really no need for a lengthy demonstration to establish the fact that Canadian society, taken as a whole, has not reached this stage of development; studies exist on the subject. Though economic conglomerates may have begun to appear (e.g., holding companies like the Power Corporation), they are not yet a characteristic of the Canadian economy. The latter has certainly reached the stage of capitalism that produces huge business corporations and concentrations of capital, as in the sector of the mass media, but it has not as yet begun the era of the conglomerate.

Nevertheless, whether we like it or not, Canadian society already participates in the effects of the post-industrial era. It is, of course, a special type of participation created by the close proximity and enterprise of the Americans, and by the heavy dependence of the Canadian economy on that of the United States. This explains why many Canadians question whether there is a real sharing of resources or whether, in the long run, the advantages to them will not be outweighed by the profits and benefits accruing to the Americans from their investments in developing this country.

The question is also worth our asking, for the presence in Canadian universities of a large number of foreign professors, particularly American professors, has given rise to considerable anxiety, such as that voiced by Professors James Steele and Robin Matthews in their brief to our Commission. Is there a cause and effect relationship between the American domination of the Canadian economy and the presence of large numbers of American professors in Canadian universities ? The link is not, of course, a direct one, but the danger exists. Moreover, Canadians tend to import indiscriminately many of the techniques and solutions developed south of the border. Perhaps the time has come to make a balance sheet in terms of Canada's future, so that conscious and explicit choices may be made. The present course of action might then be modified.

B.   THE DIFFERENCES IN CANADIAN SOCIETY

Even though we make no claim to provide a detailed analysis of the problems posed by the fact that Canadian society is not homogeneous, they must nevertheless be examined. We must show how we perceive Canadian reality in order to explain our suggestions and recommendations on the relations between universities and governments. The subject is timely in view of the present stresses and strains existing between the universities and their environment — a malaise which results mainly from a faulty perception of social reality by the university community. It also provides us with the necessary elements for evaluating certain proposals, notably the recommendation advanced in some quarters that the responsibility for financing university teaching and research should be placed in the hands of a national, if not a federal, body. Seldom has anyone gone so far as to suggest a complete transfer of jurisdiction.

As mentioned earlier, we approach this brief analysis of Canadian reality from two standpoints — the socio-cultural and socio-economic.

a) Socio-Cultural Rigidities

We should like to start by dissipating a long-standing myth, which would have it that language is no more than an instrument of communication. A vehicle for the communication of ideas, language also reflects a way of thought, of being, of living, of looking at major problems, which all add up to a culture. And the latter is reflected in a characteristic social structure.

As a result of our travels across Canada, of the public hearings and of studying the briefs submitted by the most varied groups, we are convinced that several structured societies co-exist in Canada. Their existence is the cause of a rigidity that restricts, if not prevents, a free exchange between the members of these societies.

For purposes of this brief analysis, it will suffice to identify four societies in Canada, leaving any mention of degrees of difference until we study socio-economic disparities. They are the Quebec society, the Acadian society, the Franco-Ontarians and the English-speaking society in the rest of Canada.

Firstly, the Quebec society is an obvious and undeniable reality. The province of Quebec is the only place where francophones constitute the majority and in principle control the government. This, however, in no way negates the control exercised by anglophones over the economy of Quebec. The history of the real influence of corporations such as the Bank of Montreal and the Canadian Pacific over Quebec cabinets, to which they virtually dictated the choice of an anglophone minister of finance, remains to be written, although the historian, Robert Rumilly, has touched upon it in his *Histoire de la Province de Québec*. The existence of two distinct educational systems, one Catholic and in fact mainly of French language, the other Protestant and of English language, also reflects the duality of Quebec. The two systems have been capped by two networks of universities, of which a single institution has been and remains richer than the others: McGill University, a university which developed physically in the heart of traditional Quebec, but which is the only one to have benefited from pan-Canadian and North American industrial society.

Secondly, is the Acadian society of New Brunswick, located geographically in the Northeast and Northwest of the province. Here again, cultural realities are reflected in the socio-economic situation. To see this, one has only to compare maps showing the distribution of New Brunswick's population by language and per capita income. In this regard, the lengthy brief submitted jointly by the professors and students of the University of Moncton constitutes a proof rather than a plea. Here is described the truncated system of education reserved for the Acadians until recently, and the life of a poor francophone university in an underprivileged social milieu. This has created a special problem for the University of Moncton and for New Brunswick. Let us hope that it will not be a fight to the finish between the two societies of the province, and that eventually the Acadians will be accorded the right to live in, create and develop their own culture. This means that the bicultural nature of New Brunswick must be accepted in governmental organizations, and also that the province's Higher Education Commission must give its blessing in a tangible way (i.e. by means of subsidies) to the francophone character of the University of Moncton. The difficulties created by pluralism are never resolved painlessly.

Thirdly, there are the Franco-Ontarians. In their case, we raise the hypothesis of a separate organic and structured society in the five sections of Ontario discussed by Professor Paul-André Comeau in his recent article, "Acculturation ou assimilation: technique d'analyse et tentative de mesure chez les Franco-Ontariens". [1] The existence of the bilingual universities of Ottawa and Sudbury, and the recent law allowing instruction in the French language at the secondary level, make this hypothesis credible.

Fourthly, are the English-speaking Canadians — an omnibus category rather than a homogeneous whole. In this category one can discern several ethnic groups which are not organic societies in the foregoing sense and which for various reasons speak English by choice. But the category consists mainly of the other major ethnic group in the country, people of British origin.

b) Socio-Economic Aspects

We do not claim to do the job of a geographer or economist by proposing a division of the country into regions. The task is Canada-wide, i.e. enormous, and we have not the means to undertake it. Besides, it is not necessary for purposes of the rest of this report that our description of Canadian society be definitive. It will be enough to recall that the land-mass of Canada is far from being homogeneous, no matter at what level one looks at it — whether at the level of mega-regions, provinces as at present defined, or intra-provincial regions.

Moreover, for our purposes, regions must be defined in the context of Canadian universities in order to be really meaningful. But since there are more than fifty universities in Canada, and their related communities can themselves be divided according to faculties or disciplines, only a cursory analysis can be made in the present section. Let us recall a few of the main regional differences and characteristics.

There are, of course, those pertaining to the population itself. We must not forget that Canada was populated in successive waves at different periods, and by people not necessarily descendants of the original settlers. The geographer, Jean Hamelin, explains this as follows:

> The population growth did not readily result in Canadianization. Rather than accentuating that process, the new population boundaries led to ethnic diversification: the French-

1   *Canadian Journal of Political Science*, II (June, 1969), 152.

speaking inhabitants of the Laurentides were joined by the British in the Maritimes, in Ontario and in British Columbia in the nineteenth century, and by polycultural groups in the Prairies in the twentieth. Successive waves of immigration continually changed the ethnic composition of Canada. There are, in fact, as many Canadas as these waves represented, the physical distance compounding the ethnic differences. [2]

The waves of immigrants brought with them many local traditions, especially a great diversity of religious allegiances, an important factor in understanding the problems of education.

There are also differences which spring from ecological and economic factors. These are based on the various regions, which we can group in three categories for present purposes. First are the five mega-regions: the Atlantic, Quebec, Ontario, the Prairies and British Columbia. Obviously, these mega-regions differ greatly from one another. For example, how can one compare urban industrialized Ontario to the Atlantic region, whose population is small, scattered, marginal by comparison with the rest of the country, non-industrialized and low in productivity ? In the second category are the political areas which constitute each of the ten provinces. Then there are the widely differing intra-provincial regions — e.g. Montreal and its metropolitan zone in Quebec, the Toronto-Hamilton sector and its environs in Ontario, and Greater Vancouver in British Columbia. For our purposes it is not necessary to delve into a detailed analysis of intra-provincial regions such as that given by Messrs. Camu, Sametz and Weeks, who divided Canada's territory into sixty-eight regions. [3]

The foregoing leads us to conclude that, independent of the linguistic factor, there co-exist in Canada several types of social milieu, and that these cover all the colours of the spectrum, from the traditional type of social organization based on the exploitation of natural resources, to the highly industrialized and urbanized type.

What conclusions may be drawn from this review of the linguistic and regional differences in Canada ? Since the uni-

    [2] *Le Canada* (Paris, 1969), 70-71.
    [3] P. CAMU, E. P. WEEKS, and Z. W. SAMETZ, *Economic Geography of Canada, with an Introduction to a 68-Region System* (Toronto, 1964).

versities must relate to the immediate social milieu they are meant to serve, one would expect to find great differences among them. In this respect, except for the universities in the Maritimes and those of French-speaking Quebec, historically the University of Toronto, and to a lesser degree McGill, seem to have had an unwarranted influence over the thinking of the founders of other Canadian universities.

Moreover, at present it seems unrealistic to aspire to create in all regions of the country universities which conform to the criteria of, say, the University of Toronto. Despite the attraction of this proposition in the minds of some, a University of Toronto in Newfoundland seems to us inconceivable. In that province, a university should meet the needs of a society which is less well-developed economically. In the same way, a university in an agricultural region should be quite different from a university in an industrial environment. This in no way invalidates the argument that all Canadians should benefit from the same opportunities for university education, an objective which regional co-ordination can facilitate. Of course, in all cases — regardless of the curriculum offered — the quality of teaching and research must be of the highest order and aspire to standards of international excellence.

These social realities — the cultural and economic regional variations — naturally raise a number of questions. For example, do all regions and provinces have exactly the same priorities and to the same degree ? Should they all allot the same proportion of their budget to education, to health, to other social services, to roads, etc. ? And even within the educational system itself, should priorities be the same everywhere ? Is it not conceivable that in P.E.I. the priorities should favour the secondary level, while somewhere else they should favour the junior college and, in still a third place, the university level ? Our brief trips across the country have certainly left us with the impression that priorities vary.

It is appropriate to recall that, in spite of the unwarranted influence toward standardization criticized above, the early development of some universities had been closely linked to the development of the area. This was partly true of the University of British Columbia, to judge from the brief submitted by the President's Committee of that institution. It was also true of the Prairie universities, especially in Saskatchewan, where students now complain that the contribution of their institutions to the development of agriculture has recently been slanted more to the benefit of manufacturers of agricultural machinery and less to that of the farmers themselves.

A similar link with the environment can be found in the case of l'École des Hautes Études commerciales and l'École polytechnique de Montréal, both of which have produced graduates supplying the needs of the francophone labour market. Even the University of Toronto, which is justifiably proud of the fact that its graduates occupy posts on five continents, plays a regional role. In May 1969, the *University of Toronto News* issued an article confirming this, entitled, "The Great Globe Itself is our Alumni's Oyster, but most (79,683) elect to serve in Ontario". One would also find that the majority of the University's graduates work in the centre of Ontario and in the environs of Toronto. This is not just a coincidence, of course.

According to statistics provided for us by the Dominion Bureau of Statistics (Higher Education Section) for 1968-69, with one near-exception in the figures obtained (we do not have all of them), the large universities show that the vast majority of their regular students come from the province the university serves. For example:

Université de Montréal	94%
University of Toronto	89%
University of British Columbia	87%
University of Manitoba	80%
Dalhousie University	72% *
McGill University	72%

* But note that nearly 86% come from the Maritimes.

Excluding McGill, which takes some 17% of its students from outside the country (compared with 5% at the University of Toronto and 6% at U.B.C.), this table confirms the supposition that a regional flavour is a necessity in a university institution. We do not claim, of course, that this is the only desirable characteristic, or that it should exclude a policy for the regional and international exchange of men and ideas. More modestly, we conclude with the formulation of a general rule, simple but important. A certain type of society produces a corresponding type of university destined to serve first and foremost a certain type of need. Is that not the reason why one finds the great majority of the graduates of the University of Toronto in the large urban centres ?

3. The Nature and Functions of the University

In the first two chapters we studied the dynamic relations existing between the universities and their surrounding environment. As a consequence of this inevitable and necessary interrelationship, social surroundings cannot help but have an influence on the university. We concluded that, just as one may distinguish several types of social environment, so also may one identify several corresponding types of university. From this analysis we deduced the need for dealing with the relativity of the concept of the university.

In the present chapter we shall propose a definition of the university in order to examine more closely its nature, its essential characteristics and their implications, its specific functions, and the possible uses of the university, which may or may not correspond to its reason for being. So far, we have studied the whole social fabric of which the university is a part. Now we shall study society from the point of view of that part.

A. DEFINITION OF THE UNIVERSITY

In our definition of the university we should include all the specific and essential elements of its nature that will permit us to diagnose certain problems currently arising in Canadian universities. It is an ambitious design, the sole purpose of which is to open a dialogue.

Proposed definition :

The university is a *social institution* the specific mission of which is the *transmission* and the *advancement* of *higher learning.* [1]

---

[1] Three pertinent references for comparison are:
a) The first paragraph of article 1 of the French *Projet de loi d'orientation de l'enseignement supérieur*, No. 266 (Paris, September 21, 1968): "The primary role of universities is the elaboration and transmission

Three major ideas are to be found in this definition: that of a social institution, which describes the nature of the university; that of the transmission of higher learning; and finally, that of its advancement.

B.   NATURE OF THE UNIVERSITY

a) A "SOCIAL" INSTITUTION

The university is a social institution: it is an element in the framework of institutions which structure society. It has a precise place in society which should be defined and restated periodically, just like that of any other social institution, such as marriage or the Church. Thus one should try to determine the responsibilities of the university in relation to the other institutions to which it is closely connected, especially the other levels of the system of education. One can then see that it is the outcome of an integrated system which is an articulation of the various types of educational institutions at all levels and which seeks to satisfy the varied requirements of society as a whole.

Like any other social institution, the university has its own functions, and this imposes a primary restriction on its freedom of action (currently designated as "university autonomy"). To the extent that it assumes, on its own initiative or reluctantly, roles for which it was not conceived, eventually an unbalance will result. This will affect the quality of the services it renders, [2] and will act as an indicator or self-regulating mechanism. As

of knowledge, the development of research and the training of men."
b) Article 80 of the *Loi sur l'instruction publique* of the Republic and Canton of Geneva: "The mission of the university is to provide students with the knowledge necessary for careers that require higher education, to maintain a scientific and literary culture in the country and to aid in the development of science in general."
c) The Indian Education Commission's statement of university functions, "the most important of which are *teaching*, *research*, and *extension* involving direct contact with the community". *Report, 1964-66* (Delhi, 1966), 325.

[2]   As early as 1930, Abraham Flexner, after warning the universities against the temptation of "doing a host of inconsequential things", made the following statement: "Let me concede, for the purpose of argument (and for that only), that all the things that universities do are in themselves worth doing — a very large concession. Does it follow that universities *should* do them? Does it follow that universities *can* do them? I answer both questions in the negative." *Universities* (New York, 1968), 26.

an element of the whole social system, the university performs particular functions that contribute to the survival, the proper functioning and the consolidation of that system. This is the *conservative aspect* of the university. [3]

This point of view having been noted, one might well enquire into certain attitudes prevalent in universities by asking the question: whom is the university to serve ? What are the implications of the frequent statements that insist upon a close collaboration between the university, the government and private enterprise ? [4] When crudely stated, they give rise to confusion: do they imply the idea of servitude ? Of control by a particular group ? Do they suggest that to serve private enterprise is synonymous with serving society ?

These questions are neither entirely gratuitous nor fully theoretical. There is the problem of unequal access to higher education. [5] Co-operative arrangements exist between the administrations of large private enterprises and those of our universities. [6] An example of such collaboration is that between the computer centre of a well-known university and Canadian investment organizations. The presence of I.B.M. is certainly felt in the universities. Finally, numerous study programs, particularly those in administration, tend to promote the interests of employers rather than those of workers, farmers and the less favoured. [7]

---

[3] The words of Premier Campbell of Prince Edward Island corroborate this statement: "In our view, the first and foremost responsibility of our institutions of higher education is to serve our needs — the needs of the Province and the needs of its people." *Policy Statement* (April 2, 1968), 17.

[4] For instance, what should one make of a statement like the following: "Additionally, I believe, as a representative of the universities, that we are better served by having direct representation in our university government by members of the industrial and business community than by having indirect representation by representatives of government on a political basis." Dr. G. W. HOLBROOK, President, Nova Scotia Technical College, *University Industry Interface, University Viewpoint* (A.P.I.C.S., Fourth Science Planning Seminar, May 1968), 88.

[5] See John PORTER, "The Class Bias of Canadian Education", in *U.B.C. Alumni Chronicle* (summer 1968), and *The Vertical Mosaic* (Toronto, 1965).

[6] See brief submitted by Students' Union, University of Saskatchewan.

[7] See briefs from Saskatchewan Federation of Labour and Students' Union, University of Saskatchewan.

b) An Institution for the "Transmission" of Knowledge

What are the implications of this second element of our definition of the university ?

To say that a university is an institution one of whose functions is the transmission of knowledge, is to underline the fact that it is one of the components of the system of education. What is the nature of the educational system ? The French sociologist, Durkheim, in his *Sociologie de l'éducation,* has demonstrated that it is a process by which the members of a society are "socialized" in the sense that they are taught to live in society. [8] The early socialization of the individual is generally carried out in a restricted environment, such as the family and the immediate neighbourhood. But soon this setting is not sufficient for the task, and the individual moves on to a broader environment which is more diversified and better equipped, that of the school. The system of education, then, is an instrument with which every developed society endows itself for the purpose of teaching its members how to live with one and other. The more a society develops, the greater become its needs and, in consequence, the system of education must become more diversified. [9] At the same time, individuals must constantly keep their knowledge up to date if they wish to maintain their place in society. The result is an emphasis on permanent education which, ideally, should aim at eliminating the barriers between the various forms of education. [10]

---

[8]   See also Royal Commission of Inquiry on Education in the Province of Quebec, *Report* (Quebec, 1964), vol. 2, para. 21: ". . . even though the school's primary function concerns the intellect, the whole child is involved in education. Hence the school has a more encompassing responsibility, especially at the elementary and secondary levels. It plays a major part in training for citizenship. In and through the school, the child makes his first contact with an organized society outside the family circle; thus the school should afford him the richest possible experience of social and community life. The scholastic environment must not promote individualism; it must develop in the child respect and regard for others, team feeling, communal solidarity."

[9]   See briefs submitted by the Association of Universities and Colleges of Canada, the Senate of St. Mary's University, the Senate of Mount Allison University, and the Faculty Association of St. John's College, Winnipeg.

[10]   See briefs submitted by the Département de l'Education permanente, Laval University; the Canadian Medical Association; and the Canadian Association for Adult Education (Saskatchewan Division).

One may deduce from the foregoing that the system of education, of which the university is an integral part, aims at producing complete citizens, that is citizens who (a) know and accept the fundamental values of society and know how to conform with them in their daily life; [11] (b) have acquired sufficient basic learning to feel at ease in their milieu and to be able to adapt themselves, where necessary, to a change in their particular position; and finally (c) have received the preparation necessary to assume a role (as much as possible according to their aptitudes and tastes) in the productive apparatus. [12] To what extent, then, are students wrong to denounce the fact that in the eyes of society they are only a product awaiting the government's stamp of examination approval, and to assert that the university merely serves the established social order ?

According to this analysis, the university, as a social institution, tends to prepare the members of society to fit into one or another of the social structure's many pigeon-holes. One might even refer to the *doubly* conservative role of the university (transmitting society's accepted values, and servicing the established order's needs) without, however, implying that this role is unnecessary.

Some concrete implications :

1. Is the university in the vanguard of progress or in its tow ? Without going into this question in depth, it would be well to note that during our travels and meetings we seemed to detect in the majority of university people a reassuring self-satisfaction. Could it be that they are conservative unbeknown to themselves ? Specific accusations of such conservatism have been made against them from diverse sources. [13]

---

11   The Robbins Report refers to this aim in these terms: "the transmission of a common culture and common standards of citizenship". COMMITTEE ON HIGHER EDUCATION, *Higher Education Report* (London, 1963), 7.
12   See *Mémoire des Diplômés à la Commission conjointe du Conseil et de l'Assemblée de l'Université de Montréal*, in *L'Inter* (May 1969), p. 5, art. 12: "Just as an industry exists for the marketing of a finished product, so the university, taken as a teaching centre, exists for the production of graduates."
13   Here is a particularly bitter commentary: "The university [...] has remained on the edge of this vast movement of critical evaluation and transformation: its academic and administrative structures, with the

2. Is education a social necessity or an individual investment ? If the educational system is an instrument which society
uses to ensure the socialization of its members (in order to
perpetuate, to regenerate and to develop itself), then the traditional notion of education (and university education in particular), considered solely as a personal investment, is untenable.

This traditional approach, it is true, has been largely
rejected in our society, particularly at the primary and secondary
levels of education. But it still persists at the university level:
we need only think of the arguments often invoked in favour
of a system of student loans rather than free tuition or student
allowances. If education is also a social necessity, should not
all citizens of whom the society stands in need be in a position
to get the sort of education required to fill the developmental
needs of society ? In stressing this character of social necessity,
one should not forget the rights of an individual to an education
in accordance with his tastes and aptitudes, nor the fact that
educational institutions are not simply factories for the production of graduates. This means that one must not go to the
opposite extreme and confuse the notion of social necessity with
a utilitarian (in the restricted and pejorative sense of the word)
approach to university education. Yet the need for education
comes as much from social as from individual necessity. This
should be taken into account when deciding upon policies, such
as accessibility and free tuition, so as to offer equal chances to
all citizens while minimizing the loss of human resources for
society.

Our analysis, up to this point, has emphasized only one
of the "poles of attraction" of the university, only one side of
its functions: that of the social institution which transmits
learning and is concerned with socialization and preservation.
This describes the static aspect of the university which, while
valid, remains incomplete. A university limited to this dimension would soon become petrified and outdated. It would lack

exception of a few minor changes, have remained petrified in the traditional mould. Instead of being, as it claims to be, the heart and source
of new ideas and progress, the university sets the example of an institution
that waits for crises and violent confrontations to transform it." Lecture
by Paul Gérin-Lajoie, Quebec's former Minister of Education (July 1968), 7.

the *dynamic* aspect, which involves criticism and research. Our third element, the advancement of higher learning, will concentrate on this dynamic pole of attraction.

c) THE "PURSUIT AND DEVELOPMENT" OF "HIGHER" LEARNING

As a counterweight to the conservative pole which has already been noted, the dynamic pole places an accent on the development of the critical capacity of individuals, and is indissociable from research. Thus a balance must be struck between the contending static and dynamic poles of university activity.

1) *Higher learning and the critical capacity* [14]

If it is no longer sufficient merely to transmit a given body of knowledge at the primary and secondary levels, it is even more important at the university level to "learn to learn". This implies the development of the judgment and critical capacity of students rather than the mere transmission of knowledge. It is particularly important in a society that considers itself democratic and pluralist while confronted with an accelerated growth of scientific and social knowledge; and it applies even where education is professionally oriented.

2) *Higher learning indissociable from research*

Research activity involves a special sort of critical ability. This is true of fundamental research and, less directly, of oriented or applied research, either because the difficulty to be resolved requires the solution of a more fundamental problem or because the innovation resulting from applied research gives rise to numerous other questions in the same field or in others.

If it is true that the development of the student's critical capacity is inherent in university training, it is equally true of the professor who must constantly revise and re-evaluate his own knowledge. However, we hesitate to qualify this activity as research in the strict sense, for fear of adopting too liberal a definition.

[14] See J. Percy SMITH, "Teach — Or Get Lost", in CAUT *Bulletin* (April 1969), 2-19.

Turning from the professor to the institution, the right — or better still, the responsibility — of criticism might also be claimed for the whole university community. The critical judgments expressed by official university bodies are necessary for the advancement of society, and are comparable to those of other institutions, such as the official opposition in a parliamentary regime or the various media for the free expression of opinion.

The function of criticism may be distinguished from the activity of research which, by definition, investigates the limits of knowledge. This requires us to complete the picture by considering research training, for which the university is responsible, and research itself, from which the training cannot be entirely separated. Accordingly, students preparing for a career in research must be able to participate in the life of a research centre (or group), and professors must never lose contact with the research world. Many professors must be researchers (in the restricted sense of the word) in order to be able to transmit scientific methodology to the student researchers and to ensure the development of knowledge.

3) *Conclusions*

For all of the above reasons, and because the nature of the university and the development of society appear to require them, the following conclusions may be drawn:

(1) The co-existence of conservative and progressive elements within the university explains its internal tension. Both are inherent to it by nature and must be present. [15]

(2) This internal tension is also the source of the dynamic relationship between the university and society in general, for in addition to serving the community, the university must at the same time act as a critic of society.

(3) Although the university is not the sole place where research can and should be undertaken, university activity is indissociable from research activity, part of which must be

---

[15] See Commission study no. 7, prepared by Professor Luc Martin.

undertaken at the university. Research enables the university to transcend local boundaries.

(4) Research activity should be directly related to teaching. [16]

(5) The university is strongly drawn to the conservative pole; the progressive pole must be developed by creating a favourable environment and climate for it.

(6) Among the mechanisms and procedures for creating this environment are the techniques developed for ensuring university freedom, both for professors and students, such as permanent tenure, university autonomy, university grants commissions and financial formulae.

(7) If rules of procedure or mechanisms can contribute to creating a propitious structural environment, the climate of opinion is much less tangible, and is difficult to institutionalize because it depends upon the general attitude of the interested parties or protagonists.

(8) Only a tolerant attitude of society toward the university and a tolerant attitude between the conservative and progressive elements within the university can ensure a favourable climate.

(9) The above-mentioned mechanisms and techniques and attitude of tolerance can be justified only by their protection and development of a propitious environment and climate for critical examination and free research. If they merely served the selfish interests of people in the university rather than the interests of society, they would no longer have any justification, and should either disappear or be adjusted so as to fulfill their proper functions. In chapters six and seven, then, we shall examine the efficacy of the mechanisms and procedures developed to date by our society to protect the critical and research activities of the university.

Before doing so, however, we shall briefly consider some possible uses of the university, in order to ascertain whether they always correspond to the university's primary mission.

[16]   The French draft law, *op. cit.*, 4, states: "... research, which is neither the poor nor the wealthy relative of teaching, nor its rival, must be associated with it as much as possible for their mutual profit."

4. Uses and Abuses of the University

It is not our intention to deal exhaustively and specifically with all the possible uses of the university in this chapter. Hence, we will not study in detail the briefs presented at our public hearings by the various groups — professional for the most part — that demanded a university education for their members. [1] Their problems do not fall directly within our terms of reference. We would rather concentrate on two particular aspects of university work: professional training and research.

For instance, what are the responsibilities of the university in preparing students for the practice of a profession ? Should one distinguish between the responsibility for training and the responsibility for accreditation ? Is there not a danger of conflict between the free and disinterested character of university work and the often rigid requirements of professional bodies ?

In the same vein, one might ask: what sorts of research are appropriate for the university ? How and by whom should decisions about research be made ? Is there a danger that research sponsored from outside the university — whatever the source — might run counter to the free character of university work ? Is there a likelihood of friction between the requirements of teaching and those of research ? These are major questions to which it will be necessary to return later in our study.

A. PROFESSIONAL REQUIREMENTS AND UNIVERSITY WORK [2]

As we observed in the foregoing chapter, knowledge at the university level is in constant evolution and revision. This

[1] This was the case for the following groups: Canadian Nurses' Association; Ontario Conference of University Schools of Nursing; Canadian Home Economics Association; Committee on Medical Technologists and Paramedical Personnel, Ontario Medical Association; Ontario Society of Medical Technologists; and Canadian Institute of Chartered Accountants.

[2] Generally one may refer to the briefs submitted by the following: Division of Health Sciences, University of Toronto; University of Toronto Faculty of Medicine; Canadian Institute of Chartered Accountants; Canadian Medical Association; Canadian Guidance and Counselling Association; Marilyn Pilkington (personal brief); and Mount Allison University Senate (Ch. IV).

requires great flexibility in academic structures as well as the ability to do research and teaching without external constraints. [3] This notion is opposed to that of a closed system of established knowledge and techniques; it corresponds to the dynamic pole of university work.

On the other hand, if teaching and research are conceived of as serving the immediate needs of a profession, this places certain limits on university activity from the outset. The traditional ways of doing things are largely accepted and the aim is mainly an amelioration of the existing system. It is only in the exceptional case, such as when professional knowledge runs into a blind alley, that a far-reaching revision of the system is contemplated. This cautious attitude corresponds to the conservative pole already noted. There exists, then, a conflict between the two poles or notions of university work.

The degree of conflict will be greater or lesser according to the type of profession. One should distinguish between the new professions that have developed as a result of new social needs (e.g. town planning), and the classic professions (e.g. law and medicine) that are solidly established in and recognized by existing social institutions, which grant them certain privileges and advantages. The university is one of the social institutions that grants special privileges to the members of professional bodies. For example, medical faculties have traditionally been, above all else, professional schools. They have had, and still have, a tendency to form a university within the university, and to dominate, sometimes with unwitting arrogance, the so-called para-medical professions. This example is perhaps the most outstanding, because it is here that the most acute problems have now become manifest and that immediate solutions must be found. [4]

---

[3]   These requirements are more necessary than ever, now that we live in a world of constant change. How else could we foresee the real needs of tomorrow, except by contenting ourselves with providing for them merely by referring to extrapolations based on the needs of yesterday and today ? See also: brief from Dr. Eric Beecroft, University of Western Ontario; and the *Rapport Roy*, 45: "The university must offer the conditions for a long-lasting professional training."

[4]   There are numerous studies devoted to these problems, such as Flexner's at the beginning of the century, the Debré Commission's in

The same sort of problem arises, however, in other faculties of the university where the distinction between professional training and academic education has not been clearly established. For example, in certain law faculties, conflict is always latent between the jurists and the practitioners. It also arises in the case of faculties that do not yet have a well-recognized professional counterpart, or of schools that have an explicit professional character and a close — even organic — relation with the particular professional body concerned, but where the profession is still at an early stage of its evolution, such as engineering.

There can be no question of having the tension between the two poles of university activity disappear by eliminating one or the other pole, since — as we saw in the foregoing chapter — both are valid and therefore must continue to coexist. [5] Hence, we believe it to be urgent that universities and their members become fully aware of the two potentially conflicting orientations of their work. The two could be institutionalized, if need be. For example, a professional school could be grafted onto a related "faculty", which would retain its flexibility and its capacity for free investigation and evolution. Another possibility would be to differentiate the content of courses offered in a single faculty so that two individuals could develop in different directions: one could acquire a university training in a discipline that would prepare him for research or teaching, while the other could get a more practical training that would permit professional accreditation without difficulty and would provide him with the necessary tools for the practice of his profession.

France, the Hall Commission's on health, the Castonguay Commission's in Quebec or the Bonneau Report at Laval University. The rapid evolution in this field will be further accelerated with the adoption of medicare.

   [5]   On this point the French draft law on higher education (*op. cit.*, 4), may be cited: "The university must also prepare people for the professions. This mission must be carried out fully and not incidentally. It implies that the university must be able to inform the students of the openings available to them, to guide those who want guidance, and to provide students with a practical education without compromising the culture that the university dispenses. It also assumes that the university does not regard applied knowledge as a degradation of theoretical knowledge, but rather its complement."

Parallel to making a clear distinction between a university education and training for a profession, the university should avoid assuming any responsibility for professional accreditation as such, save perhaps for the research and teaching professions if accreditation is to be required. Although, of course, there should be communication, an exchange of views, and consultation between professional bodies and the university, a faculty or a school, the university must not place itself, purely and simply, at the service of a professional body. By so doing, the university would fail in its obligations and its mission.

If a faculty or school were to place itself exclusively at the service of an institutionalized profession, the dynamic pole would then be condemned to disappear sooner or later, extinguishing the true university character of its teaching activity. The moment it is institutionalized, a professional body acquires the inertia inherent in every institution or structure: while erecting mechanisms destined to protect society, which is one of its goals, it also develops other mechanisms aimed at protecting itself and the interests of its members. It thus opposes — almost automatically — any progress or evolution that might jeopardize its own existence or the interests of its members. The faculty, school or university must maintain its autonomy not only in refusing to accredit, but also in establishing course content and the corresponding research work.

The question of accreditation for teaching should be studied more attentively. In recruiting professors, universities should of course normally recognize and accept university degrees. For other levels of education, the obligations and responsibilities of the university should be made more explicit and precise. At present, the main employer of teachers — and it also acts as accreditor — is the state. But the current tendency is to hand over the task of training teachers to the university. It is open to question whether the university is properly equipped or offers the best environment for training kindergarten and technical school teachers. This is a prior question which requires the full attention of Departments of Education before taking the decision to hand over the normal schools to the university. However, if teaching be a profession requiring accreditation, if the government be the accreditor, and if the university be the sole supplier, then the respective responsibilities of the accreditor and the supplier must be established in such a way as to ensure that the accreditor does not impose constraints upon the university that would be incompatible with its very nature. With this reserve in mind, a fundamental question must be asked: doesn't the university have a particular responsibility in the field of teacher training and isn't this training compatible with the university's nature and function ? At the moment, the reply appears to be positive in Ontario, Quebec and Alberta.

CONCLUSION

In order to preserve the dynamic pole, which is indispensable for university activity, universities must retain their autonomy *vis-à-vis* established professional bodies and must make the distinction between the traditional professions and what one might call the university professions: teaching and research. Universities must provide professional training, of course, but only within the limits dictated by the very nature of the university.

B.   HIGHER EDUCATION AND RESEARCH

At the outset it will be useful to distinguish four types of research: free basic (pure or fundamental) research, in which the very fundamentals of science or knowledge are examined; oriented basic research, with a more limited perspective, which attempts to deepen a particular sector of knowledge; applied research, which aims primarily at the immediate solution of a given practical problem; and lastly, applied studies, centering on the effective and profitable exploitation of knowledge in the production of goods and services. These categories are much the same as those employed by such organizations as the OECD, the Science Council of Canada and the *Conseil national de la Recherche scientifique de France*.

Recourse to one or more of the following criteria might help in classifying research projects according to the categories enumerated above: 1) the criterion of more or less generality;

2) that of greater or lesser freedom, the maximum amount of which indicates that a project has been conceived of and decided upon by the researchers as a function of their intellectual curiosity and of the logic of the progress of knowledge, without taking into account the possible or eventual uses of it; 3) that of more or less long-range utilization; 4) that of the user or beneficiary, i.e. the possibility or impossibility of identifying the eventual beneficiaries; 5) the public or private character of the research. Although useful, these criteria are not, however, exhaustive.

Having made these distinctions, we may now draw attention to two difficulties: 1) Is there a conflict between teaching on the one hand and research on the other (where "research" is interpreted to mean the systematic endeavour of reflection, analysis and synthesis)? This question may be asked from the point of view of individuals who wish to devote themselves to both activities, and also regarding the organization required for instruction and research. 2) Does any incompatibility exist between certain types of research — or any particular organization of research work — and the nature of the university itself?

a)   THE CONFLICT BETWEEN TEACHING AND RESEARCH

The conflict, or in certain cases the tension or rivalry, between the requirements of teaching and those of research, has several facets. Only a few will be noted here.

Let us consider, for example, the case of an individual who must carry a teaching load while doing research. The problem is more than hypothetical. As one professor testified before our Commission:

> The common assumption that teaching and research go hand in hand [...] may be true for the advanced level of the university, but [...] for young undergraduates a historian deep in his own research and writing may actually be a dead loss as a teacher. If I had spent last night writing a book, I could not be in a position to give a lecture on, say, Europe in the 1840's. That is what I am going to do this morning.

To this evidence one could add the views of a number of assistant professors who deplore not being able to finish their doctoral theses due to the weight of their teaching loads. This is another symptom of internal tension and of a conflict of interests. Our university system has already recognized this difficulty by permitting professors — to an increasing degree — to retemper their minds during a sabbatical leave of absence. But there are other ways of coming to grips with this problem, such as easing the transition from the teaching structure to that of research, both for the professors and for the graduate students. In the eyes of many, there is a danger in granting too much importance to research; it could constitute a serious threat of sclerosis in teaching at the undergraduate level. [6] It would be presumptuous to deny this possibility.

Another aspect of the tension between teaching and research is that the structural and material requirements of teaching do not necessarily coincide with those of research. On this question, we agree with the authors of the *Rapport Roy*, who wrote:

> One of the factors that has hampered the development of research at the university has been, without doubt, the confusion between teaching structures and research structures. The objectives and the means of achieving them are quite different. Preparing programs, discussing pedagogy, and distributing teaching loads are preoccupations quite different from those concerned with the elaboration of research projects. The principles followed in grouping teachers are not those used in bringing researchers together. One naturally finds various specialists in a given department whose pedagogical activities constitute a common concern; the same persons have entirely different affinities where their research work is concerned. [7]

[6] H. C. JOHNSON, Jr., "Are Our Universities Schools ?", *Harvard Educational Review* 35 (Spring 1965), 9: "The writer has suggested that the teaching function of the university will disappear unless the institutes of research and development are removed from the university structure. They should, he argues, be established and administered as distinct intellectual organizations in their own right, with their own goals, their own criteria for success, and their own financing. This would free the school part of the modern university to develop its faculty and programmes in terms of educational criteria rather than in terms of the criteria of research practitioners."

[7] *Op. cit.*, 98; see also: *Mémoire des Diplômés à la Commission conjointe du Conseil et de l'Assemblée de l'Université de Montréal* (1969), Part II.

The logical deduction, then, is that we must reconsider research from the point of view of regrouping researchers and creating special structures for them. This would also require a clarification of the role of solitary researchers and a re-examination of the practice of preparing Master's or doctoral theses in isolation. [8] One could organize research structures parallel to those for the teaching side. For example, a research centre could be created within the university.

If this suggestion is accepted, researchers — both professors and students — should be permitted and even encouraged to pass from one structure to the other. This should hold true not only for university research centres, but for any other research centre to the extent that its activities are compatible with the requirements of university freedom. [9] This in no way implies that the two categories of research centres are interchangeable: on the contrary, their aims are quite distinct, but their interests may meet at certain points.

The reason for this proposed mobility is that it would serve the interest of the whole university system: it would permit both the teacher and the researcher to apply themselves systematically and to excel in their chosen fields, and would avoid the danger noted by Chombart de Lauwe:

> At present, the professor who wishes at the same time to direct a laboratory (sometimes several !), and to participate in meetings and in planning, reform and co-ordination committees, becomes a one-man band in danger of losing his qualities both as a teacher and a researcher. [10]

[8]   On this subject, see the remarks of Paul-Henry CHOMBART DE LAUWE, Pour l'Université (Paris, 1968), 56 ff.
[9]   Read Howard Roseborough's distinction between the university and applied research centres in "University and Society", Tripartite Commission, Universities and Applied Research Institutes (McGill University, 1968), 5: "They are intellectual organizations but they are not schools in any traditional sense of the term. They are organizations with limited problems to solve, problems assigned to them by various agencies within the society and so, without any educational purpose in that education is concerned with the transmission of a cultural tradition and not with issues of community or society concern in the immediate present. The student training that occurs within them tends to be mainly of an apprenticeship type and of incidental importance to the solution of research problems." The reader might also note the distinctions made by Abraham FLEXNER in Universities, 31 ff.
[10]   Op. cit., 57.

Conclusion

From the point of view of the individual, the sabbatical leave system should be systematized, and exchanges should be organized between university and other research centres on the one hand and the university teaching structures on the other.

From the point of view of institutions, research structures should be distinguished from teaching structures. The former may be added to teaching structures (e.g. a research institute within a faculty or school), or developed as a university research centre within an institution, or else established outside the universities — whence our later proposal to create a Committee on University Research in each province.

b) INCOMPATIBILITY BETWEEN CERTAIN RESEARCH ACTIVITIES AND THE UNIVERSITY

Our definition of the university calls for this social institution, devoted to high learning, to be shared and even stretched between the two poles: socialization on the one hand, criticism and research on the other. The dynamic aspect lies, as we have noted, in criticism and in research. It is necessary, then, to ensure that research carried out at the university fulfills this requirement and is not identical with that carried out for other purposes by private or governmental laboratories. This research work is a tangible manifestation of university freedom. It is protected and accepted by the community and the state, and is financed in large measure by public funds. The German philosopher, Karl Jaspers, justifies it in the following terms:

> Thanks to the protection of the state, the university enjoys a remarkable tranquillity. Scientific research, the services rendered in mastering new techniques, the study of former times, the active part taken in the transmission of the heritage of the past: all that is excellent but not sufficient. The university only enjoys its privileged position in order that the resulting calm might lead to a better perception of the new currents and winds of change that pervade and agitate the world. The university must be the place where one becomes most aware of the present and where one may penetrate to the true nature of things. Thus there would exist at least one place where a full consciousness of what is happening pre-

vails, and from which a salutary light would shine forth upon the world. [11]

This privileged but necessary situation has certain requirements which we shall now examine, meanwhile recalling that if university teaching is indissociable from research, we cannot conclude that all research must be undertaken at the university.

What should the characteristics of university research be ? [12] The first requirement is certainly that this research be free. Applied studies do not possess this characteristic and should, for this reason, be removed from the university. Free basic research presents no such problem since it is decided upon by the researchers themselves in the interests of knowledge alone. It is unlikely nonetheless that each researcher would be allowed the freedom to undertake any research he might desire; there must be some rules governing research within the university. Stating such principles, however, is not enough: researchers must be materially in a position to devote themselves without constraint to their research. In other words, society should allocate an adequate sum for free research, which the researchers would share among themselves according to scientific priorities; and this decision on sharing should belong to the community of researchers.

The same freedom of enterprise does not apply automatically to oriented basic research or applied research. In this case, the organization of research becomes important. If each researcher were to deal individually with his sponsors, it is likely not only that the institution itself would become unbalanced by the introduction of research that does not fit into its overall plan of activities, but also that the sponsors might endanger the freedom of research by playing upon the ambitions and legitimate aspirations of each researcher.

[11]   Cited in *Message du Conseil fédéral à l'Assemblée fédérale concernant l'aide de la Confédération aux universités cantonales* (Berne, November 28, 1967), 13.
[12]   John B. MACDONALD, *et al., The Role of the Federal Government in Support of Research in Canadian Universities* (Ottawa, 1969), 7: "Basic research remains today and must remain a matter of the highest priority in universities. The primary rôle of universities, along with teaching, is the generation of new knowledge and it matters not whether the knowledge appears to be useful." See also, F. R. SCOTT, "The Law of the University Constitution", in *A Place of Liberty* (Toronto, 1964), 27-37.

In this respect, the situation prevailing in the large American universities should be emphasized. Close to 80 per cent of their research funds come from the government, each contract being decided upon by a special agreement between the researcher and the Government. The university community collectively has no role to play. A university in this position might easily become merely a research centre of the American government instead of remaining a centre for free research. [13]

It is important then, here even more than with free research, that the merit of each project for the institution and for society be judged by the university community of researchers.

A second requirement of university research is that it should have a public character. This criterion is not completely independent of that of the user or beneficiary. In the degree to which the university is a public institution serving the whole of society, it should not serve private or particular interests. This public character of university research and the criterion of the user or beneficiary may be understood in a slightly different sense. Thus, Chombart de Lauwe [14] and Ben-David, [15] among others, consider that the publication of the results of research cannot be dissociated from the research activity itself. The professors of Laval University also opted in favour of this principle, in their brief, *La liberté de la recherche.* According to them, only research the results of which can be published may be undertaken. This criterion would eliminate from the university all research contracts financed by the state which, for reasons of security or convenience, are kept secret, or contracts carried out for a private enterprise when the results are to be kept secret in order to give it an advantage over its

[13] See Clark KERR, *Métamorphose de l'Université* (Paris, 1967), Ch. II, first part. The title is "The Subsidized University", and the author concludes with this sentence (p. 76): "I am not quite certain that the universities and their presidents have always known what the government wanted; but one thing is sure: they have always followed it."

[14] *Op. cit.,* 80-100.

[15] *Fundamental Research and the Universities,* a study prepared for the OECD by Joseph BEN-DAVID. The author defines and comments on fundamental research as follows (p. 17): ". . . 'research which produces contributions to knowledge in a field cultivated by a recognized community of scientists'. This excludes the private inquiries of persons uninterested or unable to *communicate* this knowledge to others . . ." (Italics ours.)

competitors. It is not enough, however, that the results of research can be published; the potential users or beneficiaries should not be exclusively particular individuals or private enterprises.

Conclusion

Research at the university must therefore be free and of public interest, and the results must be publishable. These three characteristics clearly exclude applied studies but apply exactly to free basic research. As for oriented basic research and applied research, every case should be evaluated on its merits, and the manner in which the decision on research is made plays an important role in maintaining freedom. We are thus led to recognize the need for universities, either individually or collectively, to have a large measure of independence from social forces, whatever they may be.

PART II

The University and Government

5. University Autonomy and Academic Freedom

A. INTRODUCTION AND CONFUSION

From the literature on university autonomy one discovers that the phrase is used with quite different meanings. These cover a whole spectrum, from the notion of a state within a state to mere decentralization within a bureaucratic structure.

Illustrations of these differences abound. For instance, the highly respectable American Committee on Government and Higher Education — chaired by Milton Eisenhower and containing such members as James B. Conant and R. Sargent Shriver, Jr. — came up with this direct statement:

> Each intrusion [into autonomy], even if a minor one or made with beneficent intent, is erosive. Thus an enlightened society must be alert to them at the outset, and attitudes and practices must be built which will regard *all intrusions as unwise and impossible*.[1]

Similarly, in its brief to our Commission, a Canadian university used the authority of J. S. Mill to defend its call for almost unlimited autonomy. [2] It was surprising to find that this *laissez-faire* attitude is shared by a provincial premier: he told us that universities should be "free to destroy themselves".

This kind of interpretation of autonomy is hard to take seriously; yet it must be taken seriously because it shows, in a pristine form, the ideological foundation upon which more moderate claims for autonomy are based. Basically, it reflects both the sectarian tradition of universities, which feel they have almost sacred missions, and *laissez-faire* liberalism, which con-

---

[1] Italics ours; AMERICAN COUNCIL ON EDUCATION, *The Efficiency of Freedom* (Washington, 1959), 8.
[2] Brief from the University Council, Notre Dame University. An appendix quoted J. S. Mill as follows: "A general state education is a mere contrivance for moulding people exactly like one another: as the mould in which it casts them is that which places the predominant power in the government, whether this be a monarch, a priesthood, an aristocracy, or the majority of the existing generation, in proportion as it is efficient and successful, it establishes a despotism over the mind ..."

siders "the state" as an enemy. The sanctity absolves the absence of rational justification, while the liberal ideology provides a convenient weapon against the hand that feeds. What is not realized, of course, is that this kind of intransigent attitude provokes, inevitably, a similar response by governments. Thus "on the . . . government side the proposition goes: democratic government *equals* responsible government *equals* detailed central control *equals* complete institutional compliance" — an equally simple and misleading set of propositions.[3]

Even more reasonable demands for institutional autonomy show an uncertain foundation. It is generally agreed that, while the state has some rights in the sphere of higher education, the universities should possess autonomy in certain key areas. Control over admissions, academic staff and instructional programs are most frequently cited as the essential ingredients of genuine university autonomy.[4] Indeed, in Manitoba the Universities Grants Commission is specifically forbidden to deal with admissions — an exclusion specified in its Act, we were told, on the insistence of the University of Manitoba. Unless the above-mentioned position of absolute opposition to any governmental intervention is taken, the justification for university control of these areas is usually sought in the necessity to preserve academic freedom. Yet it is seldom very clear why and how they affect academic freedom. It is certainly not clear that all aspects of them do. Thus to claim complete autonomy regarding admissions is either naive or wrongheaded; for universities do not in fact have this autonomy today and, more important, ought not to have it. This becomes obvious when

---

[3]   J. L. MILLER, *State Budgeting for Higher Education* (Ann Arbor, 1965), 29.
    [4]   The International Association of Universities has listed these three, plus 4) research and 5) the allocation of financial resources "within wide limits", while the British Robbins Committee has listed the same three plus 4) the balance between teaching and research, and 5) a vague area called "the shape of development". See *University Autonomy; Its Meaning Today* (Paris, 1965), vii, and COMMITTEE ON HIGHER EDUCATION, *Higher Education Report* (London, 1963), 230. The brief to our Commission from the Committee of Presidents of the Universities of Ontario has an even longer list (p. 5): it repeats the Robbins list and adds no. 5 from the IAU list. See also Fred SCHONELL, *The University in Contemporary Society* (speech delivered to the Tenth Commonwealth Universities Congress, Sydney, 1968), 8-9; and ERIC ASHBY, "Self Government in Modern British Universities", 7 *Science and Freedom* (Dec. 1956), 6.

one breaks down control over admissions into its various component parts: does it mean control over the numbers of students
attending universities ? Does it mean establishing standards
for admission ? Does it mean establishing quotas for the professional schools ? Does it mean control of fees ? [5] The answers
to these questions will show that the state already controls
some aspects of admission in so far as they overlap governmental responsibility for social policy. It is also clear that
because admission policies form an inextricable part of general
social policy on educational opportunities, governments ought
to have a say in their determination.

An example of such a policy regarding admissions would
be a requirement that there must be no discrimination on
grounds of race, creed or colour. From this point of view,
Professor E. Maher did a study for us of Canadian university
admission forms, and found that many of them require unnecessarily detailed information, such as the applicant's religion or
photograph. This not only invades the applicant's privacy but
could give him the impression that he might be discriminated
against, and even provides a basis for such discrimination. We
support Professor Maher's conclusion, and recommend that such
information should no longer be required.

Upon analysis, the case turns out to be not much different
in the question of academic staff. Here it is necessary to differentiate between the selection, promotion and retention of staff
on the one hand, and general personnel policies and working
conditions on the other. Salary levels and scales, staff structure
and staffing ratios are all of obvious interest to government
because they are closely related to the total cost of universities.
Similarly, matters such as staff welfare benefits could easily be
regulated by the state, or even included in government social
insurance plans, without necessarily hurting the academic
functions of the universities. [6] Moreover, a number of faculty

[5] See the brief from the Students' Union of Dalhousie University
for complaints about the unilateral action of universities on fees.
[6] The case for government intervention is even stronger for non-
academic staff if boards of governors refuse to allow them to unionize,
or if the universities compete with the provincial governments themselves
for such staff. As some students said to us at the CUS national seminar
in 1968, "Why shouldn't the universities be model employers ?" A
provincial minister asked us, "Why should we allow the university to
compete against us with our money ?"

members believe that faculty associations should establish direct negotiating processes with government representatives on these matters. For example, it is argued that since a portable pension scheme would have to be backed by the respective governments, this should be negotiated with them.

As to what is taught at universities, that too is lurking in the twilight between the lights of the universities and the darkness of government. Obviously, there are differences between decisions on what major programs should be offered — whether graduate, professional, etc. — and on what is the academic *content* of such offerings. The government, no doubt, must have a say before a medical school is established; it should be far less influential as to what is taught in such a school.

Perceiving that the old arguments will not do — perhaps "sensing" rather than "perceiving" would be more accurate — the universities have now developed a new line of defence: collective autonomy. [7] The phrase refers to the autonomy of a collection of universities in a *system,* not that of an individual institution. It is true that the co-operation of the universities in a system may reduce the scope of the areas in which a government may feel moved to intervene in order to secure co-ordination. But aside from this, the phrase can be just as misleading as when the word "autonomy" is applied to individual institutions. The interest and role of the state, even in the three areas just discussed, must still necessarily be large.

The decomposition of the term "autonomy" reaches its limits (i.e. disappears) when it becomes nothing more than a convenient term to oppose bureaucracy:

> [when] proponents of institutional autonomy [. . .] base their arguments [. . .] upon 1) the general necessity for decentralized administration in any organization as large as state government, and 2) the unique and varied character of the programs in colleges and universities which makes it important that higher education be free from detailed administrative controls . . . [8]

[7] Used as the title of the second annual review (1967-68) of the Committee of Presidents of Universities of Ontario.
[8] MILLER, *op. cit.,* 25.

Gone are the high-faluting incantations, academic freedom is forgotten, and all that matters is fear of bureaucratic incompetence. On this basis, should the bureaucrats ever develop sophisticated enough techniques to control universities, there would be no compelling reasons why they should not use them.

The circle of confusion is thus closed. But not completely: the term "autonomy" is also used internally in universities, where it adds to the general confusion; for, as all academics know, the hoary problem of the autonomy of departments and faculties is more difficult to solve than most other university problems. It may even be that this *internal* autonomy is largely responsible for the loss of *external* autonomy: by institutionalizing the "multiversity" character of the modern university, it prevents the university from being an autonomous unit simply because it is no longer a unit.

It is clear from our discussion that modern universities cannot expect to be completely or even greatly autonomous from government. Because "autonomy" is properly thought of as an *absolute* rather than a *relative* quality, the term is very misleading as applied to universities. We were therefore tempted to strike it from our vocabulary and to recommend that henceforth it be stricken from the vocabulary of the university community. We would have substituted the word "independence", since one can more easily speak of *degrees* of independence. But because then it would have been impossible for us to discuss the uses and abuses of the word "autonomy", we have not yielded to this temptation.

B.   THE SOURCES OF CONFUSION

The confusion in the claims for autonomy may be traced to several sources. One of these is a minor source of confusion, but two of them are of major importance. The minor one arises from a lack of clarity regarding *who* — or what body — possesses the autonomy. This is due to the existence of lay boards of governors as the supreme governing bodies of universities. For, strictly speaking, the autonomy so vigorously defended is deposited in a body whose very purpose and justification is to keep an eye on the academics. Indeed, lay boards have been entrusted with financial responsibilities exactly because it was thought necessary to have responsible citizens oversee the execution of this public trust.

It is no denigration to say that the boards have used their financial power to keep the "ivory tower" in touch with "the world of reality" — as the usual cliché has it. But the board was also intended to act as a buffer *against* "the world of reality". Who is to draw the line between the admittedly desirable function of keeping scholars informed of changing public attitudes, and an abuse of such a function to the point of infringing upon academic freedom ? This has been somewhat less of a problem in Canada than in the U.S., for at least two reasons. First, the British tradition of academic autonomy probably moderated the American influence of heavy lay domination; second, Canadian lay boards have been notorious for their lack of ability to collect money and thus to claim greater say in academic affairs.

An aspect of this minor source of confusion, overlooked in many discussions, is that in Canada several provincial governments already appoint the majority of members on boards of governors. Hence the autonomy of universities with such boards rests on the good will of the government and on the political climate of the province. In practice, however, these universities are almost as autonomous as the so-called private universities.

The two basic sources of confusion are more serious. For the sake of convenience in exposition, we shall call them "conceptual" and "functional" confusion.

a)   CONCEPTUAL CONFUSION

The confusion between institutional autonomy and academic freedom occurs so often as to be baffling. Most knowledgeable and otherwise astute observers or practitioners fall into the trap of identifying — either explicitly or implicitly — these two concepts. A good example is the following quotation from a Princeton scholar-administrator, one of the more articulate and shrewd observers of academic life:

> In every country in which public funds are the main
> source of support for the universities, the question of the
> effects of this source of support on *academic freedom* is quite
> properly high on the list of significant issues. In the case of
> Britain it can be stated categorically that the heavy depen-
> dency on direct parliamentary grants has not had any adverse
> effects at all on the *autonomy of universities* with regard to
> the selection of staff and students. [9]

True, the two concepts are related — but as much by close
historical association as by logical necessity. It serves society
and scholarship little if the logical relationship between them
is obscured.

Institutional autonomy is the relative ability of a university's governing body to run the university without any outside controls; academic freedom is the ability of professors and
students to pursue their lines of inquiry without any political
or social pressure. In the Commonwealth countries and in the
U.S., institutional autonomy is usually justified as a safeguard
for academic freedom. Yet, *a priori*, the linkage is not direct.
The mere interposition of a few well-intentioned, wealthy and
usually government-appointed men between the sources of
financial support and those who benefit from it is hardly likely
to be a sufficient protection for academic freedom. It is no
accident that the 1967 handbook on *Academic Freedom and
Tenure* of the American Association of University Professors
practically ignores institutional autonomy and relies instead
on legalistic, procedural protections. Furthermore, these protections were devised more against university administrators
and lay boards than against outside intervention.

Indeed, it is possible to argue that the present confusion
between autonomy and academic freedom has worked to the
disadvantage of the professors and students by making it possible
for university presidents and governing boards to call upon the
image of institutional autonomy and integrity in actual opposition to the exercise of individual academic freedom. It may be
that academic freedom would be better protected if university
autonomy were limited by the governmental adoption of a proce-

[9] Italics ours; W. G. BOWEN, *Economic Aspects of Education*
(Princeton, 1964), 57.

dural law for its protection. Perhaps it should even be protected in Canada's constitution, as it is in Western Germany: "Art and science, research and teaching shall be free." [10]

As Lord Bowden has pointed out, academic freedom is enjoyed in Western Germany despite the almost complete absence of university autonomy:

> The finances of every German university are controlled in detail by a senior official of the government called a Kurator, who lives in the university offices with the bursar. Estimates have to be prepared in extraordinary detail and approved by the state government before the university can spend a penny. The annual estimates for the University of Aachen, which I have seen, were as big as a couple of volumes of the London telephone directory. Once estimates have been approved it is impossible for a professor to change an order for a gross of pen nibs to a similar order for paper clips without asking the man from the ministry, whose operations can sometimes be a great nuisance to the academic staff. Despite the very complicated structure of academic committees with their senates and rectors, financial power is firmly in the hands of the government whose representative has to be consulted and satisfied throughout the year.
>
> Nevertheless, despite all this, and despite the fact that German university professors are all civil servants, German universities and their staff preserve a degree of academic freedom and individual autonomy which is in some ways more absolute than anything we know in England. Every professor reigns supreme in his own department and cannot be coerced by anybody. He is appointed for life and he can study and lecture about any subject in which he is interested, whether it is of the slightest importance to his students or not. [11]

Since academic freedom can be abused by those who enjoy its benefits, complete autonomy is not desirable even when universities are governed by the scholars themselves. In the article just quoted, Lord Bowden goes on to give an illustration of how academic decisions were taken in German universities under the guise of academic freedom that — in the interest

[10]   Basic Law of 1949, Art. 5, sec. 3.
[11]   Lord BOWDEN, "The Universities, the Government and the Public Accounts Committee", VI *Minerva* (Autumn1967), 30. Also, on the striking similarity between the positions of university faculty and academic public servants in Canada, see *Commission study* no. 18.

of the students and society — should not have been taken. A better example is given by C. D. Darlington, who shows how Oxford and Cambridge, though frequently cited as models of both academic freedom and autonomy, abused both, and had to be reformed by the state. In the eighteenth and nineteenth centuries, Oxford and Cambridge were governed by academics who "were left to their own devices and emoluments in entire freedom with the result which Gibbon has described, 'steeped in port and prejudice', neglecting their statutes, their studies and their students". [12] Academic freedom, then, must be socially oriented and perpetually earned rather than claimed as a matter of divine right.

A topic often neglected in discussions of autonomy and freedom is freedom of research. The problems here involve differentiating between the limitations placed on freedom of research by the total of funds available and the conditions attached to those funds; and between freedom and the abuse of freedom in research. In the first differentiation, one cannot expect government to make unlimited funds available for whatever costly research happens to strike the fancy of scholars. But if funds are denied or reduced with a punitive aim, then obviously academic freedom has been infringed. A corollary, far less explored, is the "positive" infringement of academic freedom through financial inducement: "The earmarking of university funds or state appropriations for research to be conducted under tightly drawn terms and conditions can pose the same threat to academic freedom as can research funds provided for by the federal government or by the large foundations." [13] The difficulty is that scholars are not organized collectively to protect freedom of research. But the university as an institution

---

[12] Further: "Self-determination had meant self-propagation . . . . It had entailed a genetic continuity which was freed from the control of the environment. No adaptation was necessary. Evolution ceased. Each branch of learning preserved its own inviolable doctrine as the Ark of the Covenant of the Lord." C. D. DARLINGTON, "Freedom and Responsibility", *Science and Freedom* (June 1958), 13.

[13] C. V. KIDD, "The Implications of Research Funds for Academic Freedom", in WESTERN INTERSTATE COMMISSION FOR HIGHER EDUCATION, *Campus and Capitol* (Boulder, 1966), 613. See also the brief from l'ASSOCIATION DES PROFESSEURS, UNIVERSITÉ LAVAL, *La Liberté de la Recherche*.

can play this role. Thus in this sphere there is a direct link between autonomy and freedom.

In the second differentiation, an example of the abuse of freedom in research is the increasing tendency for professors to spend their research time as paid consultants to government and business, or as professional practitioners. Some even use university premises for running a consulting firm as a business enterprise. The university as an institution has a legitimate role to play in limiting such abuses. [14] For instance, it could place a limit on either the income that professors may derive from work done outside the university or on the time that they may devote to such work.

b)   FUNCTIONAL CONFUSION

If the confusion between autonomy and freedom is great, the confusion between autonomy as a necessary tool for protecting academic freedom and as a convenient excuse for opposing outside control of any kind is even greater. The problem here is that universities often claim autonomy in order to protect areas that are not essential to academic freedom and should not be protected. Thus universities should not claim autonomy for areas that are of vital interest to the state and society. Though many of these areas are of great academic significance, most of them are not directly related to the exercise of academic freedom. In a later section, we try to establish principles by which the need for autonomy in these areas may be judged.

Also, there are activities within a university that — by any stretch of the imagination — are not in need of academic freedom. A good example is athletic activities: it is hard to see how a football game, though undoubtedly worthwhile and re-

---

[14]   As C. V. Kidd has observed: "A scientist who is a faculty member has certain obligations to the university which involve a short-range, voluntarily accepted set of limitations upon his freedom of action as one of the prices to be paid for the establishment and maintenance of a strong university over the long run. A scientist who ignores the rules of the game is not sustaining freedom against tyranny, or protecting science against administrators, but simply failing to exercise the responsibility without which freedom is meaningless. These observations are pertinent to faculty members who invoke academic, scientific, or any other kind of freedom to do whatever they want to do." *Ibid.*, 617-18.

warding, can have any need for academic freedom. Of a similar nature are some of the frankly vocational programs such as secretarial science, home economics and physical education. Most contract research commissioned by outside agencies can be placed in this category as well.

Ironically, these and similar endeavours have been included in the university gambit mainly as a result of the desire — and pressure — to "serve the community". The danger is that while this "service" is rather well paid, it often hampers the institution and the staff in carrying out their proper functions and, as a result, increases the probability of governmental intervention. [15] For if autonomy is needed to protect academic freedom, the university must be performing functions that require this freedom. And the protection that is sought ought to cover only those functions.

A question that ought to be raised here is the place of academic freedom within the general sphere of civil rights. Some people argue that academic freedom has little relation to other freedoms. Basing his conclusions upon the rather miserable record of German and Soviet scientists, and of American scientists during the McCarthy era, when both civil liberties and academic freedom were threatened, E. Shils wrote:

> None of the totalitarian countries witnessed a forceful and wide-spread insistence of the academic profession on their liberties. [...] Even in the United States, where the danger of remonstrance was far less — and where the threat to liberty was of course smaller — our professors as a whole did little to protect their liberties. [...]
>
> A true passion for science or scholarship does not easily combine with an active concern for justice and liberty in general. [16]

[15] On this whole point see the well-argued position of M. Ross, *AUCC Proceedings : Annual Meeting 1967*, Vol. 2, 62-79.
[16] Further: "There is really a great tension between consecration to science and the exercise of civil responsibilities, even where it is civil responsibility on behalf of the scientific community.
"Then, there is sheer cowardice, the desire for safety, which can be given an honourable face. No one who has witnessed his own behaviour or that of his colleagues in situations threatening to academic freedom will contest the contention that this phenomenon is all too common. When the force of cowardice coincides with the pressure of professional specialization and the scientist's love of his subject and his distrust of

This may have been written during a period of especially moody introspection by American scholars; but there are cynics who would say that what was not achieved with loyalty oaths has been accomplished by lucrative research contracts. "The lust for knowledge", like all immoderate passions, may be fully satisfied only by the acceptance of support for research that diminishes academic freedom. The result, so say the cynics, is that the halls of academe contain precious little worth defending that has not already been voluntarily surrendered.

C. A JUSTIFICATION FOR SUBSTANTIAL AUTONOMY

We do not fall into this cynical trap. It is our firm conviction that academic freedom is alive and well and living in Canadian Universities. We do, however, reject the notions of the university as an "ivory tower", or as a "state within a state", possessing all but sovereign powers. These notions have been dead for a long time and are long overdue for a funeral, not only because the interests of the larger state must be safeguarded and promoted, but also because the main purposes of our universities cannot be realized apart from society and without the means that society, via its government, allots to them.

As explained in Chapter 3, we view the university as a *social* institution that performs special functions for society. It is because of these functions that university staff need academic freedom. There are two implications of our definition. One is that, because the university is a social institution, the ultimate judgment about how well it performs its functions must rest with the larger community. Secondly, the universities must actually exercise their special functions. It will not do to claim academic protection and freedom for these functions when the actions of universities and academics betray their absence. [17]

We also reject the notion of universities as a royal crown on top of the educational pyramid. If, as we believe and as practically all government policies proclaim, it is the aim of

the dilettante who meddles in realms beyond its boundaries, the total enfeeblement of the defence of academic freedom is considerable." *Science and Freedom* (June 1958), 23-24.

[17] On this point, see Luc Martin's study for our Commission, especially pages 2, 5-16.

our society to provide education for all to the limits of their abilities, then a university education for those who are qualified is as much a social right as is an elementary education. We agree that, because of the nature of university functions, the relationships of the government to universities must necessarily differ somewhat from those with other levels or kinds of education. But these differences must not be construed as a justification for preferential treatment or an élitist mentality.

Instead, university autonomy must seek its main justification in the protection of genuine academic freedom. As we have shown, it would be possible for academic freedom to exist even in the absence of institutional autonomy. But since institutions exist within a specific historical evolution and a given political culture, it is necessary to anchor the instruments for the protection of academic freedom to our existing institutions. [18] For this reason we are convinced that, at present, and in the foreseeable future, substantial institutional autonomy is needed as an instrument for the preservation of academic freedom. For, in its best form, it can shield the academic community from not only the actuality but even the fear of illegitimate outside pressures.

This acceptance of the need for autonomy does not invalidate the interests of the state. It merely acknowledges that traditions and present circumstances thus condition an acceptable and well-functioning system of government-university relations. That Canadian traditions and attitudes call for the retention of considerable autonomy needs not be dwelt on. Anybody who ever visited the universities of the Maritime provinces could hardly have avoided noticing the strong historical roots of the individual institutions and — the growth from the roots — their deep distrust of each other. Financial necessity and common sense should have dictated a closer co-opera-

---

[18] This differentiation between political cultures is well remarked upon by Bowen: "The British experience has demonstrated that, at least under certain conditions, it is possible to transfer a larger share of financial responsibility to the central government without curtailing the most elemental aspects of academic freedom." Then he warns: "Please note that it is not being argued that a similar transfer could be made with similar effects (or lack of effects) in the United States. The record of U.S. experience with oaths, affidavits, and other more subtle forms of pressure is not particularly encouraging in this regard." *Op. cit.*, 57. See also Michel Brûlé's study for our Commission.

tion, but both seem somehow irrelevant under these conditions. [19] Similarly, Canada's new universities not only cherish their fresh academic gowns but are possessed of profound suspicions of other and older institutions. The result, in practical terms, is that the discomfiture these traditions and attitudes would suffer and, in turn, cause the political leaders to suffer, makes it very unlikely that a wholesale transformation of the systems of higher education will take place.

More important, perhaps, is the fact that the governments — as presently organized and working — are simply not prepared to assume direct responsibility for higher education. This does not mean that they could not take it over. But it does mean that if universities were to continue to perform their proper functions and to enjoy the protection of academic freedom, the governments would have to develop some new and different institutional structures and styles of work. This they are not at present capable of doing. We therefore advocate the retention of substantial autonomy both to protect academic freedom and to prevent the proliferation of inappropriate, monolithic bureaucracies.

This preservation of autonomy, however, imposes two responsibilities on the universities. One is to see to it that the purposes for which the autonomy is used are indeed in evidence and safeguarded. Secondly, the universities must be responsive to society's needs without becoming "service stations" or facsimiles of a modern supermarket. [20] This is not an easy task, but

[19] The situation is not much different in other provinces, though in none did the geographic, financial and cultural needs for co-operation seem greater than in the Maritimes.

[20] This postulate is so generally accepted that it has the overtones of a cliché. See W. Logan: "Society has come to accord a wide measure of independence to universities. This privilege, however, is not based on any natural law or on any irrevocable grant, but has continuously to be earned and merited by a never-ending process of adjustment to changes in society which have come to stay." *Universities : The Years of Challenge* (Cambridge, 1963), 12. See also the Robbins Committee: "Effectiveness in this sphere can only be achieved if a nice balance is kept between two necessities, the necessity of freedom for academic institutions and the necessity that they should serve the nation's needs." *Op. cit.*, 228. Perhaps the main problem is not whether universities will undertake to accomplish this balance, but whether the government ought to be the judge of its accomplishment.

the penalty for failure will be a take-over by the state with obsolete, inadequate and inappropriate machinery.

D.   ESSENTIAL AND PRUDENTIAL AUTONOMY

To declare for autonomy, of course, does not solve the problem of government-university relations. It is one thing to say that universities ought to have a certain amount of guaranteed independence; it is another to be specific about the "certain amount". Basic principles help. If our postulate of academic freedom as the main justification for autonomy is valid, then, naturally, the areas covered by autonomy ought to be related to that concept. But in real life it is not always possible to make sharp, logical distinctions between those areas that directly affect academic freedom and those that do not. There is a whole crepuscular zone of matters which are not directly related to academic freedom but which — for reasons to be given later — it would not be prudent for the state to invade.

We therefore suggest that the areas claimed for autonomous decision-making by universities should be divided into two categories. One covers those areas that are essential to academic freedom, and the other covers those that prudentially should belong to universities, or at least should be shared between them and the state. The first may be called areas of "essential autonomy", while for the second we have devised the term "prudential autonomy".

Examples of each area will illustrate the difference. The actual hiring, promotion and retention of academic staff, because of their close relation to academic freedom, are matters for essential autonomy. For reasons already given, so are decisions about what kinds of research and of influence from the professions are appropriate for universities. On the other hand, the state could regulate various personnel and administrative practices of the universities without directly infringing upon academic freedom. In fact, many state governments in the U.S. *do* regulate such matters as accounting, budgeting and building design, and even make central purchases for universities.

American experience demonstrates that such governmental control, while seemingly compatible with the exercise of academic freedom, often leads to administrative inefficiency and, as a result, to a lowering of faculty morale. This inefficiency seems to be inherent in the nature of centralized bureaucratic organization: decisions of considerable importance to universities are necessarily delegated to low-grade clerks who often have no understanding of the nature of higher education, and who are junior to the university administrators with whom they deal.

Prudential autonomy should be considered in the light not only of the above danger but also of the disproportionate distribution of power between governments and universities. The state is in possession of awesome powers — indeed, in a very real sense, public universities are creatures of the state. Often, therefore, it is enough for a government to direct a mere inquiry to the universities for it to influence decisions within the universities and/or the whole university system. For instance, Glenny shows how information-gathering alone (with the implicit assumption of publication) exercised such an influence in New Mexico. [21] Indeed, that this kind of subtle but powerful influence can penetrate into the very heart of academic freedom, was shown by the recent case involving the award of a research fellowship by the academic panel of the Canada Council to a university lecturer who had been active in student protests and who was alleged to have Marxist views. In this case, the fear of criticism by members of Parliament seems to have been enough to cause his award, which otherwise was a routine one, to be reviewed by the whole Council. Later, a number of MP's did criticize the award, thus implying that a scholar's political views should be considered in awarding research grants. [22]

[21]   L. A. GLENNY, *Autonomy of Public Colleges* (New York, 1959), 96-7.
[22]   We give two additional examples from the U.S. During the McCarthy era a group of educators suggested to the American Council on Education that "professors set up some kind of investigatory agency to probe the political reliability of their colleagues [...] to ward off improper and indiscreet interferences by committees of the Congress and of the State legislatures". And in the same period, the Association of American Universities — a body comparable to the AUCC, i.e. composed mainly of administrators — called upon the professors' "obligation of being diligent and loyal in citizenship". The first example is from F. MACHLUP, "On Some Misconceptions Concerning Academic Freedom",

It may be that in order to balance the great power of government, the universities should possess, in addition to those areas affecting academic freedom, some area of jurisdictional competence that could be used as a defensive weapon against inadequate financial support — if need arises. Perhaps the area most suitable to the purpose is control over the number of admissions. The number of students admitted is socially important, while a decline in the staff-student ratio is of great academic significance. To be able to limit the number of admissions would permit the universities to raise a public discussion of their case. At the same time, it would not be too powerful a weapon if their case could not be publicly justified, because they would have to bow to public opinion. [23]

What is amazing about the existing relationship of governments and universities, with its unequal distribution of power, is how little the state has actually used its power. As the brief to our Commission from Professor Edward F. Sheffield put it:

> It is customary to criticize governments for eroding the autonomy of the universities. The nature of governments' responsibility to the people is such that they must act in ways which render the universities less than wholly autonomous. It needs to be noted, however, that governments have the power to interfere to a far greater extent than they do. Fortunately they realize, most of the time, that to be strong a university must be free. So governments suffer the universities to fumble their way to doing voluntarily, slowly, what could be done by government fiat much more quickly.

in Louis JOUGHIN, ed., *Academic Freedom and Tenure : A Handbook of the American Association of University Professors* (Madison, 1967), 168; and the second, from "The Rights and Responsibilities of Universities and their Faculties", a statement by the AAU, *ibid.*, 200.

[23] A variation on this proposal was suggested by Sir Douglas Logan, Principal of the University of London, to the annual meeting of the AUCC in 1967, when he advocated that universities should "regain control of their own budgets" through charging higher fees. But "of course I am not suggesting a complete cessation of all government grants to universities. Far from it. After all, the civilized state has an obligation to offer its citizens attractive opportunities for higher education, particularly in fields which are of little interest to industry. And so I finish my remarks on this age-old theme of 'universities and the state' with a variation of the old exhortation attributed to Colonel Valentine Blacker: 'Put your trust in God, my boys, [but] keep your powder dry.' In this context, "keeping your powder dry" means insisting on retaining the right to charge the full rate for the job even though this right, like many others, would be exercised only in the last resort." "Universities and the State", *AUCC Proceedings 1967*, vol. 2, 168.

This point was also made to the Commission by the students from Memorial University. Perhaps the desire of governments to keep universities "strong" is one explanation; perhaps another is that, because universities have emerged only recently as multi-headed hydras with insatiable appetites, governments are not yet prepared to handle them. In any case, this surprising phenomenon cannot be expected to last much longer.

6. University-Provincial Relations

Art has been described as the discovery of truth through lies: here we hope to discover truth through errors. In the Appendix to this Report we give information on the various provincial bodies for dealing with higher education. Most of these bodies are new, and their relations with government and universities are changing very rapidly. It may well be that by the time the Report is published they will have undergone significant changes; they will certainly have been modified to some extent.

Rapid change is only one problem: a more difficult one is to distinguish between local situations and aberrations, on the one hand, and the basic difficulties that confront university-provincial relations. It is often too tempting to ascribe current difficulties to local peculiarities of institutions, practices or personalities, without going through the more difficult process of analysis to see whether the problems are of a more profound nature. [1] Of course local aberrations can aggravate a wide-spread *malaise* — just as a good set of institutions and procedures can ameliorate it — but this does not invalidate the attempt to separate the two. It seems unreasonable to say, as we were frequently told by the academics in one province, that nearly all their problems of government-university relations were due to a change in one of the key personnel of the university commission. [2] For even if such an appraisal of the situation were correct, it would point to a faulty procedure for the selection of the personnel. Also, if the change of one man can have such wide-spread and deep repercussions, it would seem that the system as a whole could stand closer scrutiny.

We are aware that in many provinces the system of government-university relations is only now emerging. It may

---

[1] A similar temptation, seemingly given in to by the majority of briefs presented to us by university-based organizations and individuals, is to attribute all ills to the lack of money. This faith in the efficacy of finance is touching, but hardly well-founded.

[2] We use "university commission" as a generic term to mean the body interposed between a provincial government and its universities.

therefore be too early to judge the appropriateness of current mechanisms and practices. In New Brunswick, for example, we were told that the new Higher Education Commission had moved "from crisis to crisis" and had not had time to settle down properly. Similarly in other provinces, the policies and procedures needed for properly fulfilling the functions of a university commission may still be missing. This is mainly because the new commissions have to answer questions about the universities from the point of view of the provincial system as a whole — a job nobody did before. And this takes time, as often only experience of the past can illuminate the path to the future.

If, then, we seem to be harsh in some of our following observations, we do not make them out of an unseemly desire to ferret out all the follies and foibles of Canadian higher education — a task best left to fiction writers — but out of a conviction that only if errors are exposed, can their causes be eradicated.

A. THE SOURCES OF PRESENT PROBLEMS

a) THE LACK OF CLEAR AIMS

If there is a single cause which is to be blamed for the shortcomings of present government-university relations more than any other, it is probably the lack of clarity about the aims of higher education. It is a cumulative matter, ranging from the uncertainties of universities themselves about their intended and actual roles in society, through the bewildering and awkward attempts at inter-university links and organizations, to the so-far restrained, but impatient and inconsistent, attempts of provincial governments to deal with universities and with the whole system of higher education. To make matters worse, the uncertainties at each level are compounded by the absence of established policies and procedures for relations between the various units and levels.

By lack of clarity of purpose we do not mean the great normative justifications for education generally, or for universities specifically. Nobody can possibly argue with the proposition that a university ought to search for "truth, beauty, goodness". [3] Nor will anybody deny that education is in some way related to the economic welfare of the country, though the economists are not quite sure how or why. The problem arises when one contemplates the possible purposes of the so-called multiversities. For if the definition of a modern university as a "mechanism held together by administrative rules and powered by money" [4] is correct, then the purposes may well turn out to be very different from those of the past, and will have to be justified by very different arguments. Indeed, if such is the case, perhaps the whole traditional terminology associated with universities is irrelevant. Regardless of the validity of these observations, the fact remains that modern universities are not sure what their specific purposes should be.

Even if everybody agreed on the general moral, intellectual, spiritual and even economic values of higher education, this still would not dispose of the question of what kind of priority these values should have in governmental spending. Neither would it settle by what process the claims of the system of higher education should be placed before the government for decision, nor by what process the government should attempt to verify the justifications given for these claims. Part of the trouble lies in the fickleness of public opinion and thus of the justification for public expenditure. If the very survival of national welfare and sovereignty were thought to depend on our technological ability to "catch up with the Russians" (or "the Americans"), then the expenditure on higher education could be very high indeed. But this particular justification might fade and another less powerful one might take its place. Thus the desire for economic growth, desirable though it may be, is not of the same emotional and political intensity. In suffering from these changes in public opinion, the academics get a sample of what politicians must face as a matter of course.

Often governments, frightened by future needs and problems, established a body intended to deal with them but instead it became an instrument to satisfy immediate demands.

---

[3] MAYO, *Commission research study* no. 11, 28.
[4] Clark KERR, *The Uses of the University* (New York, 1966), 20.

The universities have responded with similar half-way measures, adaptations and reforms. The result is often a jerky tug-of-war between the various conflicting interests both inside and outside the universities. [5]

The absence of any clear understanding about the purposes of universities and of the systems of higher education, then, is reflected not only in the failure of the universities to develop a satisfactory voluntary system themselves, but also in governmental policies regarding higher education, the way in which these policies are determined, the contradictory spheres of jurisdiction between the university commissions and individual institutions, the confusion between the various mechanisms of government for dealing with post-secondary education, and the unsettled nature of the systems of higher education generally.

b)   THE PROBLEMS OF UNCERTAINTY

The uncertainty about the role of universities has been brought to sharp focus by the confluence of two developments. One is the changing nature of the universities. This has both quantitative and qualitative aspects. Quantitively, the number of high-school graduates has been increasing, and many more of them have been going on to university. This double increase has occurred rapidly, thus adding the dynamic problem of rates of change to an already significant problem of numbers. Also, the composition of the university population has been changing: there has been an equally rapid growth of graduate and professional schools. Finally, the "uses of the university" have changed. For a number of technological, social, political and economic reasons, universities have not only expanded their activities in traditional fields, but have been asked — or undertook of their own accord — to engage in practically any human endeavour that took society's or a university's fancy. These activities range from new fields of professional and vocational training through

---

[5] There may be something to be said for this approach to conflict resolution. As we were told by a university president with a distinguished public service record, it is better to see the conflicts resolved in a struggle between different bureaucracies than to have one bureaucratic structure imposing a dead level of uniformity on the varied institutions of higher learning.

such varied student services as vocational guidance, counselling, nursing and psychiatric services, to facilities such as computing centres, faculty housing, parking garages, nursery schools, restaurants, banks, stores and even hotels. The result, of course, is the proverbial multiversity: a city, if not an empire — and often a law — unto itself.

The second development has been the result of the first: these expanded functions, serving an increasing number of people, have sky-rocketed the cost of this "education", and governments have been frightened by rising and projected costs. [6] Their resultant policies and legislation have often been based solely on this financial consideration. However, the repercussion of this development on the universities has been to force them to re-examine themselves and their relations to society, to government and to each other. An unkind, but perhaps accurate, way to sum up these two developments would be to say that, as higher education became an important item in the budgets of governments, they became concerned about it and, as a result of this concern, the universities re-discovered their capacity for self-examination.

Part of the difficulty with government-university relations, then, can be traced to money: it made the government notice higher education and it awoke the universities' conscience. But important as financial considerations may be, the most important problem it to ascertain the *purposes* for which the money is to be spent. Here lies the real crux of government-university relations: neither the government nor the universities are certain about what these purposes are or ought to be.

Developments during recent years show the various aspects of this uncertainty. These developments followed a somewhat similar pattern throughout Canada. The insularity of individual institutions rendered them inadequate to cope with their increasing functions and numbers. As they faced increased pressures from government to economize through co-operation,

[6] A recent "scare" projection issued by the federal Department of Finance, no doubt designed to frighten the public too, purports to show that, by 1994, expenditures on education will consume the whole of Canada's Gross National Product ! See *Canadian Press* story, 14 June 1969.

the institutional leaders made attempts to co-ordinate their activities. Almost all of these efforts were based on the principle of "voluntary co-operation" and, on the whole, resulted in little more than talks about co-operation. This was mainly because the institutions themselves were caught in the midst of internal reforms, which undermined the legitimacy of such efforts or at least made them difficult, for external adjustments did not keep pace with internal reforms. Moreover, the government, the only body that had the power to do so, failed to provide the necessary framework within which both meaningful co-operation could take place and governmental responsibilities could be borne.

In provinces where the government finally established an institutional structure to express the state's interests and responsibilities (e.g. either a special section within a department of education, an advisory committee or a separate ministry for university affairs), its effort was mainly in response to specific problems, usually to introduce economies and equitable treatment of institutions. Also, the effort was tempered by the reluctance of the political leaders to become embroiled in unnecessary controversies — which popular mythology had loaded in favour of the universities. (Thus: academic freedom equals autonomy, equals educational, spiritual and economic progress; while governmental control equals suppression of freedom, equals retardation of progress.) The result was that, while this direct intervention by government induced the universities to co-operate a bit more, and introduced a politically convenient buffer for the government, it did not establish the necessary institutions and procedures to tackle the larger and more important problems.

That we are still facing these problems across the whole spectrum of higher education is indicated by the creation in 1968-69 of study commissions on higher education in three of the provinces: British Columbia, Alberta and Ontario. In order to find a solution to the problems, it is necessary to understand why most of the attempts to meet the changing demands of higher education have failed to achieve their objectives.

B. THE FAILURE OF VOLUNTARY CO-OPERATION

Voluntary co-operation among universities failed because of its characteristics and because, even if it could work, a collection of institutions cannot adequately express or safeguard the interests of the state in the sphere of higher education. It may seem foolhardy to attack voluntary co-operation. Like "motherhood", "patriotism" and all other social virtues, co-operation is, of course, a "good thing": it brings to mind responsible men of good will pursuing selflessly the *summum bonum* of the whole community. If this is accomplished "voluntarily", the effect is even better: voluntary association is, after all, a foundation of our free social intercourse. Moreover, the opposite of "voluntary" co-operation is "forced" co-operation, and we all know that force is a "bad thing".

In fact, however, the voluntary co-operation of universities has seldom been "voluntary" or even "co-operative". As a rule, whatever co-operation there is has been brought about by pressure from government; practically all "voluntary" co-operative arrangements now in existence derive their efficacy from either a direct or indirect threat of governmental sanctions. [7] In Ontario, for example, it is common knowledge that the very idea of voluntary co-operation through the Committee of Presidents was suggested by the government's Committee on University Affairs. [8] The most successful co-operative effort, the procedure for accreditation of graduate programs, derives its force from the very real threat of the Committee on University Affairs not to support the establishment of any graduate program without this accreditation.

There are, however, exceptions. In one province, the attempts of university heads to incorporate their committee met with an early opposition from the government; in another province, the premier, probably ascribing to the university presidents some of his own political astuteness, discouraged them from collaborating because — so we were told — he feared they would "connive" against the government. In both

---

[7] The experience has been the same in several American states. See L. A. GLENNY in LOGAN, ed., *op. cit.*, 88.

[8] See the COMMITTEE's *System Emerging* (Toronto, 1967), 1.

cases, it seems to us, the fears of the government have been unwarranted. In the former case, the heads of the two most important universities "didn't talk to each other", though they shared the same city; while in the latter case, the suspicions that each university has for the others would have made any "conniving", never mind co-operation, very unlikely.

a) Autonomy as a Cause

It is the very notion and tradition of autonomy which prevents individual institutions from co-operating in any but a superficial way: each has power over areas that it would have to give up, or at least share with the others. Not unlike the sovereignty of a state, autonomy makes it difficult for each institution to delegate this power, and each fears that common decisions will not be enforced — a fear similar to that of sovereign states *vis-à-vis* the United Nations. As with such sovereign states, their unequal size makes agreement on the composition of any inter-university body difficult. [9] Furthermore, the executive head of each institution is bound both by his responsibilities towards "his" institution and by the natural human tendency in such circumstances to defend its interests.

To carry the analogy of autonomy and sovereignty a bit further, just as a state (especially a small one) is not likely to trust international, voluntary sanctions to prevent the predatory actions of its neighbours, so a university is not likely to trust a voluntary inter-university body to punish a less-than-scrupulous member of this body. Who would apply such sanctions, and how ? One has only to pose the question to see the shaky foundation upon which hope for voluntary co-operation rests.

A number of illustrations could be given; two will suffice. In one province a collective decision of presidents, after a study, recommended the establishment of a professional school at one university, but the government decided to have it located at another. The explanation of this move seems to lie not in the government's following a "master plan" (it had none), but in

---

[9] Note the complaint from the University of Toronto that its representation on the proposed Council of Ontario Universities would be too small, U. of T., *Staff Bulletin* (March 20, 1969), 1.

the close links of the premier to the second university and its president. Needless to say, the suspected duplicity of this president by his presidential colleagues did not encourage future trust and co-operation. This example shows both the difficulty of making decisions that are binding and the inability of a voluntary body to punish the violators of such decisions. It is a reflection on all concerned that the episode was never made public.

In another province the university presidents had agreed to postpone any future expansion of graduate programs until a survey had been made and a joint decision on allocation arrived at. However, the biggest university — which was already holding a near-monopoly on graduate programs, and had some new ones in very active planning stages — decided to break the agreement. As the dean at one of the other universities told us:

> It's the honest guy who gets clobbered — because he obeys the voluntary restrictions — while the bad guy goes ahead and does what he wants. As you know, once faced with a *fait accompli*, it's very hard to change anything. I will never be caught in this bind again. [10]

The strength of the tradition of autonomy in preventing co-operation has meant that collective opposition to real or anticipated governmental pressure has been the basic reason for any successful co-operation. The point was admitted with remarkable candor by President Dunton, while chairman of the Ontario Committee of Presidents:

> FULTON: The Canadian system [in Ontario] sounds almost like an embryonic [federated] university.
>
> DUNTON: It has the beginnings of it.
>
> FULTON: The universities have to have a terribly strong central machinery.

[10] This case also illustrates a point made earlier: that internal changes have made external relations difficult. It was a question of secretive presidents single-handedly arriving at an agreement and then the president of the largest university trying to get it approved retroactively by his senate, which had by now been reformed in such a way that he could no longer be sure of its support. Thus, while on substantive grounds the presidential decision may have been well justified, the procedures through which they arrived at it were not acceptable.

> DUNTON: Yes. The *universities are trying to develop a
> central machinery before the government develops its own.
> This is going to be the race.* We are trying to develop among
> ourselves the research capacity to know what we are doing,
> which nobody knows at present. [11]

Because of this motive for voluntary co-operation, there has been
a tendency on the part of inter-university bodies to protect the
status quo — to distrust and oppose governments in their efforts
to safeguard the public interest and develop new forms of
post-secondary education.

b)   LESSONS FROM THE FAILURE

The main lesson from all this is very simple: "convenants
without swords are but words . . ." Universities, like all other
human organizations, are selfish, and without sanctions will
not co-operate in any but a trivial sense. Since the only agency
of society that can supply the necessary sanctions is the government, it must provide the framework within which this co-operation can take place. Nothing will stimulate co-operation so
much as a governmental assurance that any desirable co-operative arrangements agreed on will be enforced.

Even if voluntary co-operation could achieve all that its
proponents claim for it, it would not be desirable to leave to
collective inter-university bodies the right to decide on questions
that are of basic concern to the government. If, as we believe,
it is an essential of a democratic society that people have a
clear understanding of who is responsible for what policies —
so that those responsible can be held accountable — then decisions on these questions should be openly assumed by the
government. It is of course possible to argue about the scope
of such questions, but it should not be difficult to concur in the
principle.

The dismal record of voluntary co-operation in the face
of the need to safeguard the vital interests of the state should
not lead to the conclusion that the problems faced by systems
of higher education can be solved only through direct govern-

[11]   Italics ours; *Conference on Higher Education in Industrial Societies*
(Boston, 1969), 56.

mental intervention to enforce co-operation. While it is true that *voluntary* co-operation has been both chimerical and propagandistic, co-operation as a result of governmental persuasion is not. Given the large size and number of universities in most provinces, local traditions of independence, and especially the distinctive characteristics of university functions, it is clear that direct governmental intervention would result in neither better education nor more efficient administration. What seems desirable and necessary is to "educate" the universities for co-operation. To use a favourite term in the jargon of professional educators, it is up to the government to provide the proper "educational environment".

C. THE UNIVERSITY COMMISSIONS

a) THEIR CREATION AND NATURE

It was because of the realization that universities themselves would not and could not solve the problems facing higher education, that the governments of most provinces — often after study by a royal commission — established a continuing body for this purpose. Usually attached to the ministry of education, its functions are to help the government decide on policies and grants for higher education and in some cases to allocate these grants. All provinces with more than one university established such a body. Those that had only one university — Newfoundland and Saskatchewan — did not think it necessary to do so because they felt that the university's board of governors adequately performed these functions. Prince Edward Island, however, provided for such a body in 1968 even though it was at the same time uniting its two universities under a single board of governors. These intermediary bodies have different names, of course, but for convenience of exposition we shall refer to them all as university commissions. (See the Appendix for details of their names, composition and powers.)

Unfortunately, the creation of the university commissions has not succeeded in removing many of the difficulties already described. This is not a criticism of these bodies or of the governments that established them. No doubt their creation solved many problems or facilitated the solution of others.

Nevertheless, as new institutions of government they introduced a new element into the process of decision-making; an element that, in turn, has created new uncertainties and, for the time being, a kind of "crisis of confidence" between the universities, these new bodies and governments.

Whether these bodies should have been created or not is an interesting but probably by now a "purely academic" question (though we were told in one province that the government did not wish to establish a university commission because of the "bad experience" of other provinces). Given the popular attitude in most provinces, shared by responsible politicians, that the universities ought to be treated differently from other educational institutions, and given the existence of similar bodies in both the U.S. and the U.K., it seemed unavoidable that they should be resorted to in the Canadian provinces. As the former Principal of Queen's University, J. A. Corry, put it:

> Watching [the British University Grants Committee] for a long time, we concluded that an independent commission standing as a buffer between governments and universities would secure the support and ward off the dangers.

> It was a civilized means and an effective instrument as long as university grants took a relatively small part of government budgets and were not seen to threaten other powerful bodies and blocs of opinion that have a stake in wide access to the public purse. But that day has vanished as new universities are established, as higher education per force becomes more complex and more expensive, and costs rise in what seems an astronomical fashion. [12]

With his usual perspicacity, Dr. Corry has not only explained the main reason for the creation of such commissions, but also pointed to the main reason why they are facing difficulties: while they were set up to do one thing, the evolution of higher education is forcing them into doing others. A number of problems have been created by this development, but it is possible to separate them into two broad categories. One covers the relations of the university commissions to government, the other their relations to the universities.

[12] J. A. CORRY, "Universities, Government and the Public", *Queen's Quarterly* (Autumn 1968), 427.

b) IMPLICATIONS OF THEIR ADVISORY FUNCTION

In most provinces the university commissions are only advisory bodies to the government. However, in three of the provinces (New Brunswick, Manitoba and Alberta), they also have executive powers, the main one being that they decide on the distribution among the universities of the total grant allocated by the government. In the two provinces with no university commission, the board of governors of the single university performs the advisory function, and also the distributive function in the sense that it allocates the government's grant among the faculties of the university (and between the two campuses of the University of Saskatchewan). Leaving the executive powers aside for now, there are some serious implications for government-university relations inherent in the advisory function of the university commissions — at least, as it is presently performed.

Perhaps the chief implication is that an advisory function tends to obscure responsibility. There is an understandable temptation on the part of a government to "hide behind" its university commission while actually dominating it. Whether governments get rid of this temptation, as Oscar Wilde would say, by yielding to it, is difficult to determine with certainty. Clearly the university community often suspects that they do. [13] Thus, it is hard to accept the boast of one of the older university commissions that its recommendations have never been turned down, as evidence of the excellence of its recommendations. One suspects that instead it must have "read the mind" of the government. Since the deputy provincial treasurer is a member of the commission, this should not have presented any great difficulties. As we were told at one of our hearings by the president of an old and respected university:

> My main objection to the [commissions] is that initially they were established to divide a certain sum of money among the universities; they have advised the government that the universities need more money, but I don't think that they have done so nearly enough or courageously enough — or certainly have not done so in such a way that they would ever make

[13] The Ontario Confederation of University Faculty Associations states flatly that the Ontario Advisory Committee on University Affairs "is in the pocket of the government". Brief to our Commission 131.

any statement that would be unpopular with the government. Or if they did, none of us knows about it.

Some covering up by the commissions for governments has been inevitable. Conventional wisdom has it that an advisory body, if it is to be a viable organization, has to have the confidence of those whom it advises. This may mean confirming the prejudices of those in power — even if only confirming minor prejudices in order to dislodge more important ones.

Another far-too-usual aspect of the advisory function of commissions is secrecy, to be discussed more fully later. Perhaps the most serious implication of advice given in secret is that it may simply be ignored, and the body giving it will have little influence. Because of this secrecy, the body cannot appeal for support to its clientele or to the general public. This may help to explain why the two advisory bodies for higher education in British Columbia, the Financial Advisory Board and the Academic Board, have been so weak and ineffectual. [14]

Part of the problem of the advisory function lies in the very wide spectrum that the phrase "advisory body" covers. At one end of the spectrum, it could mean bodies like the Science

[14]   After outlining the recommendations of the Macdonald report of 1962 on higher education in British Columbia, Dr. John Chapman made the following observation about the 1969 scene in that province:

"Now, how has this worked out ? I should think it would be correct to say that the Financial Advisory Board has been faced with the almost impossible task of dividing among the three universities the money allotted to it by the government. It has been denied the role of advising the government on the needs of the institutions and in fact has managed to do very little except receive brief attention as it tries desperately to carry out its painful duty.

"The Academic Board, made up of two representatives from each of the universities and three members appointed by the Lieutenant-Governor, has, with minor exceptions, been concerned with aiding the development of the colleges and has had virtually nothing to say about universities.

"It is probably true to say that no province in Canada has such an undeveloped co-ordinative and advisory structure for higher education as does B.C. As a consequence, we do not have adequate relations with government, no effective secretariat (the Division of University and College Affairs established in late 1966 in the Department of Education is grossly understaffed and has the majority of its time occupied by dealing with student loans and bursaries), 'ad hoc' and differential financing and only little in the way of co-ordination between the institutions and most of that at the departmental level. In short, we do not have a higher educational system but a collection of institutions." *UBC Reports* (February 27, 1969), 2.

Council of Canada and the Superior Council of Education in Quebec. These are advisory in the sense that they form, as it were, an extension of the representative and consultative system of democracy. They are usually free to publish documents and recommendations in their sphere of interest, [15] and are composed of representatives of the bodies which would be affected by any policy changes of the government in that sphere. While they hope, of course, that their recommendations and reports will be implemented or at least influential, they do not have any executive functions. They are often a convenient amalgam of representatives of pressure groups that the government cannot handle as well individually; the bringing together of these representatives thus facilitates their resolution of conflicts when the government seeks advice.

At the other end of the "advisory body" spectrum is the advisory capacity of a deputy minister. Obviously, his advice is in a different category from that of the above bodies. His responsibility in offering advice is sobered by the realization that his department may have to administer the policy decided on by his minister or the cabinet. Consequently, the relationship between a minister and his deputy is of a different kind from that between the minister and other advisory groups. The university commissions fall somewhere between the two extremes. This helps to explain the uncertainty surrounding the acceptability of their advice and the extent of their powers.

c) The Expansion of their Powers

Historically, the university commissions emerged out of a process which saw the early establishment in some provinces of a committee to give the government advice on the total sum to be allotted to universities, and on how this sum should be distributed. At this stage the body was purely advisory and its advice could easily be ignored. But soon, in order to avoid accusations of political favouritism, the government came to accept its advice almost automatically on the allocation of grants, and it therefore made the effective decisions on allocation.

[15] In fact, the Superior Council is required by law to submit an annual report to the legislature.

Grants commissions were then created in other provinces with the actual executive power to decide on these allocations.

Governments at first tended to interpret their defence of the public interest in higher education to mean merely the protection of the public purse. Hence the original motivating force behind the creation of a commission was often purely financial. [16] It was with this aim in mind that the legislation was drafted, the commission membership assembled and procedures established. The result was that, as the commission's tasks changed, its jurisdiction had to be stretched. This introduced new problems. For instance, the membership was often unsuited for the new tasks, and was either changed or had to be educated by the universities and by an expert staff. Also, the procedures for dealing with the university community had to be modified. Some provinces added academics or academic administrators to the commission's membership — a move that may have introduced more realism into its recommendations but did not greatly diminish the suspicions. Indeed, this often put the dilemma of the commissions into sharper focus, for it implicitly recognized the need for *academic* advice when making financial recommendations or decisions.

The qualitative break in this evolution came when it was realized that the government could not control the future development of universities if it only attempted to distribute money to them in sufficient and equitable sums. It must establish some form of control over their planned expenditures. Hence the university commissions have been encouraged to move into this area, and are now, either through legislation or simply by virtue of their financial powers, in effective control of

---

[16]   U.S. experience was similar: "The impetus for the establishment of agencies to co-ordinate state-supported colleges and universities has in the main come from the wishes of the legislatures to economize, increase efficiency and limit programs, or from the short-sighted, if not selfish, aspirations and concerns of individual institutions. The more positive purpose of promoting a better, more vigorous system of higher education has usually been overlooked. Of the states included in the present study, only in Texas and Wisconsin has this positive objective been mentioned in the law, and even here investigation reveals that the controlling motivations which actually led to co-ordination were the more expedient ones that operated in the other states." L. A. GLENNY, *Autonomy of Public Colleges* (New York, 1959), 22-23.

new academic programs, facilities and schools, as well as new capital expenditure.

This expansion of powers has intensified the problems in the second broad category: the relations of the commissions with the universities. In a sense, their basic problem now is the same as the one that individual universities face:the falsity of the claim that, because the board of governors seems to have mainly financial powers, it does not make any significant academic decisions. Or to put it differently, what are the implications of the recent change from narrowly financial grants commissions to broadly educational commissions ? What problems are inherent in this change and how can these problems be solved ? Further, how can the responsibilities of the university commissions be reconciled with the responsibilities of individual universities and their boards under current legislation and practice ?

d) IMPLICATIONS OF FORMULA FINANCING

A general problem springing from the increasing functions of the university commissions is the danger that they will use the haziness of their jurisdiction to enter into essential or prudential areas of university autonomy directly, or — more likely — do so indirectly by initiating policies that have repercussions in these areas. In this latter category, perhaps the most contentious policy — and one that is likely to become a battleground of the contending parties in the near future — is formula financing. Adopted first in Ontario, formula financing has spread rapidly to most other provinces with university commissions. [17] Although ostensibly an objective method of financial support designed

[17] Versions of it are used also in Alberta, Manitoba, New Brunswick and Nova Scotia. By now there is a substantial body of literature on the subject. The best Canadian defence and explanation of its virtues is to be found in the publications of the Ontario Committee on University Affairs and in the speeches of its Chairman, Dr. D. T. Wright. The original proposal can be found in the OCUA's report to the Minister of University Affairs: *A Formula for Operating Grants to Provincially Assisted Universities in Ontario* (Toronto, Ontario Department of University Affairs, 1966). A good critique is contained in the brief of the Ontario Confederation of University Faculty Associations to our Commission, especially pp. 19-20, 27, 31-2, 100-123. In the U.S., perhaps the most useful source is J. L. MILLER, *State Budgeting for Higher Education : The Use of Formulas and Cost Analysis* (Ann Arbor, Mich., 1964).

to preserve university autonomy, it has serious implications for academic policy.

Formula financing takes many forms and covers a multitude of virtues and sins. In principle it can be likened to an equation which says that for x type of services you will get y dollars. The equation can be either very simple or very complicated. In a sense, any generalized policy which states that if conditions x prevail you will get y dollars, can be said to be a formula. The formula used by the university commissions in Canada is in principle simple: it provides for a grant of so many dollars per student in various types of program according to their cost. Thus all one needs to know in order to calculate the total grant to each university is the number of students in each program and the relative cost of each program. On the other hand, some of the formulas used by state boards of higher education in the U.S. are complicated mathematical expressions of detailed relative costs, and are really part of a process of program budgeting for the purpose of reviewing and determining the budgets of individual universities.

In principle, therefore, formula financing is nothing new. What it does is to express in a numerical fashion the policy of the government (or of the agency administering its funds). This is both its strength and its weakness. It is its strength because it proclaims publicly — and usually in a binding and thus predictable fashion — that if the universities follow such and such a policy, they will get so much. This is such a great advance over the previous unpredictable and often arbitrary way in which universities received money from the government — and still do in some provinces — that it tends to blind people to the fact that it also expresses *governmental academic policy* which masquerades under the mask of a *mere financial formula*. Because the expression "formula financing" evokes mathematical certainties, the policy is often presented as the very embodiment of objectivity. Thus even such an astute observer as President Bissell of the University of Toronto has said that "a formula, in itself, is merely a method of achieving objective rather than subjective distribution". [18] What President Bissell could have

[18]   *University of Toronto News* (May 1969).

meant, at best, was that formula financing applies uniformly the subjective evaluation expressed by the formula.

Basically, any financial formula must contain two elements, regardless of its base. First, it must reflect some relation to cost, and second, it necessarily contains an element of value judgment about this cost. Thus, even if the formula employed is based on *actual* costs and merely equates these with the needs of the universities, what the government (or its agency) is in fact saying is that this is the kind of cost we sanction. In other words, it is making a value judgment about academic matters; for by sanctioning the present costs, the government is at least approving and probably encouraging the conditions upon which the estimates of cost — and they are seldom more than that — rest. Thus in Ontario, for example, since the formula pays more for honours students, it discourages universities from considering the abolition of honours programs or even from modifying them drastically. There are good arguments for abolishing honours programs; if they are retained in Ontario it will be as much because they have been built into the formula as because of the academic arguments for their retention. Certainly a university is not likely to experiment with new approaches that may bring it less money under a formula. This incentive to diseconomy is often overlooked by those who argue that formula financing leads to economies within universities. Nor is a university likely to initiate any new, expensive program. Thus, by equating past costs with future needs, formula financing is actually a guardian of the *status quo*.

The issue becomes even more obvious when one considers that the weights in the formula could be adjusted to incorporate value judgments that differ from the actual past costs. Thus the weight given to graduate students could be increased in order to encourage the growth of graduate schools. It may be that the formula *should* contain such judgments on social values; but if it does, they should be made consciously and for publicly stated reasons. If the university commissions begin making surreptitiously-assumed value judgments by juggling the weights, this means that they have assumed a role which they were not intended or equipped to perform. On the other hand, if they adjust the weights openly it means that, rather than merely distributing funds equitably among the universities, or even playing the role of "honest broker" between the universities and the government, the commissions have actually assumed a role of leadership in higher education.

It is our contention that the university commissions ought to assume this leadership, but in order to do so their position *vis-à-vis* both the government and the universities must change. In terms of their present composition, powers and procedures, the existing bodies are not in a position to perform such a socially critical function. It may be that a formula can be used as a tool for such a function, but, if so, it must become an instrument of conscious change rather than of unthinking preservation.

D.   CRITICISMS OF PRESENT PRACTICES

a)   THE LACK OF CONSULTATION

In many ways the practices and procedures of the university commissions are still based on the original assumptions that led to their establishment. Because they were at first considered as only advisory and as concerned mainly with financial matters, consultation with universities was not thought to be necessary. But now the commissions are becoming increasingly concerned with matters of educational policy and planning. Full consultation with not only university heads but also provincial faculty and student organizations has therefore become a prerequisite for satisfactory procedures and policy. It is thus disheartening to find in at least one province that even the university presidents are not informed about such basic policies as whether or not the commission employs formula financing. Equally discouraging is the practice in another province of not conveying information to anybody but the heads of institutions. In fact, the commission in question may even decide not to release information sought by them.

It would seem that most university commissions are reluctant even to meet with representatives of the universities collectively. It is true that in some provinces this is partly a result of the lack of an inter-university organization. Thus, in one province, though the commission has been in existence for a couple of years, the presidents of the universities still have not met among themselves. But it is mainly a result of the fact that most commissions have preferred to deal with the universities in the same way that the universities themselves have operated: in secrecy and eternally dividing and divided. If this habit can be broken, the situation will improve, even if no other steps are taken. It is our understanding that the Universities Grants Commission of Manitoba has taken a step in this direction by adopting the principle that the universities within the province will have a chance to comment upon each other's major projects.

The problem of consultation with organizations of professors and students will lose some of its thorns once universities reform themselves internally and thus remove at least one layer of suspicion that prevails in this area. It is obvious that faculty, students and, for that matter, non-academic staff, should participate when matters directly affecting their interests, such as working conditions or student aid, are being decided. Since faculty and students also have a vital interest in matters of general academic policy, they should not only be consulted on province-wide decisions regarding these matters but also participate in these decisions. How such participation is best achieved may depend on conditions prevailing in each province. [19]

Regarding the government's role in consultation, it is amazing in how many instances the very establishment of the university commissions was accomplished without any meaningful consultation with the universities. No other organizations or groups in society would have been treated the way

[19] In New Brunswick, the Act which established the New Brunswick Higher Education Commission stipulates that one group represented on the nominating committee for the Commission shall be "the heads of such organizations of university teachers as are recognized by the universities for the purposes of negotiations with respect to employment and conditions of professional service". Ironically, had there been consultation with university officials, it is very likely that this clause would not have been included. It is the first, and so far only, legal recognition of the right to negotiation on the part of the faculty, and it will be interesting to see whether it will be used by the faculty to claim this right, or amended by the government to remove the recognition.

universities were when the Acts creating the commissions were passed. Labour unions, business organizations, animal lovers, utopian sects — they all would have been consulted before legislation affecting them was passed by the legislature. Yet in several provinces the universities were ignored, and in others, only a token and hasty hearing was afforded to presidents and governing boards. In one province, universities learned about the establishment of a committee to investigate them from newspaper reports. Needless to say, such an attitude on the part of the government is hardly conducive to co-operation.

b) Secrecy

Among the problems which can be bracketed under the category of "style", or the way of doing things, perhaps the most disheartening is the aura of secrecy which pervades so much of the activity of university commissions and even governments. In most cases the secrecy is unnecessary and, in a democratic society, indefensible; in the academic community, with its oft-proclaimed commitment to freedom, it is incomprehensible. No doubt, this secretiveness is part of a prevailing Canadian political attitude. [20] But one would expect the univer-

---

[20]   See D. C. Rowat, "How Much Administrative Secrecy ? 31 *Canadian Journal of Economics and Political Science* (November 1965), 97-98. See also Hugh Lawford's criticisms of government secrecy in the study prepared for our Commission. The following is a similar observation about the operating style of American state systems of higher education:

"Some state agencies have published for the use of college administrators, and occasionally faculty members, data which are believed to be of value to those directing operations. These published data are not usually seen by the whole faculty — perhaps because some of the administrators do not like it when a particular release places their institution in an unfavourable light. This aversion to publicity becomes an issue between the central agency and certain institutions when the data are released for general public use. One president stated that 'matters in which the Board [of higher education] and staff are critical of an institution should be kept within the family'.

"In all systems, public airing of conflicts and dissensions among the institutions is discouraged. At least three of the agencies make particular efforts to prevent publicity unfavourable to the system or an institution. All except the routine releases are checked and reviewed in Oregon and New York, the two systems with information offices. Iowa brings the institutional publicity officers together to encourage joint efforts and agreement on system matters. In the states with voluntary systems, differences of opinion are never made public; there is no minority report. The impression of sense of unity is often further supported by the use of the word 'system', or 'university', in the title of the central

sities and university commissions to take the lead in changing this attitude.

In none of the provinces, whether they have a university commission or its functions are performed by a board of governors, do the provincial bodies publish their proceedings, nor are they open to the public. Often this strengthens the suspicion that these bodies do not defend the interests of the universities properly, and that they are "in the government's pocket"; it also prevents the university community from discovering the rationale upon which their recommendations or decisions have been based. This is a most serious shortcoming, one that violates both common sense and democratic decency. Recommendations or decisions which affect such a large and important segment of public life should be made on grounds that can be publicly defended. And they *should* be publicly defended, for the same reason that "justice should be not only done but seen to be done". With so much at stake, the traditional policy of "quiet diplomacy" between officials of the universities, the commissions and governments will no longer do. [21]

We believe that much of the present fear and suspicion that the commissions and universities have of each other is attributable to this general climate of secrecy and lack of open communication. It may be that our present political system is incapable of coping with a sudden shift to openness. But certainly much greater openness is desirable and should be experimented with. At the level of the commissions, the advisory function may argue against making their meetings public, but it should allow for the publication of their minutes, perhaps after a suitable lapse of time so that the government can receive and consider any recommendations first. In the two

agency, and on all publications and press releases." GLENNY, *Autonomy, op. cit.*, 73. Though written in 1959 about the experience of the United States, this comment describes fairly accurately the situation prevailing in most Canadian provinces.

[21] On the inadequacy of "quiet diplomacy" by the president and board of governors of the University of Saskatchewan during the recent controversy with the provincial government over control of the University's budget, see John C. COURTNEY, "The Government-University Controversy in Saskatchewan, 1967-1968", 17 *CAUT Bulletin* (December, 1968), 19-33.

provinces without a commission, the meetings of the university's board of governors should be subject to similar policies because the board plays a somewhat similar role. Here the possibility of open meetings is even greater (except for certain matters which must be considered *in camera*).

It is our impression, however, that most university commissions, boards of governors, university administrators and faculty will not voluntarily initiate a policy of public accessibility to their transactions of business. Perhaps the best way to pierce this wall of darkness, therefore, would be to subject it to the light of provincial legislatures. The inclusion of university affairs within the scope of an education committee of the legislature would probably be the best way to achieve this end. Another important advantage of such a device is that it would familiarize many provincial politicians with university affairs. This is neither a revolutionary nor a particularly novel proposal. As Quebec's Parent Commission argued:

> Why is it so dangerous and improper for education policy to be discussed openly before the electorate and the Legislative Assembly ? A better informed public opinion would look askance upon it being treated as a mere political football. In quite a different spirit, the political parties should inform us of their programs in education, and governments should give an accounting to the public of how they have exercised their mandate in a field so vital to the general welfare. To place education in the very forefront of political issues will invest it with the importance it should have. [22]

We therefore recommend that provincial governments which have not already done so should create a committee of the legislature on education, and that this committee should include university affairs in its scope.

c)   FINANCIAL PROCEDURES

With regard to government-university financial procedures, perhaps the complaint we heard most frequently was the awkward timing of budgetary decisions. Partly due to the

---

[22] ROYAL COMMISSION OF INQUIRY ON EDUCATION IN THE PROVINCE OF QUEBEC, *Report, Part One : The Structure of the Educational System at the Provincial Level* (Quebec, 1963), 81.

differing fiscal years, partly due to bureaucratic red tape, government grants to universities are not confirmed until late in the winter or early spring. This delay causes hardship to the universities and probably hampers many of their attempts to improve themselves. While recognizing the binding effect of the parliamentary sessions, we feel that it should be possible to reduce this financial uncertainty. We therefore recommend that the provincial governments should allow the universities to anticipate their annual grants by committing expenditure up to a certain margin and in specified areas before the budget is approved in the legislature.

The universities also complain that, for purposes of planning, they need to know how they will stand financially several years hence. In many other countries the government commits minimum capital and operating grants to universities for a three-year or five-year period, with the possibility of later revision upward according to unanticipated increases in numbers of students or costs. Since a number of these countries have a parliamentary system of government, the requirement of annual legislative approval of budgets need not be a bar to such a commitment. We therefore recommend that, in order to promote orderly planning within universities, the university commission and/or provincial government should commit minimum grants to universities for both capital and operating costs over a three-year or five-year period, with the additional amount of the grants to be adjusted each year in accordance with changing circumstances.

Another complaint related to financial procedures is that an increasing amount of information, and in increasingly diversified form, is being sought by the university commissions. More important, the information is often sought without stating the purpose for which it will be used. This is another illustration of the lack of clarity on the part of the governments and the commissions as to what their purposes are in the area of higher education. Since the universities do not know as much about themselves as they should, when asked for information they are often confronted with having to undertake special internal surveys. Faced with the vague but obviously potentially powerful jurisdiction of the commissions, the universities may either try to avoid direct answers, or try to confuse or delay their answers. This may irritate the commissions, and a feeling of hostility may be built up. Also, in some cases the information sought has been based on preconceived notions about universities that do not reflect the kind of familiarity with higher education one would expect. Yet decisions must be made about the kind of information needed for the proper functioning of the whole system of higher education. It is our impression that wise decisions will not be made until the jurisdiction of the university commissions — and, of course, of the universities themselves — is more clearly defined.

d) CONCLUSION

We have come to the conclusion that the rules and style of the game will have to be improved if some of the existing suspicions and hostilities are to be diminished and cease to harm higher education. One of the most offensive habits of the university commissions and governments alike is to make a decision or a change in policy without giving the universities at least a prior chance to comment on it. In one province, the situation is so bad that, as we were told by the premier himself, all the plans for higher education are in his head. The result is to encourage everywhere in the academic community the soul-destroying habit of trying to "read the premier's mind" — a habit so deeply ingrained by now as to create one of the strongest impressions that the Commission was subjected to. In this case, it may well be that nothing short of a change in government will improve the situation. But even in other provinces, there are too many cases of unilateral decisions for comfort. The style of the game is not likely to be improved until all of the participating parties know what game they are playing and can agree on the rules — on what their respective rights and duties are.

7. *The Reconciliation of Interests*

A. THE PUBLIC INTEREST IN HIGHER EDUCATION

In the post-war era, justifications for governmental interest in and support of higher education have ranged from the requirements of national security to those of economic growth; from the necessity of survival in a technological age to the preservation of cultural identity. [1] More recently, in conjunction with the rapid increase in public expenditure on higher education, the universities have begun to be viewed as important social institutions. Democratization, equalization of opportunity, and a faith in higher education as a corrective of social maladjustment (such as poverty and the unjust distribution of income) have been advanced as reasons for increasing support of university education.

When social goals such as these are pursued through universities, the implications for the universities are portentous. As Dr. Corry put it:

> The universities have moved to the public domain. Those who feel threatened by their hungry presence want to cut their pretentions and their cost and we shall see more of this very quickly. Those who expect direct benefit from universities, particularly governments, want to be assured that the directions they will take will serve the beneficiaries most effectively, and with the least possible duplication of courses and effort. *Not only costs, but content, organization, enrolment, kind and quality of service are public issues.* [Italics ours.]

> In the language of the lawyers, the universities are now revealed as "an industry affected by public interest", the phrase used to explain and justify governmental regulation of public utilities. The universities have become a public utility of a most important kind. Sooner or later, all industries so identified so far have become subject to governmental regulation. [2]

---

[1] A handy summary of the various justifications is contained in the opening pages of the Bladen Report, *Financing Higher Education in Canada, op. cit.,* 1-9.

[2] J. A. CORRY, "Canadian Universities — from Private Domain to Public Utility", *U.B.C. Reports* (February 27, 1969).

The problems we wish to attack in this chapter, then, are: How can the public interest and the interest of the universities be best served in the area of higher education ? What institutions and procedures can be most useful in the pursuit of these interests ? In the long run, what is in the best interest of the universities is probably also in the best interest of the public (and vice versa). But it is important to distinguish between the long-run public interest and the expression of that interest through a particular government. Thus, at specific points in time, what universities *believe* to be in their best interest and what a particular government *thinks* is in the public interest, are often in conflict; it is our intention to propose institutional and procedural mechanisms through which such conflicts may be resolved in the best interest of the public, and may even be prevented from arising.

First, it will be useful to identify the vital areas of public and governmental interest. Basically, they appear to fall into two categories: (1) a general delineation of the university's role in society and a responsibility for protecting this role; and (2) a specific allocation of financial and other support to higher education within the total educational efforts of the society.

Under the first category, it is the responsibility of the government to provide the necessary policies for the achievement of society's goals in so far as they affect higher education. Thus, providing equal educational opportunities and planning to meet manpower requirements are governmental responsibilities that have far-reaching implications for universities. [3] While the

---

[3] Cf. Premier Robarts' statement: "It is the task and the purpose of this government to provide whatever opportunities are necessary to enable each individual, through education, to develop his potentialities to the fullest degree, to employ his talents to the greatest advantage, and we plan to accomplish this through free choice, not by coercion and regimentation of our fellow citizens." ONTARIO DEPARTMENT OF EDUCATION, *Working Papers* for Inter-provincial Conference on Education and Development of Human Resources (Montreal, September 8-19, 1966), 61. Compare this with the following statement of the Deputy Minister of Education for British Columbia, G. Neil Perry: "Returning to our main theme again, we might say that the economic aims of education are to increase the elasticity of supply of manpower, or more generally, to ensure that the output of the educational system at any time would correspond tolerably closely to the changing manpower requirements of the economy." G. Neil PERRY, "The Political Economy of Education", in R. SHEARER (ed.), *Exploiting Our Economic Potential: Public Policy and the British Columbia Economy* (Toronto, 1968), 95.

phrase "educational planning" lacks precision, [4] it is probably the best way to describe briefly and comprehensively the kind of activity that the government must undertake to fulfill its obligation to society in the realm of higher education. In the most immediate sense, it means that the government must decide "who shall pay in what way for whose education" — i.e. how the costs of higher education are to be distributed and how accessible the various degree programs are to be. [5] It also means that the government must decide on the priority to be given to higher education in competition with other levels of education and other social goals, such as helping the old and the sick and the poverty-stricken. [6]

While the basic policies affecting universities are formulated by governments in this broad context of the university's role in society, it is the second category of governmental interest through which universities feel the institutional consequences of decisions arrived at in the broader context. It is here that governmental policies, procedures and structures affecting education have an immediate relationship to the universities and, equally important, where universities' reactions are felt. Thus, once the

[4] Indeed, some have denied it any meaning at all: "There is widespread agreement today in academic and governmental circles that public decisions regarding education should be made 'planfully' rather than *ad hoc*. This consensus extends beyond saying that government should be the principal financial supporter and even beyond saying that administration of education should be centralized in one or a few agencies equivalent to a ministry. It is widely agreed that public decisions regarding education should take into account policies and developments in other sectors of the society and vice versa.

"But there is no equally firm agreement on precisely what 'planning' is or should be. Clarity is not aided by recognition among scholars that no government has ever 'really' planned comprehensively, except possibly in war-time. Certainly at present there is nothing like 'the theory of planning' and even less is there 'a theory of educational planning'." ANDERSON and BOWMAN, "Theoretical Considerations in Educational Planning", in VERDA and LAYWERYS (eds.), *Educational Planning*. Another contribution in the same book states (p. 58): "There does not exist as yet any simple and generally agreed definition of educational planning." Philip H. COOMBS, "What Do We Still Need to Know About Educational Planning ?"

[5] For professional programs the government has delegated much of this responsibility to the professions — a residual remnant of medieval monopolistic privilege that recent changes in social policy are slowly eroding away.

[6] For an illuminating analysis of the trends in governmental spending, see the study done for our Commission by the Institute of Intergovernmental Relations, Queen's University (Research study no. 13).

general portion of public expenditure is allocated to higher education — a decision that only the government can make — the problem of how and by whom the resources are divided among the institutions becomes the focus of interest. Though the general standing of higher education in the priorities of government is of greater impact and importance in the long run, in most provinces the "division of the pie" creates more immediate strains and problems. Obviously, there is a connection between these two categories of decisions. Yet a change in the priorities of governmental expenditures comes about as a result of a shift in general public opinion and/or a significant change in the social system, while changes in policies within the field of education are more frequent and more subjected to the direct influence of interested parties. What we are proposing in the following pages, therefore, concentrates on the second category of governmental interest. [7]

B.   ALTERNATIVE PROVINCIAL MECHANISMS

If our analysis in the preceding chapter is even approximately correct, the basic problem of university-provincial relations is the role of the intermediary bodies. As we explained, these bodies originally came into existence to advise the provincial governments on the financial resources to be allocated to the universities and on the division of these resources among them. The situation has changed to such an extent that it is now the responsibility of provincial governments to ensure that there is co-ordination among the institutions of higher education and comprehensive planning of their future development. Rather than exercise a negative power of veto, governments must play a positive and constructive role. In our view, therefore, because exclusive intervention by government is undesirable, intermediary bodies are needed not only to perform the advisory and allocative functions of the existing university commissions but also to assume these newer functions of co-ordination and planning.

---

[7] There is at least one more aspect to this problem: the likelihood of governments wishing to control the timing of university expenditures as part of a fiscal policy to balance general economic conditions. Because the expenditure on higher education has become a significant proportion of governmental budgets, it is very likely to be subjected to this consideration.

An alternative way in which these functions could be performed would be through the creation of a unified university system within each province, governed by a single board of governors or trustees. Besides governing and co-ordinating the individual campuses within the system, the board could also perform the advisory and planning functions. There are several examples of such a structure elsewhere, especially among state governments in the United States. It was recommended for Ontario by the Spinks Commission, [8] and there are good arguments in its favour.

Under such a system, undoubtedly, the governing body would have more than sufficient power to accomplish its tasks. On the surface, therefore, planning and co-ordination would be accomplished with greater ease. Moreover, experience in the United States indicates that such a system need not result in undue uniformity or even to uniformity much greater than that already in existence. [9] A single governing board could consciously plan and provide for variety and experimentation, whereas the existing provincial grants formulæ allow for no variations in student-cost units from one campus to another and may be just as likely to lead to a "dead level of uniformity".

Yet we have rejected such a solution, at least for the foreseeable future, because we think that in most provinces a co-ordinating and planning commission, rather than an all-encompassing governing board, is more in harmony with the present needs of both the government and the universities. We recognize, however, that the arguments against a governing board may not be equally applicable to all provinces and all situations. These arguments may be summed up under four categories.

[8] COMMISSION TO STUDY THE DEVELOPMENT OF GRADUATE PROGRAMS IN ONTARIO UNIVERSITIES, *Report* (Toronto, 1966). The new multi-campus University of Quebec does not constitute such a structure because it does not include the six previously existing universities; the advisory Council of Universities has jurisdiction over it as well as the other six. Moreover, in addition to the governing board for the whole University, each campus also has a governing council of its own. On the other hand, the legislation creating the University provides that, by mutual agreement, any of the existing universities may join the University of Quebec. It is therefore possible that eventually there will be a master governing or co-ordinating board for all or most of the universities in Quebec.

[9] GLENNY, *Autonomy, op. cit.*, 224.

The first concerns administrative centralization. The experience of American states having a governing-board system with a large number of campuses shows that the individual institutions have very little self-government. While it was intended that administration should be decentralized, in practice this is rare; on the contrary, governing boards have tended to centralize their administration. [10] Secondly, single governing boards tend to pay too much attention to day-to-day administration and not enough to planning and co-ordination. [11] Thus the canons of both administrative decentralization and comprehensive planning are often violated.

Thirdly, a single governing board would tend to stifle local initiative by creating the impression that only the central agency can sponsor innovations. Of course, the central agency should have a say in any drastic or dramatic departure from the inherited doctrines of academe; but it is important to create conditions that encourage the initiation of plans and proposals for change. By taking away — both legally and *de facto* — the powers of initiation from the local units, the single governing board plugs up the fountain of initiative at which universities must refresh themselves if they are to play their proper role as critics of society.

Finally, there are some provinces in which historical conditions make it imperative — at least in the foreseeable future — that the trappings of local, institutional autonomy be preserved if the system is to develop in a peaceful and orderly fashion. One can think of provinces where a strong, centralized board would bring many economic, and perhaps even academic, advantages — mainly by overriding strong parochial and religious suspicions. But probably the social cost incurred in the process would be too great; it is not at all clear that allegiances and prejudices which are deep within the soil and the soul would disappear through an administrative reorganization.

[10]   *Ibid.*, 242.
[11]   Robert O. BERDAHL, *Statewide Systems of Higher Education* (pre-publication draft), Ch. 4.

C. PROPOSAL FOR A CO-ORDINATING COMMISSION

All in all, therefore, while we recognize both the temptation of logical neatness and the seemingly greater economy and efficiency of the single governing board, at least for provinces with three or more university campuses we recommend instead a co-ordinating and planning commission with a statutory base, a semi-autonomous status and substantial powers. Our conclusion is based mainly on our study of the Canadian situation, but also on experience elsewhere, especially in the American states:

> The co-ordinating board (commission, council, committee), often referred to as the "super" or "higher" board, is rapidly gaining ascendancy over all other methods of co-ordination. While the single governing board arrangement has gained only three new adherents in over thirty years, no less than thirteen new co-ordinating agencies have been formed in the past four years and several existing agencies have been given co-ordinating powers. The total in existence is now twenty-one. [12]

What we are proposing, then, is that the existing university advisory committees and grants commissions should be reconstituted. To correct their previous shortcomings, they should have the scope, powers, personnel and procedures proposed below;and to highlight their new status and functions, we suggest that they be renamed University Co-ordinating Commissions (UCCs).

a) SCOPE

Provincial governments will have to face the question of the co-ordinating agency's scope, that is, whether it should include other post-secondary institutions within its jurisdiction. There is no easy answer to this question, partly because the provincial systems of post-secondary education vary so much from province to province and are changing so rapidly. The main difference among the provinces is the extent to which education in the other post-secondary institutions *precedes* or is *an alternative to* a university education. The extreme examples of what we might call the *prior* and *parallel* systems are in

[12] Lyman A. GLENNY, "State Systems and Plans for Higher Education", in Logan WILSON (ed.), *Emerging Patterns in American Higher Education* (Washington, 1965), 91.

Quebec and Ontario. In Quebec, students must go through the new system of post-secondary colleges before they can go on to university, while high-school graduates in Ontario can either enter a university directly or go to one of the new community colleges. Most other provinces have a mixture of the two systems, with high-school graduates having three choices: they can enter a university directly, or first go through a junior or community college, or enrol in a technical institute or college. Since university-oriented students in the parallel segment of community and technical colleges should be able to transfer easily to the universities, all provinces have the problem of co-ordinating the course programs in their junior and other post-secondary colleges with those in the universities.

In our view, the question of the extent to which the other sector of post-secondary education should be a prior or a parallel one is vital because it affects the level, standards and accessibility of university education. Since it is beyond our terms of reference, we recommend that it be made the object of special study and public discussion.

Whichever way this question is answered, it seems that the need for the independence of the university system would be greater than that of the other sector of post-secondary education because of the special nature of universities. The ideal mechanism for the supervision and co-ordination of the universities, therefore, may not be as suitable for other post-secondary institutions. For this reason we feel that, on balance, the co-ordinating agency should not include other post-secondary institutions within its scope. Where the parallel post-secondary segment is small, however, and the government is prepared to grant it the same degree of independence as the universities, the advantages of co-ordination may be great enough for it to be included.

Some provinces, such as Ontario, Quebec and Alberta, which have a relatively large sector of other post-secondary institutions, have created a separate supervisory agency for this sector. In most other provinces this sector is also expanding rapidly, and a similar agency may be created. There is therefore developing the problem of co-ordinating the work of this agency with that of the university commission. One way of helping to meet this problem would be to have the chairman or some other member of the commission also serve as a member of the other post-secondary agency, and vice versa. An alternative would be for the government to create a co-ordinating committee composed of key representatives from both agencies. This mechanism has been used with considerable success in California for many years to co-ordinate the state university and college systems, and has been adopted recently in New South Wales, Australia.

b) POWERS

That the creation of a body responsible for the co-ordination and planning of higher education ought to be anchored in law is based on two considerations. Firstly, while the advisory capacity of such a body need not be limited, both advisory and executive functions should be spelled out by statute for greater certainty and the better protection of both the university community and the commission itself. The university community would thus be assured of the limits of the commission's powers, and the commission, by having statutory independence, would be less liable to charges of "being in the government's pocket". Secondly, in return the universities would be more willing to give up some of their previous claims of jurisdiction, while the government, apart from seeking the advice of the commission, could legitimately delegate to it some executive power. Or to put it in the words of a provincial premier: "We are convinced that this concept of a university commission will work only if each of the original parties — the universities and the government — transfer some parts of their traditional authority to the [. . .] commission." [13]

The question of what powers a new UCC ought to receive from the government and the universities cannot of course be answered in detail. The powers should, however, be based on its need to plan, to co-ordinate and to preview proposed programs.

[13] Letter from Premier Duff Roblin to Professor I. M. Rollo, Past President of the Association of the Academic Staff, University of Manitoba, June 20, 1967, as quoted in the brief from the University of Manitoba Students' Union, 13.

Because of the inherent stubbornness of established institutions, the major emphasis should be placed on planning. For reasons given below, the inevitable conflicts among the universities themselves and between them and the co-ordinating agency should take place, and be reconciled, at the planning rather than the executive stage. In this later stage, the power of the co-ordinating body should be limited to that of a policeman, a function easily performed if that body controls finances and if the earlier resolution of conflicts has resulted in a consensus among all participants. [14]

If planning can be described as the chief co-ordinating function of a central agency supervising higher education, preview is probably its most important instrument of control. If the powers of the co-ordinating agency are not to be used only in a negative or punitive way, it must have some prior opportunity to bring proposed costly programs into harmony with a general plan before extra money is granted for them. Whether this should be done through a "voluntary" accreditation procedure by the universities but backed by the financial policy of the central agency (as in Ontario for graduate studies), or whether the agency itself should assume responsibility for passing the judgment, is debatable. The first way gives wider participation in decision-making, while the second may result in more successful control. In any case, there should be a method through which costly new programs can be taken into account by the central agency before they are established, without being sprung on it at a late stage with no prior warning. This kind of occurrence would be rare if the province had a plan in which the participating institutions could see the reflection of both justice and their own aspirations.

The chief purpose, therefore, of the kind of agency we recommend would be to elaborate and supervise a master plan

[14] The practical working out of the relationship may take some time. As one of the most experienced American administrators put it: "In this area of working relationships between central state planning agencies and individual public institutions of higher education, I believe we are at present simply feeling our way. I doubt that we have found any definite solutions. Rather, I would guess that we must look forward to many years of experimentation." John D. MILLET, "State Planning for Higher Education", 46 *Educational Record* (Summer 1965), 227.

for universities. Consequently, the powers given to such an agency should be based on this purpose. Because we believe that conflict in higher education, as in all vital areas, is inevitable, it is our view that the most propitious battleground for such conflict is in the field of planning; by taking place in this field, the conflicts can be more peaceful and, above all, more creative. In addition, since they would be resolved in the realm of the future, the interplay of selfish interests would not be so strong. Hence, more rational justifications might prevail, and less legal authority might be needed to gain agreement.

At this point a word of caution may be in order. It is generally conceded that the joining of planning and executive functions in one body can often lead to a neglect of planning or to the inclusion in the planning of elements that are more concerned with administrative convenience than with social and academic goals. This was one of the reasons why we rejected the idea of a single governing board. The executive functions of the new university commissions should therefore be limited mainly to those necessary for developing and enforcing a master plan. The universities in each system should be able to develop enough leadership and co-operation to meet the remaining needs for co-ordination. To separate the planning and executive functions would require the creation of two overlapping bodies. A better alternative would be — and Canadian political tradition has lent itself to this — the provincial creation every five or ten years of a review committee with a membership broader than that of the university commission. In this way the social goals of the master plan could be reappraised and kept in tune with the times.

Another power often mentioned as desirable for the proper co-ordination of higher education is the power to review the budgets of individual universities. We recommend that the power to preview and approve detailed budgets should not be given to the UCCs. First of all, experience elsewhere indicates that where such a function is performed by the co-ordinating agency, it is frequently done badly and with little concrete value. Secondly, it is exactly this kind of power that poses the temptation to meddle in the administration of individual institutions and to ignore the far more important job of planning. Finally, the activities of financial review lead to the creation of a large bureaucratic superstructure at the centre and, worse still, the domination of this bureaucracy by non-academic values. It is dubious whether the state benefits from such activities in the short run; it cannot but suffer in the long run.

We therefore propose instead that the provincial governments should make a total annual sum available to the UCCs and that the UCCs should be required to use a general formula, like that already employed by some of the existing university commissions, for distributing a large proportion of this sum to the universities for both current and capital expenditures. This would make a detailed review of expenditure requirements unnecessary and would avoid suspicions of arbitrariness or favouritism in the allocation of grants.

However, the formula should not be used to distribute all of the money granted to a UCC for the universities. As explained in Chapter 6, such a formula does not take sufficient account of the variations among universities in size, age, traditions and programs, and tends to create an undesirable degree of uniformity. Also, since it is based on the existing level and balance of expenditures among programs, it discourages desirable changes and experiments. For instance, by taking into account only students in credit courses, it may prevent an expansion of non-credit courses for adults. We therefore recommend that only a major portion, say 75 per cent, of the total allocation should be required to be based on the formula. The remainder should be granted at the discretion of the UCC, after receiving proposals from the universities and consulting with university organizations, in order to take special circumstances into account and to promote desirable new developments. Also, the formula and its proportion of the total allocation should be revised every few years after consultation with university organizations, perhaps at the time that the proposed multi-year commitment of provincial grants is renewed.

In the absence of a detailed preview of university budgets, the financial accounts of universities should be made public, and the provincial governments should have the right of post-audit inspection. Whether the accounts are audited by the provincial auditor is of no great consequence, but certainly they should be submitted to the legislature and made subject to potential examination by its committee on public accounts. Moreover, the UCCs may well have an important part to play in helping to design a better and more uniform accounting system for universities.

We recognize that the above proposals regarding financial techniques, like our other proposals regarding mechanisms of provincial supervision, may not fit the special circumstances of particular provinces. We therefore conclude our discussion of finance with some general considerations that should be taken into account regardless of what particular techniques are adopted. Any method of finance contains value judgments, and is more than a mere mechanism. One should therefore define at the outset what objectives it is to serve and what circumstances it should take into account: whether it will give priority to the needs of individual institutions or to those of the whole system, whether the universities in a particular province have had a long and strong tradition of independence, the extent to which they are at different levels of development, whether the bicultural element exists, whether some universities need special catching-up grants, etc. One must then choose the particular techniques that best suit the circumstances. Whatever the techniques used, it is important that the allocation of grants should be made in accordance with explicit criteria which are publicly known and periodically debated.

Student aid is another possible area of jurisdiction for the UCCs. Regarding this important aspect of modern higher education, it is necessary to differentiate between administration and policy. Because of the danger of the UCC becoming primarily an administrative agency, the administration of student aid should not be under its direct jurisdiction. However, policy regarding student aid necessarily looms large in the planning of higher education and should therefore be among its advisory powers. Because the social consequences of decisions in this area are so great, the UCC should not necessarily expect the government to take its advice in this field. If the government announces a different policy, the UCC should then take this policy into account when developing its master plan.

As for other advisory powers of our proposed co-ordinating body, because its executive powers would be narrow, its advisory powers should be broad. There are of course important matters of policy regarding higher education that should ultimately be decided by the government — for instance, the creation and location of new universities and professional schools, and the general principles of university government to be followed in the charters of individual universities.[15] But to prevent parochial, partisan or arbitrary considerations from entering into decisions on such matters, a government should have the advice of a well-informed, dispassionate body, and should take its advice most of the time. Indeed, we favour a provision such as the one for Quebec's new Council of Universities which *obliges* the minister of education to seek the advice of the Council on the principal steps he proposes to take regarding the universities, though such a provision would be hard to enforce.

If the UCC's advice is given within the framework of a master plan to which the government has been a party and has given its blessing, one can expect both the UCC's recommendations and the government's response to them to be in harmony with the plan. This is one of the great advantages of a master plan. It helps to ensure that a government will make its decisions within a comprehensive, logical framework rather than on an *ad hoc* basis of political expediency in reaction to pressures of the moment.

c)   PERSONNEL

Regarding the personnel of the co-ordinating commissions, a matter of considerable importance is the size of the commission itself. There seems to be a consensus among observers that commissions with more than fifteen members decrease in their effectiveness. [16] Meetings are difficult, subcommittees must be formed, administrative and detailed problems tend to dominate

15   For an analysis of inconsistent variations found in the charters of Ontario universities, and a good argument for greater uniformity on important matters of principle, see the brief to our Commission from Mr. Tim Reid, M.P.P.
16   Cf. Arthur D. BROWNE, "The Institution and the System: Autonomy and Co-ordination", in *Long Range Planning in Higher Education* (Boulder, Colorado, 1965).

discussions, pressure for institutional representation increases, and eventual domination of the commission by the supposedly subordinate chairman or executive secretary are some of the problems arising from large membership. Consequently, we recommend as a limit a membership of fifteen.

Of greater importance is the problem of the commission's composition. While the commission should have statutory independence, it should also have the government's confidence. Consequently, the membership should have a majority of governmental appointees. At the same time there should be a stipulation — as in the statute for Quebec's Council of Universities — that some of them are to be appointed after consultation with representative organizations in the fields of business, labour, culture and the professions. This would not only assure a wider public participation in the shaping of the educational system but also give assurance that appointments will not be politically partisan. Moreover, since the commission will deal with matters which are of direct interest to the universities and for which an intimate knowledge of university affairs is required, a large proportion of the members should be from the academic community. In some provinces no provision has been made for academic representation on the existing university commission, and during our hearings in these provinces this was one of the most frequent complaints we heard from university, faculty and student representatives alike. In contrast with this is the provision for Quebec's Council of Universities that a majority must be from the academic community. Of seventeen members, nine are appointed after consultation with the authorities, faculty and students of the universities. Yet note that the requirement is "after consultation with" rather than "on the recommendation of."

We conclude that the academic representatives should compose up to half the membership of a UCC. If they are actually appointed or nominated by the academic community, a reasonable balance of membership would be approximately a third appointed directly by the government, a third appointed after consultation with interests outside the universities, and a third from the academic community. The UCC might be a body of twelve, with four of each. Thus there would be an equal meeting of minds from the three vital elements concerned — government, society and the academic community.

Experience with university commissions in other countries indicates that incumbent university presidents should not be appointed to such a commission, because they would find it difficult to think in province-wide terms and would be under suspicion of favouring their own institution. Experience elsewhere also indicates that universities should not be represented directly on the commission.

> This representative arrangement insures a close working relationship between planners and operating officials, but it can also tend to temper the planning activity to proposals acceptable to individual institutions. [17]

Also, even if representatives of all of the universities were included on the commission, the larger ones would still feel that they were under-represented. Be the provinces blessed with many universities or few, therefore, institutional representation is both an unnecessary and undesirable complication of an already difficult situation. Instead, we recommend that the academic representatives be nominated by the provincial committee of presidents and the provincial organizations of faculty and students.

There is some question whether the members appointed directly by the government should include senior civil servants, such as the deputy ministers of education and finance, and whether specific provision should be made for their inclusion, as with some of the existing university commissions. Because of their close association with the government, their inclusion might detract from the independence of the commission. Also, because they would serve over a long period of time, they, along with a government-appointed chairman, might even come to dominate it. On the other hand, the government's views should be represented on the commission, and since these officials would be in the minority, they would not dominate it if the other members assumed their full responsibilities. If the proceedings of the commission are made public, as proposed below, any

[17]   John D. MILLET, *op. cit.*, 226.

suspicion of domination could be easily verified. Moreover, their inclusion, especially the deputy minister of education, would contribute greatly to the co-ordination of higher education with other segments of the educational system and other governmental activities, and would give the commission the benefit of their long experience and wide knowledge of provincial affairs. We therefore conclude that at least the deputy minister of education and/or the head of the departmental branch for higher education should serve on the commission, but that if the government also appoints the chairman, it should not appoint more than two senior civil servants to the commission.

To prevent "hardening of the arteries" within the commission and possibly even the domination of higher education by a kind of oligarchy, the appointment of all members should be for a specified period of time and, depending on that period, renewable for no more than one term. A public service of four to eight years is probably all that should be asked of public-spirited men.

A closely related problem concerns the nature of the positions of chairman and executive secretary. The problem is so complex, and depends so much on personalities, that one cannot easily reach firm conclusions. Those who oppose the appointment of a full-time chairman, with the rest of the membership only on part-time basis, fear the domination of such an agency by its head. If he is appointed by the government, as with most of the existing university commissions, this may mean domination by the government, or at least the suspicion of such domination. Moreover, if he is the only full-time member of the commission, leadership and power tend to be concentrated in his hands, and too much depends upon his competence and personality. The whole system of higher education may come to be shaped by the ideas of one man. All the eggs of higher education are placed in one basket, so to speak. For these reasons we think that the commission should choose its own chairman, following the practice of the great majority of university boards of governors. But because there is a similar danger of a full-time executive secretary dominating the commission, we feel that, as a counter-balance, the chairman should serve full time.

The question of whether a university commission should have a large staff of its own or instead be served mainly by the staff in a government department has been hotly debated, especially in Ontario and Quebec. We have concluded that the commission should have an expert staff for its own purposes; if it is too dependent upon departmental staff, it may be dominated by the government. At the same time, there should also be a staff and special branch or section in the province's department of education which is particularly concerned with co-ordinating higher education with the other educational sectors, and the two staffs should work closely together. At first there will very likely be a gray zone between their fields of jurisdiction, and a period of adjustment will be necessary. Because of the need for co-ordination with other educational sectors, we think that a separate department of university affairs, as in Ontario, is unwise, even though in Ontario this need is partly met by having the same minister for the departments of education and university affairs.

Regardless of whether the commission has its own staff, a serious danger is the domination of the university commission and of higher education by a bureaucracy that is too narrow in its view. In the past there has been a tendency for the section on higher education in the provincial departments, and even for some university commissions, to be staffed with administrators from the lower levels of education who have little knowledge of universities. In future there will be an additional problem: co-ordination places great emphasis upon economy, efficiency and physical facilities, and central planning now requires sophisticated accounting, statistical and computer techniques. There will therefore be a danger that the administration of higher education will be dominated by narrow financial and engineering experts rather than by broadly-educated, humane administrators who understand the special nature of the university and its relation to society. This is why, in a later chapter, we recommend special programs of broadly-based graduate training for prospective administrators in the field of higher education.

d) PROCEDURES

For a number of important reasons we recommend that the legislation reconstituting the university commissions should make mandatory the publication of their proceedings, decisions, recommendations and studies. In the first place, such a requirement would make clear that the commission is not "in the government's pocket". Secondly, since the commission's recommendations and reasoning would be made public, if the government chose to ignore the advice of its expert body, it could do so only for good reasons that it would be willing to give and defend publicly. This would dispel any suspicion that the government had been influenced by arbitrary or narrowly partisan considerations.

By securing the confidence and co-operation of the universities, a more open process of decision-making would also reduce the need for direct intervention in their affairs. It would assure the universities and their component parts that a commission is "doing its home-work". It would deprive the press, the public and the government of any grounds for believing that universities are afraid of public scrutiny. And it would break down some of the mistrust (a certain amount of which, however, is unavoidable and healthy) that separates government from the universities, the universities themselves, and the various elements making up the university. Finally, it would educate not only the public and the government but also the academic community itself on the future needs of higher education. As in all good educational situations, full information would provide its own disciplinary corrective.

The above recommendation is also in line with our previous proposal that provincial legislatures should take more interest in higher education and should scrutinize it in their committee on education. We recognize that there is a danger in such scrutiny. Provincial legislators may take too much interest in the internal affairs of universities and may make such critical comments on the views or actions of individual scholars as to inhibit their academic freedom. The role of the legislator should rather be to study and debate important general principles and policies affecting higher education: the future development of the universities, their role within the whole educational structure, policy on accessibility and student aid, and similar topics. The UCC's published reports and documents, which would deal with such issues, would provide a good basis and focus for this study and debate.

Closely linked with the idea of openness is that of consultation and participation. Greater openness and wider participation in decision-making will become even more imperative as modern managerial and computer techniques penetrate higher education. The question will be: who is to control these techniques and to what uses will they be put ? If the universities are to retain an effective say in the determination of their goals — the objectives which the techniques should be employed to serve — a conscious effort will have to be made by the central decision-making agency to secure a broader consensus.

A procedural principle that the university commissions should adopt, therefore, is that of consultation with all universities on proposals that originate in one of them but that will affect the others. Program preview ought to include not only a scrutiny of such proposals by the commission itself, but also an opportunity for other institutions to voice their possible opposition to such proposals.

Because systems of higher education have grown in both size and complexity, it is not surprising that the various segments of the academic community have developed different interests and points of view. Before the growth of universities, it was possible to encompass these interests within a simple co-ordinating framework. Now it is necessary to devise formal channels of communication through which they can be expressed. Such formal links will have to be sponsored and fostered by the co-ordinating agency if it wishes to receive the benefit of the great variety of useful advice that the component parts of a "multiversity" have to offer. To expect that realistic planning, decision-making and co-ordination can take place only through contacts with institutions as units, especially as represented only by their legal heads, is short-sighted; the greater the complexity of higher education, the greater must be the complexity of advisory sub-systems. The links of legal authority must not be confused with those for information inputs. Channelling all flow of information to the co-ordinating agency through one funnel can lead only to ignoring important interests and leaving them unnecessarily dissatisfied.

Among the most important of these interests are the faculty and the students. Partly because of the present way in which universities are at present governed, these groups do not feel that the university heads and governing bodies adequately represent their views. It is true that university government is being reformed in the direction of greater faculty and student participation. But even after this reform has taken place, the faculty and students will still have interests quite distinct from those of universities as institutions. The faculty and students therefore need vigourous province-wide organizations to represent their interests. In some multi-university provinces such organizations still do not exist, and we recommend that they should be created. We also recommend that the university commissions should adopt the procedural principles of keeping these organizations fully informed, hearing representations from them at any time, and consulting with them on all important decisions and recommendations and on any other matters that directly affect their respective interests.

Since "the rules of the game" must be reciprocal, the university community also has some procedural obligations to a university commission. In order to preserve its independence, credibility, and proper role as a buffer between the universities and the government, universities and university organizations must not by-pass the commission by going directly to the government. During our travels, several examples of such short-circuiting were brought to our attention. For matters falling within the competence of a university commission, university heads and organizations should always in the first instance deal with the commission, and should make representations to the government only as a last-resort appeal against a decision or recommendation of the commission. Similarly, since it is always easy for an institution or organization to imagine that it has been dealt with unfairly, the government has an obligation not to encourage ill-founded appeals.

D.   CONCLUSION

A guiding consideration behind our proposals in this chapter has been the need to create conditions of mutual trust. In our view, the answers to important questions of social and academic policy must arise from the ongoing clash of the various interests involved, and must be continuously revised. Rather than try to find final answers to such questions, we have instead concentrated on proposing machinery and procedures through which the contending parties can reconcile their interests, develop mutual confidence, and more peacefully resolve their conflicts. Once these conditions are established, the substantive problems can be more easily discussed and solved.

In our opinion, such conditions will not exist until the powers and procedures of the provincial supervisory bodies are clearly set forth and known to all, until the provincial governments have confidence that the nature and powers of these bodies are adequate to protect the public interest, and until the various segments of the university community feel that their interests are fully protected by their representation on and access to such bodies.

PART III

Problems of Federalism

8. The Role of the Federal Government

A. THE CONSTITUTIONAL PROBLEM

In Part I we showed that in Canada, as elsewhere, the concept of the university is relative. It varies in time and space, since the university is a reflection of the surrounding society that it serves. For this reason we have stressed two aspects which are peculiar to Canadian society, i.e. the socio-cultural and the socio-economic differences within the country. We see these as basic factors; but the extent to which the spirit of the country's constitution is respected must not be overlooked.

a) WHAT DOES THE CONSTITUTION SAY ?

One should begin by referring to section 93 of the B.N.A. Act. This section has the English word "education" in its title, while the various French translations generally use the term *enseignement*, which has a narrower meaning, if not a more technical one. The section is quite precise, allowing little latitude of interpretation: only provincial parliaments may legislate in this field, subject to guarantees mentioned in paragraphs (3) and (4), concerning Catholic and Protestant religious minorities and their confessional schools.

But what is the scope of the meaning of the word "education" ? How should it be interpreted ? In our judgment, it should be interpreted — to resort to judicial language — in a liberal sense, to include the whole domain of education. To our knowledge, no judicial rule of interpretation allows one to restrict its scope. And this is consistent with our view that the university is (or should become) an integral part of the whole system of education.

Some arguments and testimony may be invoked in support of this interpretation:

1. The historical argument: As Mr. Ralph Mitchener noted in the December 1968 C.A.U.T. *Bulletin* (pp. 54-55), it is interesting to compare the text of the 1864 Charlottetown Conference

Resolutions with that of the 1866 Quebec Resolutions. While in 1864 higher education had been separated from the rest of the educational system, in order to entrust jurisdiction to the federal parliament, by 1866 this distinction had disappeared and the provincial parliaments inherited the whole domain. Even if university education at the time did not seem as important as it is today, it is nevertheless difficult to sustain the thesis that the framers of the B.N.A. Act of 1867 had not intended to include higher education in section 93, or had forgotten to do so.

2. The juridical argument: The *obiter dictum*, too easily forgotten, by Chief Justice Duff of the Canadian Supreme Court, should be brought to mind. In 1938 he affirmed — in *In re the Adoption Act* [1] — that the word "education" had been used in its broadest sense, and he reiterated that section 93 was a touchstone, a cardinal point of the Federal Compromise.

3. Mr. Pierre Elliott Trudeau took the same position in an article in *Cité libre* (February 1967), entitled "Federal Grants to Universities". This article was translated and reproduced in *Federalism and the French Canadians* (1968).

We may therefore conclude that from the beginning, as the Canadians of the time understood the need, a compromise was struck, based on societal differences having a three-fold dimension: confessional, cultural and regional.

Nevertheless, the question of jurisdiction over higher education has been the subject of considerable, often heated, debate during the last few decades. The advocates of federal intervention often derive their arguments from the reports of the Rowell-Sirois (1939), Massey (1951) and Bladen (1965) Commissions. These reports stress such arguments as the cost of education and the provinces' limited resources, the distinction between education and culture, and the national, even universal, role of the universities, which "serve the national cause in so many ways, direct and indirect, that theirs may be regarded as the

---

[1]   *Supreme Court Reports*, 1938, 402.

finest contributions to national strength and unity". [2] The Quebec autonomists have presented rebuttals in the report of the Tremblay Commission. [3] The members of this commission have concluded that provincial jurisdiction is exclusive, and that it is the duty of the federal government to direct its general and fiscal policies in such a way as to allow the provinces to play fully and completely the roles that fall to them under the constitution and that are required by the public good.

Present-day federal participation in the field of higher education is based mainly on three arguments. The first is the alleged unlimited power of taxation and spending of the federal government, a highly political problem recently discussed at the federal-provincial constitutional conference of June 1969. Concrete examples of the use of this power are the federal-provincial agreement of 1966, whereby the federal government finances part of post-secondary education (a critical analysis of this agreement follows), financial aid for students in the form of bursaries and loans, and grants for the health sciences. The second argument, also discussed elsewhere, is the federal government's interest in research. Although one cannot deny this interest, neither the federal government not its agencies should be allowed to intrude unduly into the operation of universities, or to paralyse a plan for their rational development prepared at the level of a province or mega-region. The third argument is the federal claim of exclusive jurisdiction over television broadcasting. The debate becomes more and more strident as this field of communications expands and as the federal government seeks to extend its regulatory activities to educational television.

b)   Conclusion

We hold the view that the grant of powers in section 93 of the B.N.A. Act coincides with the realities of Canadian

[2] Royal Commission on National Development in the Arts, Letters and Sciences, *Report* (Ottawa, 1951), 132. In the same vein: the personal brief submitted to our Commission in March 1969 by Dr. Henry Hicks, President of Dalhousie University.

[3] Royal Commission on Constitutional Problems, *Report* (Quebec, 1956), Vol. II, ch. VII.

society. We therefore intend to discuss not only the problem of federal-provincial co-ordination in areas where it is needed (e.g., research and manpower), but also how regional economic disparities may be alleviated without transferring jurisdiction to the federal level. [4] We are going to propose that the role of the federal government should be restricted so as to conform to the requirements of both the constitution and the facts of Canadian society. At the same time, we will recommend increased interprovincial co-operation and co-ordination at the regional and national levels.

B.   THE FEDERAL-PROVINCIAL AGREEMENT OF 1966

The federal-provincial financial agreement of October 1966 marks a major change in the relations between universities and governments. Before that time the federal government had been making large general grants to the universities outside of Quebec. As a result of the agreement these payments were stopped, and since then all general government support to the universities has been paid to them by the provincial governments. Though the implications of this shift in the nature of state support are far-reaching, they have not yet been fully realized by the academic community and even by some provincial governments in English-speaking Canada.

The federal grants to universities began in 1951 at the rate of 50¢ per capita of the population in each province, paid in accordance with student enrolment, and were raised in later years. From the beginning, however, the government of Quebec opposed the grants as an unconstitutional federal intervention in the field of education, and for several years instructed the universities in Quebec to refuse the money. As a result of protracted negotiations, in 1959 the federal government finally agreed instead to increase its corporation income tax abatement for Quebec under the general tax-sharing arrangements, from

---

[4] In the briefs to our Commission that supported federal intervention, the majority of the authors saw in it the opportunity of getting financial aid from another source, and thereby also escaping complete control by provincial departments of education. Very few authors openly extolled a transfer of jurisdiction: when questioned by the members of the Commission, most of them admitted that they were mainly thinking of dollars.

9 per cent to 10 per cent, and to pay the province any difference between this and the value of university grants that would otherwise be payable. Thus henceforth Quebec's government was free to make its own decisions regarding the level, nature and allocation of state support to universities.

The situation in 1966, then, was that the universities in Quebec received all of their general state support through the provincial government, while those in the other provinces were also receiving grants from the federal government through the medium of the AUCC. For the year 1966-67 these grants were raised from $2 to $5 per head of population, and were distributed to universities under a new enrolment formula which weighted students by degree, program and level, and which gave a supplementary grant for out-of-province students. [5] In that year the federal grants to universities outside Quebec totalled nearly $70 million and constituted about 16 per cent of their income. The remainder came from other types of federal support (about 11 per cent), provincial governments (about 45 per cent), student fees (about 20 per cent), and private sources. [6]

a) FEDERAL WITHDRAWAL FROM DIRECT INTERVENTION

At a federal-provincial conference in October 1966, the federal government made a set of proposals which, in effect, accepted Quebec's long-standing opposition to direct payments to universities. In presenting these proposals, Prime Minister Pearson spelled out the nature and extent of the federal government's interest in education and related fields. [7] He stressed that, under the Canadian constitution, the development of the pattern of education throughout Canada was a matter of provincial jurisdiction. At the same time, education — and particularly higher education — was obviously of profound importance to the economic and social growth of Canada as a whole. In view of the federal government's primary responsibility for employment and economic activity generally throughout Canada, it had

---

[5] See Ralph MITCHENER, "Education", in *Canadian Annual Review 1966*, 356.
[6] Based on figures given in *DBS Daily* (Oct. 29, 1968), 4.
[7] PRIVY COUNCIL OFFICE, *Federal-Provincial Conference Ottawa, October 24-28, 1966* (Ottawa, 1968), 6-21.

"specific and particular responsibilities to which higher education is relevant". Because of this, and its broad interest in the adequacy and equality of educational opportunity, the federal government proposed to assist the provinces in meeting the costs of education at the post-secondary school level. This was where the costs were rising most rapidly and dramatically, as had been emphasized in the Bladen Report.

He added that "this does not mean that the federal government can or should impose on the provinces any views as to how much money should be spent for education or in what way it should be applied". Both of these were matters for provincial decision, to be determined by provincial governments in the light of their own provincial needs and priorities. The fiscal contributions made by the federal government should be made in such a way that they did not influence the institutional structure of education within a province. This was a reason why the federal government felt that shared-cost programs such as those of the technical and vocational training agreements should not be continued. They inevitably pushed a province in the direction of developing those institutions for which costs could be shared.

He also pointed out that the level of federal support for education should have a realistic relation to the rise in the educational costs of the provinces, and should increase automatically as these costs rose. The lack of such a relationship had been a very real difficulty with the previous system of operating grants to the universities. The increase in provincial population and in education costs were clearly two very different things, especially in the area of post-secondary education where the cost increases were most dramatic.

The Prime Minister also declared that major areas of federal jurisdiction and interest directly related to education were cultural affairs, research, scholarships and bursaries to individuals, and adult occupational training.

b) The Nature and Impact of the New Scheme

The result of agreement on the federal proposals was that the federal government cancelled its general payments to universities, and phased out its support of technical and vocational training at the secondary level, except for adult occupational training. It substituted instead a fiscal transfer to the provinces for the general support of post-secondary education as part of the federal-provincial fiscal arrangements for the five-year period 1967-1972. Following the precedent of the special agreement with Quebec in 1959, the federal government transferred to all provinces a tax abatement of four points on personal income tax and one point of corporation income tax. The income from these points, plus a payment to equalize it in accordance with the general fiscal arrangements, is then adjusted to yield to each province the *greater* of (1) $15 per capita of the provincial population or (2) 50 per cent of the recognized operating costs of post-secondary education within the province.

Where a province receives the per capita payment, the amount automatically increases each year in accordance with the national increase in post-secondary expenditures across Canada. For 1968-69 the per capita amount was about $18.75. This alternative was provided in order to support more than 50 per cent of the cost for provinces whose post-secondary expenditures are low. Three of the provinces, Newfoundland, Prince Edward Island and New Brunswick, are receiving the per capita payment. A province must shift to the 50 per cent option in any year in which it would gain thereby, but once having done so may not revert to the per capita amount. This provision seems to have been designed to encourage the poorer provinces to spend more on post-secondary education.

Especially for the seven provinces on the 50 per cent option, the way in which "post-secondary operating expenditures" were defined was of critical importance in determining the value to them of the fiscal transfer. In the Federal Provincial Fiscal Arrangements Act, 1967, and its subsequent regulations, post-secondary education was defined as that for which junior matriculation or its equivalent is a prerequisite. This means that the arrangements recognize the operating costs of grade 13 in New Brunswick, Ontario and British Columbia, and those of grade 12 in Newfoundland, Nova Scotia, Quebec, Manitoba,

Saskatchewan and Alberta. [8] Operating expenditures exclude the following items: student financial aid; any capital debt or depreciation charge except the purchase of library books, periodicals and related items; alterations; ancillary enterprises such as residences, student unions, cafeterias, book stores, university presses, teaching hospitals and health services; overhead expenditures of provincial government departments; and all rental charges except for computer, data processing and photo copying equipment. Also excluded are income from assisted, sponsored or contract research, whether from federal or other sources, and any other federal payments for post-secondary education to either a province or its educational institutions, such as for hospital schools of nursing. An amount of 8.5 per cent of total operating costs is allowed for furniture, equipment, and the repair or renovation of buildings.

It is important to note that the new scheme includes the actual transfer of tax revenues to the provinces. Thus in 1967-68 the amount transferred, plus the accompanying equalization payments, came to about $240 million, while the additional educational adjustment payments were about $160 million. Hence the total value of the fiscal transfer for that year was about $400 million (see Table I). This figure is slightly higher than 50 per cent of the total recognized costs of post-secondary education, because it includes payments higher than 50 per cent to the three provinces on the per capita option. The provincial share of the remainder is much lower than 50 per cent because the total includes expenditures out of income from student fees and private sources. Post-secondary institutions other than universities and colleges account for about one-quarter of total recognized costs.

The impact of the new scheme upon both the universities and the provinces in English-speaking Canada was immediate and profound. From the viewpoint of the universities, it meant that all of their general state support now came from one source, which was by far the largest source of revenue. Hence their focus regarding the adequacy of their total revenues shifted

8   John B. MACDONALD and others, *The Role of the Federal Government in Support of Research in Canadian Universities* (Ottawa, 1968), 74.

almost completely to the provincial governments. In provinces
with more than one university, it was in the interest of the
universities that state support should be allocated among them
on an equitable and non-political basis. The provinces, too,
recognized this need, and speeded up their creation of special
bodies for allocating or advising on the allocation of grants.

In provinces such as Ontario and Nova Scotia, which had
a number of private and sectarian universities, another effect
was to accelerate their transition to public institutions. Under
the old system, the fact that they received part of their state
support from the provincial government and part from the
federal government tended to obscure the fact that the majority
of their funds came from the state. Now it became much
clearer to both the provincial governments and these universities
that they were in fact public institutions and had a direct
responsibility to serve the public interest. However, our impression is that parts of the academic community in some of these
universities still are not fully aware of the significance of this
transformation.

Another important result of the new agreement is that
provinces are now able to plan and budget for the development
of secondary and higher education as a co-ordinated system.
They can do this much more easily than they could before,
when universities were receiving less than half their revenues
from the province and tended to regard themselves as not
part of the provincial system of education. Our impression is
that much of the academic community and even some provincial
governments have not yet adjusted to the opportunities presented by this new situation.

c) University Criticisms of the Scheme

In their briefs to us, many academic groups in English-
speaking Canada were critical of the new sole dependence
upon provincial governments for general state support, on the
ground that this weakens the autonomy of universities. The
frequently-heard conventional wisdom was that "two masters
are better than one", since this reduces the danger of complete
domination by one. While we recognize that there is validity

in this argument, it is important to ask how much autonomy is necessary and why it is desired. Some academics told us frankly — and we have the uncomfortable feeling that many more share their view — that what they really meant by "two masters" was "no master" — a policy of divide and rule. [9] The implication is that either they do not see much need to serve the public interest or, like Plato's philosopher-kings, they feel more capable of interpreting the public interest than the elected representatives of the people.

One can argue that the need for a single level of government to supervise universities in order to guide their development as part of an articulated educational system is important enough to override the preference for "two masters". In any case, the view that "two masters" really means "no master" is no longer true. Now that state support to higher education has reached such a high level, one could not expect either the provinces or the federal government to make large grants to universities without some form of supervision to ensure that they serve the public interest. From this point of view, two masters may be worse than one because of divided control and lack of co-ordination. When federal support was relatively low and in the form of general-purpose grants, this was not a serious problem. But as we shall see in the next chapter, the problem is now beginning to arise in an acute form through the federal government's greatly increased financial support for research.

---

[9]   The following are extracts from the testimony of a leading Maritime university president at one of our public hearings: *President :* "I feel pretty certain that there is much less likelihood that the federal government would interfere with the policies of running the universities than would the provincial governments — if only for the reason that the federal government is more remote [. . .]. Now I think that the provincial governments should support the universities as well. In other words, in this instance, I would rather have two masters than one [. . .]. One reason why I say that I would like to have direct federal grants, as well as provincial grants, instead of having one person to control them all, is that by dividing our opponents or masters [. . .] we may be a bit stronger in dealing with each other [. . .]. There is less likelihood of the government that is farther away — which pays us on an acceptable formula — breathing down our necks than there is of the government that is close to us."
Commissioner : "In other words, more money and less control ? "
President : "You are no more subtle than I, my dear friend. I cannot disagree with you."

Another frequently heard criticism from the universities is that under the new arrangement the provinces are not obliged to spend the full amount of the fiscal transfer on higher education. Prime Minister Pearson made a particular point of this in presenting the federal government's proposals. While it is true for the three smallest provinces, which are on the per-capita option, it is not strictly true for the other seven, because the total of their additional adjustment payment depends upon the level of their operating expenditures for post-secondary education. If such a province spent less on post-secondary education, for each dollar of reduction it would lose a dollar from the federal treasury, so the impact of the scheme is the reverse. While technically these provinces are not obliged to spend on higher education, the effect is like that of a shared-cost scheme: they are attracted into spending even more because half the cost of any *additional* recognized expenditure is paid by the federal government.

A closely related university criticism is that the provinces may choose to spend more of the fiscal transfer on other types of post-secondary education. This is undoubtedly true. On the other hand, the nature of the system of post-secondary education within a province is legitimately a decision to be made by the provincial government, and there is no good reason why the universities should not have to compete for public money with other post-secondary institutions. It should also be noted that, in presenting the federal proposals, Prime Minister Pearson stressed the danger of the previous technical and vocational agreements distorting the educational structure in favour of post-secondary technical institutions. Under the new scheme a province no longer has a stronger incentive to establish and operate this type of institution. The effect of the new agreement, then, is to favour universities somewhat in relation to post-secondary technical education.

A special problem created by the agreement was that of support for the sectarian universities and colleges. Under the old arrangement the federal government had been making payments through the AUCC to all of its member institutions, a number of which were sectarian. Several of the provinces, including Ontario and the three most westerly ones, had refused to make grants to such institutions. The discontinuance of federal grants meant that they were in serious financial difficulties. The solution adopted by most of these provinces has been to pay them operating grants equal to about half of what the grants would have been if they had not been church-related, on the ground that this represents approximately what they would have received had the federal grants continued. However, the fact remains that while some provinces, such as Quebec and Nova Scotia, support sectarian institutions at the same level as non-sectarian ones, others do not. In the latter case, there is strong pressure upon the sectarian institutions to sever their church connections, and also pressure from them for full provincial support.

A special committee of the AUCC board of directors presented a brief to our Commission based on a study of church-related universities and colleges. Among other things it pointed out that, of the 59 institutions holding membership in the AUCC, 40 were at one time either church-sponsored or supported. Many have since either severed their connections with churches or established much looser connections. Though 24 still have some connection with a church, none of them is strictly sectarian in the sense of requiring members of the governing board or the president to be from the sponsoring church, or giving preference to church members in selecting staff or students, or imposing religious instruction.

"By and large", says the committee, "the remaining church-related institutions attempt to serve the Canadian population as a whole, and for all practical purposes they are doing the same work as the universities and colleges which are not church-related." The committee also stresses the need to encourage diversity and variety among institutions of higher education. Hence it urges full public support of church-related institutions provided that the public interest is adequately represented in their governance and academic policies, and that the principle of public accountability is maintained.

We question whether such institutions deserve "full" public support in the sense that they should receive state support at the same level as public non-sectarian institutions. However, we agree with the proposal, and recommend, that provincial governments should define and make known the conditions required for support from public funds, so that church-related institutions wishing to receive such aid may meet the stated conditions. Since the committee's recommendations have already been published, [10] and since a special commission has been set up by the Catholic institutions to study their problems in detail, we make no further recommendations on this subject.

d) PROVINCIAL AND GENERAL CRITICISMS

From the provincial point of view, a serious criticism of the new scheme is the difficulty of estimating the eligible costs, and the consequent inability to predict the full financial implications of the scheme. Another, arising from the difficulty of confirming the costs, is the time it takes to reimburse the provinces and to produce final figures. Though serious, these may be only short-term problems. More serious criticisms are the lack of prior consultation with the provinces and the continuing unpredictability of federal action, which may at any time interfere with provincial priorities. Without warning, the federal government suddenly shifted its support from secondary technical and vocational training to post-secondary education. The effect of withdrawing federal operating support from the previous program was virtually to require the provinces to pay the federal share, since it is almost impossible to cut back drastically an ongoing program. [11]

The technical and vocational scheme had already demonstated the undesirable effects of federal initiatives taken without adequate consultation, and of massive cost-sharing plans. [12]

[10] The brief has been approved by the AUCC board of directors and extracts from it were published in 10 *University Affairs* (July 1969), 22-23.

[11] A provincial minister of finance told us that, since the federal government may walk out of a program at any time, his government had decided to play the game prudently, and not be trapped into overspending on higher education, in case it might later have to pay the federal share.

[12] The timing and nature of the scheme were particularly inappropriate for Quebec. See G. Bruce DOERN, "Vocational Training and Manpower Policy", XII *Canadian Public Administration* (Spring 1969), 68-69.

Yet for most provinces the new arrangement is essentially a shared-cost scheme, since each *additional* dollar spent by the provincial government within the prescribed limits is matched by a federal dollar. It therefore suffers from the disadvantages characteristic of any cost-sharing plan for a limited purpose. First, it constitutes federal intervention in provincial affairs in the form of defining the limits of the costs to be shared. Thus the basic definitions were decided on without prior consultation. Second, the scheme presents the problem of defining "inclusions and exclusions": services included within it are highly favoured compared with closely related ones which are not. In this case the key definitions are "post-secondary" and "current operating costs". Since the average number of years of post-secondary schooling varies from province to province, it is impossible to arrive at a definition of "post-secondary" which is fair to all provinces. Similarly, the dividing line between current and capital costs, or between central and ancillary services, is not an easy one to draw.

A third disadvantage is that the federal government must have evidence of the amounts actually spent on items falling within the definitions. This not only requires most provinces to submit certified and audited statements of cost to the federal government, but also requires them and all of their post-secondary institutions to keep accounts in accordance with the definitions of eligible costs. Also, the Fiscal Arrangements Act, 1967, gives the federal Comptroller of the Treasury the power, after consultation with the appropriate provincial authority, to examine any financial return for a secondary or post-secondary institution. Indeed, out of fear that some provinces may stretch the accounting definitions to include additional eligible costs, the federal government may even be tempted to ask selected universities if it may examine their accounts without this prior consultation. Thus the scheme is hardly conducive to confidence and trust between governments or between universities and governments. As Professor E. F. Sheffield said in his memorandum to our Commission (p. 2):

> The insertion of the shared-cost feature of the arrange-
> ment launched the federal government into a process of
> categorizing and scrutinizing expenditures which made a

mockery of the theory [of enabling the provinces to assume their constitutional responsibilities in the field of post-secondary education] and introduced unnecessary complexity in its application.

Even more serious is that a shared-cost scheme creates "forced draft" spending on services within the limits of the definition, and a consequent reduction of funds spent on other provincial services. Thus, although Mr. Pearson pointed out that the total value of the federal transfer was intended to cover increasing capital costs, the effect of the scheme is to favour expenditures on current costs and is likely to leave the growing capital needs of post-secondary institutions inadequately provided for. Similarly, it puts a high premium on provincial spending for post-secondary education relative to other levels of education and other provincial services, and is likely to distort the pattern of provincial spending. For instance, in a particular province, it may be desirable to spend more on elementary or secondary education, or on the economic development of the province, than on post-secondary education.

It should also be noted that the definition of current operating costs includes costs paid for from student fees. Since in seven provinces every two-dollar *increase* in cost paid out of student fees is matched by a federal dollar paid to the provincial government, some of these provinces may be tempted to favour an increase in student fees. The strength of this temptation depends partly on what proportion of student fees a province is indirectly paying in the form of student aid. The temptation would be neutralized if it were paying as much as half.

Another criticism of the shared-cost portion of the scheme is that it provides inadequate equalization to the poorer provinces. In other words, provinces which are able to spend more on post-secondary education get more money from the federal government. Proportionately, the poorer provinces are unable to spend as much and hence lose the matching federal dollars. If they do spend more so as not to lose federal dollars, this is likely to distort their pattern of spending even more seriously than in the wealthier provinces. A complicating problem is that a province such as Nova Scotia may have a disproportionately high number of out-of-province students, and therefore much higher costs for post-secondary education. Even though the federal government shares these costs, the province must still find the money for its own share.

A general criticism of the scheme is that the extent of federal support is not clear. From the viewpoint of the federal government, the cost of the new arrangement is the whole value of the tax transfer plus the equalization and education adjustment payments, minus the cost of its former support of secondary technical and vocational education. On the other hand, since it actually transferred tax sources, and stressed that provincial revenue from the scheme need not be spent on post-secondary education, the provinces can argue that only the equalization and/or education adjustment payments, or even that none of this revenue, can legitimately be claimed as federal support for post-secondary education. Hence, while the federal government claims that it is paying for half the cost of post-secondary education, the provinces tend to give it little credit for expenditures in this area. As a result, the public are confused about the actual extent of federal support.

Another problem, which results from the open-ended nature of the scheme, is that it may cause over-spending on post-secondary education by both levels of government. It encourages more expenditure at the provincial level and places no limit on the matching expenditure at the federal level. In view of the rapidly rising costs of post-secondary education, this places a heavy strain on budgets at both levels of government. The total of eligible expenditures under the plan increased by 25 per cent in the second year, and was expected to increase by at least 25 per cent in the third year (1969-70), to about $1.25 billion (see Table I). Though the whole impact of the scheme is to favour greatly the expansion of post-secondary education, it is impossible to determine objectively how much should be spent on this level of education in relation to other levels and other governmental services.

e)   CONCLUDING PROPOSALS

A proposal which would help to solve the problem of possible over-spending on post-secondary education would be to place a ceiling on the federal share based on a rising dollar figure per capita, or per capita of the post-secondary age group. A ceiling such as this was placed on the federal contribution to the capital costs of technical and vocational training. As with the technical and vocational scheme, however, this proposal would not solve the problem of the poorer provinces being unable to match the federal money and thus to reach the federal ceiling, nor would it meet most of the other basic criticisms of a shared-cost scheme.

These criticisms could be met by removing entirely the cost-sharing feature of the scheme. This could be done by extending the provision for increasing dollars per capita that is now enjoyed by three of the provinces to all of the provinces. However, the relative number of people in the post-secondary age group differs considerably from province to province, and hence the expenditure requirements per capita for each province are different. The per-capita plan could, therefore, be made much more equitable by basing the per-capita amount on the post-secondary age group rather than on the whole population of a province. [13] Under such a revision of the scheme the provinces would be free to spend the federal adjustment payment on other levels of education or other governmental services, according to their own priorities (though they would probably be forced by post-secondary needs to spend the bulk of it on post-secondary education). Such a revision would therefore go far toward meeting the objection that the scheme is an invasion by the federal government into the provincial field of education. But it would not meet this objection entirely because the federal adjustment payments would still be mainly intended to support expenditures and to equalize opportunities in a specific area of provincial responsibility: post-secondary education.

We therefore propose that the existing scheme should be abandoned, and instead that federal support for provincial

[13] We are indebted to H. W. Kitchen for his presentation of this proposal, and his demonstration of its more equitable impact, both in *University Education in the Atlantic Provinces : the Next Decade,* a study done for the Atlantic Development Board in 1968, Ch. VI, and at one of our hearings.

expenditures should become more general and unconditional while at the same time federal equalization of provincial financial abilities should be made more thoroughgoing. This could be achieved through a further transfer of tax points to the provinces, and an accompanying revision of the general federal-provincial equalization arrangements designed to grant additional aid to the poorer provinces. However, since these equalization arrangements are based only on differences in provincial revenue-raising ability and do not include differences in expenditure requirements, they could not, in their present form, grant sufficient aid to the poorer provinces. Mr. Pearson admitted this in presenting the 1966 proposals. The equalization formula would therefore have to be revised to take into account the differences among the provinces in their expenditure requirements. One index of these differences, of course, would be the number in the post-secondary age group relative to provincial population. The implementation of our proposal would place the provinces in a strong and relatively equal position to pay for post-secondary education while at the same time allowing them to retain full constitutional control over the field of education.

C. REMAINING AREAS OF FEDERAL INTEREST

As we have seen, one of the main objectives of the federal government in its proposals of 1966 was to demonstrate that it did not wish to have any direct control over higher education. In several remaining areas, however, federal programs or grants still have a strong impact upon the nature and development of universities. In most cases this impact has a distorting effect, either because it develops some fields at the expense of others or because it does not accord with provincial priorities. Our recommendations are therefore designed to restrict the federal role in areas bearing directly on higher education and to improve federal-provincial co-ordination in areas of joint concern.

The most important of these areas is the support of university research. Here the impact of federal support is so great and so complex that we have devoted a whole section of the next chapter to the problem. In most other areas the impact is less direct because the support is given either in the form of payments to the provinces for shared-cost programs or in the form of student aid. In either case, however, the impact is great. The shared-cost programs involve ear-marked payments by the provinces to the universities for particular programs, while student aid affects not only a province's priorities regarding accessibility to education but also the nature and total number of students at universities.

a)   HEALTH AND WELFARE GRANTS FOR UNIVERSITIES

One of the most long-standing federal schemes involving payments to universities is the program of health and welfare grants begun in 1948. It is designed to expand the training of professionals in the various fields of health and welfare. Through it the federal government shares with the provinces half the cost of payments to post-secondary institutions and hospitals for new training programs, staff salaries, travel expenses and teaching equipment. With the imminent introduction of a Canada-wide program of health insurance, these grants have been stepped up considerably. In 1966-67 the federal share of the grants was nearly $2 million. [14] A more recent program is the Health Resources Fund, to provide capital aid to medical colleges and similar institutions. It was established in 1966, to be matched by provincial funds for specific projects, with a projected total of $500 million to be granted over a fifteen-year period.

Although under these programs the projects for which federal aid is approved must be proposed by the provinces, the federal grants have the usual distorting effect of any shared-cost program: they encourage over-expenditure in the particular areas for which the cost is shared. Also, since these grants are made mainly through provincial departments of health, they tend to divorce health science faculties from the rest of the university and to prevent a co-ordinated consideration of a university's operating and capital requirements. In fact, we gained the impression during our hearings that the grants under

---

[14]   EDUCATION SUPPORT BRANCH, DEPARTMENT OF THE SECRETARY OF STATE, *Federal Expenditures on Post-Secondary Education, 1966-67, 1967-68* (Ottawa, 1969), 16, 18. Succeeding federal expenditure figures in this section, except for doctoral studies, are also from this publication.

the Health Resources Fund program are so large [15] that already they have had the effect of distorting the building programs of universities. We heard complaints that the program was creating luxurious quarters for the medical sciences, with a continuing costly upkeep, in relation to other university buildings and equipment.

We have therefore come to the conclusion and recommend that the federal government should discuss with the provinces the advisability of withdrawing from its grants for health and welfare training programs, either phasing out or greatly reducing its capital grants for health sciences, and making an equivalent transfer of tax revenues and equalization payments to the provinces. We also recommend that all capital grants for the health sciences should become part of an integrated system of provincial support to the universities.

b) STUDENT AID

In 1967-68 the federal government provided about $37 million worth of aid to university students under several different programs. These programs are not co-ordinated and have varying effects upon the university system. For instance, the Central Mortgage and Housing Corporation has been providing extensive capital assistance to universities since 1960 in the form of loans for the construction of student residences. It also makes loans to student co-operative organizations. In some cases its loans are provided through a provincial agency, such as the Ontario Student Housing Corporation.

The most general federal provision for student aid is the Canada Student Loans Plan, which began in 1964. Under the Plan the federal government guarantees loans made by chartered banks and designated credit unions on the basis of certificates of eligibility issued by the participating provinces. The government carries the cost of interest payments while a post-secondary

---

[15] An example is the grant of $34.2 million to McMaster University, announced by the Department of National Health and Welfare on May 31, 1969, toward the building of a $66 million health complex, containing a college of health sciences and a teaching hospital, to be completed by 1971.

student is in full-time study and for six months afterwards. Quebec operates its own scheme but receives in compensation a federal grant roughly equivalent to its share of the federal interest payments. Student use of the Plan has grown rapidly. In 1968-69 some 120,000 students borrowed over $70 million. Loans were expected to reach about $95 million in 1969-70, and the cost of the Plan for administration and interest payments, including the compensation to Quebec, about $11 million. In Ontario it is used by about one-third of all post-secondary students. [16]

Certain other forms of student aid are granted indirectly through the provinces under shared-cost programs, notably the health and welfare training scholarships and awards begun in 1948 for medical, nursing, physical education, welfare students, etc. In 1966-67 the federal share of these health and welfare grants was $4.4 million. Grants made directly to students include awards to the children of war pensioners and war dead, Indians, and students from the Yukon and Northwest Territories (totalling about $2 million in 1967-68). Grants to students also include awards for graduate study by the federal research councils (the National Research Council, the Medical Research Council and the Canada Council), and by a small number of other federal departments and agencies. For M.A. work the total value of these grants in 1967-68 was about $1.4 million, while for doctoral studies they totalled about $13.3 million. [17]

Another large category of federal student aid is that given by the Canadian International Development Agency (formerly External Aid Office), and a smaller amount by the Department of External Affairs, for foreign students studying in Canada. In 1967-68 the cost of this aid was about $9.4 million, including $1.2 million for doctoral studies. Although the Agency makes contracts with the universities for special group training pro-

---

[16] "Student Loans a Sound Investment", *Globe and Mail* (May 8, 1969).
[17] This last figure has been calculated from information given in the EDUCATION SUPPORT BRANCH's *Federal Expenditures on Research in the Academic Community, 1966-67, 1967-68* (Ottawa, 1968), but is only an estimate since awards for doctoral study are not in all cases separated from other research expenditures.

grams and provides university operating grants of $500 per Commonwealth scholar, it makes no direct payment to the provinces or the universities for the cost of educating other foreign students which it supports. Since fees represent only about 20 per cent of this cost, the provinces are paying a large share of it through their general support to the universities. Except where a research grant covers part of the cost, the same situation pertains to the large number of graduate foreign students supported by awards from the National Research Council, and to a much smaller number supported by the Canada Council.

The effect of the Student Loans Plan is to set a general social policy in the field of education regarding the nature of student aid and of accessibility to higher education. Also, federal aid to special categories of students favours these students relative to others (e.g. potential teachers), and makes it virtually impossible for a province to design a co-ordinated, fair system of student aid. We therefore feel that the federal government should withdraw from all forms of student aid except for categories for which it is specifically responsible, such as Indians, the children of veterans, and foreign students brought to Canada under its external aid program.

The Macdonald Committee has taken the view that grants by the federal research councils to graduate students are a form of assistance to research. [18] But these grants have the effect of encouraging the development of new graduate teaching programs or the expansion of existing ones, and of requiring the provinces to pay a very large share of the tremendous resulting cost. Yet the grants are given without any consultation with the provinces or reference to their plans for university development. When this factor is combined with the impact of federal support for research, the provinces have difficulty in controlling the development and cost of graduate studies. For this reason we propose the withdrawal of federal support even from graduate

18   John B. MACDONALD and others, *The Role of the Federal Government in Support of Research in Canadian Universities* (Ottawa, 1969), 202.

students, and the substitution of planned provincial programs of graduate aid. [19]

In summary, then, we recommend that, in order to enable the provinces to decide their own educational policies and priorities, and to develop and finance integrated programs of student aid, the federal government should propose to the provinces that it withdraw from all forms of student aid, except for categories of student for which it is specifically responsible, and make an appropriate compensating transfer of tax revenues and equalization payments to the provinces. We also recommend that the federal government pay to the provinces a sum equal to the cost to them of educating foreign students supported by federal agencies. Since the provinces also have a responsibility for foreign students and Quebec already has a program in this area, federal policies regarding foreign students should be worked out in consultation with the provinces and their university commissions.

c) MANPOWER TRAINING AND FORECASTING

Other more general areas of federal interest which touch upon university affairs are the contribution of education to economic production, and manpower training and planning. One of the main reasons the federal government gave for its general support of post-secondary education in the agreement of 1966 was the contribution of higher education to production, even though the importance of this contribution relative to that of other levels of education is not specifically known. The federal government also makes large shared-cost payments to the provinces for specific types of manpower training. Since the agreement of 1966, however, it has shifted its support from regular school or post-secondary programs to short courses for

[19] We recognize, however, that the preparation of a Ph.D. thesis may be considered as much a contribution to knowledge as to graduate training, and that federal grants to Ph.D. students to enable them to write their theses, like grants to post-doctoral students for research, may be considered by many people as support for research. Also, assistance at this level does not have the same impact upon the growth of graduate programs since the student would already have entered a Ph.D. program and would have completed all but his thesis before receiving the federal support. There may therefore be a case for federal grants to Ph.D. students who are working on a thesis.

re-training, so that the effect on higher education has declined. In 1967-68 it made capital grants for manpower training at the post-secondary level of $12.5 million, and operating grants of $6.1 million, a decline from $11.2 million in the previous year.

Because of its interest in economic production, the federal government is naturally concerned with forecasting and meeting manpower requirements, and because of the presumed importance of high-level manpower it is especially interested in the supply of university graduates. For instance, the Economic Council of Canada has stressed the need for meeting high-level manpower requirements. [20] Also, the Department of Manpower and Immigration has recently taken over from the AUCC "Operation Retrieval" — a program designed to attract Canadian graduate students at foreign universities back to jobs in Canada, and the Department is now doing studies of high-level requirements.

The provinces have a parallel interest in provincial economic production and the related manpower requirements. Because of their control over educational institutions, they are also deeply involved in meeting manpower needs, and especially in providing guidance to prospective university students about career possibilities and long-term needs for professional manpower. It is therefore important that the federal and provincial authorities concerned should co-ordinate their manpower policies and programs. Among other things, in order to avoid duplication of effort and to ensure prediction on a common base, they should co-ordinate the forecasting of the long-term requirements for professional manpower.

d) OTHER AREAS OF INTEREST

Although the federal activities discussed above are the ones having the most direct impact upon universities, a number of others are also related to university affairs. For instance, the federal government operates three military colleges, on which it spent $13.6 million in 1967-68. The colleges have programs similar to those of the universities, and the largest of them, the

[20] See its *Second Annual Review* (Ottawa, 1965), 94-95.

Royal Military College, grants degrees and is a member of the AUCC. The federal government recruits much of its professional personnel from among university graduates, and each year representatives of the civil service commission visit campuses for this purpose. Also, the new bilingual language policy for civil servants is likely to encourage and improve the teaching of a second language at Canadian universities.

Some of the ways in which federal activities touch the universities arise out of its general programs and interests, which are only incidentally concerned with the universities as such. Thus the federal government has a general responsibility for providing statistical information through the Dominion Bureau of Statistics. Though the Bureau's function is restricted to collecting and providing statistical information, good comparative statistics are of vital importance to research and planning for higher education. The Bureau is aware of the need for improved statistics on education. It recently commissioned a study of requirements in this area,[21] which proposed that the staff of its Education Division should be strengthened, and that it should work closely with the information systems committee of the Council of Ministers of Education. The Bureau is now trying to implement these proposals.

The federal government also has a general interest in stimulating and supporting a Canadian cultural identity. On the other hand, the provincial governments — especially that of Quebec — wish to support a provincial identity. One aspect of this division of interest is the recent debate with the provinces regarding control over educational television, which involves the subtle distinction between "informing" and "educating" adults. The result of this debate is obviously of importance to the universities. Since it is part of a broader constitutional debate, however, we make no recommendations on the subject other than to suggest that the respective jurisdictions in this sphere should be clarified by constitutional amendment.

Another aspect of this interest in a Canadian identity, of particular relevance to universities, is the recent concern over

[21] David C. MUNROE, *Statistical Services in Education for Canada* (Ottawa, 1968).

the high proportion of foreign professors being hired in Canadian universities. Curiously, federal tax policy has actually encouraged this development. The federal government has reciprocal tax agreements with a number of countries, including the United States and Britain, which grant a complete tax exemption of up to two years to foreign teachers who at the time of arrival state their intention to return to their home country, even though they may later decide to remain in Canada. Since the justification for this exemption appears to be doubtful, we recommend that the federal government should discuss with the provinces whether these agreements should be continued in their present form.

Another area in which federal interests touch the universities, but in a very vital spot involving academic freedom, is the preservation of national security. In addition to defence research, to be discussed later, another indication of the influence of the military establishment on Canadian universities is the federal financing of several chairs of military history. Of more direct concern are surveillance of professors and students by security officers of the RCMP, and decisions by the Minister of Manpower and Immigration on the admissibility of foreigners invited to teach or lecture in Canadian universities. In recent years, the CAUT has on several occasions complained about these investigations and decisions, and has made proposals for improving the methods and procedures used. Both the CAUT and the AUCC have presented briefs on the subject to the Royal Commission on Security. Related problem areas are the security clearance of students or university personnel seeking government employment or research contracts, and access by scholars to government information.

All of these problems are complex, since they involve drawing a delicate and difficult line between the interest of the state in national security and the interest of the university and society in freedom of information and of the individual. Recognizing their importance, we commissioned Professor Hugh Lawford to do a special research study of them. [22] Because his long report was completed very late in our project year, we

22   *Security and the Universities*, Commission study no. 19, 196 pp.

have not had time to digest it or make detailed recommendations on these problems. However, we hope that his thorough analysis will make a valuable contribution to their solution, especially since the Royal Commission's Report, as published in abridged form in June 1969, had little to say on the subject.

Aside from these general ways in which federal interests and programs affect the universities, it has been argued that the federal government has a legitimate role to play in a special area affecting education: that of supporting Canadian unity through protecting and supporting the French language and through providing for inter-language student exchanges. Thus the Royal Commission on Bilingualism and Biculturalism has proposed federal grants to support francophone teachers' colleges and universities in minority language areas. [23] Similarly, an AUCC committee has recently proposed that the federal government should launch and pay for a program of exchanging students between francophone and anglophone universities. It has also been argued that the federal government should promote the interprovincial mobility and exchange of students generally, and should pay the extra cost where the number of out-of-province students is greater than average. However, federal programs in any of these areas would be regarded as an intervention in the provincial field of education.

We therefore recommend that the federal government should take no action on any of these matters, unless this is done through prior discussion with and the full agreement of all provinces, and their full agreement to any necessary constitutional amendment. We should also like to stress that similar action could be taken by the provinces themselves through interprovincial cultural agreements and the machinery for interprovincial co-ordination recommended in Chapter 10.

[23] ROYAL COMMISSION ON BILINGUALISM AND BICULTURALISM, *Report, Book II : Education* (Ottawa, 1968), Part II.

TABLE I

Estimates of Post-Secondary Education Basic Fiscal Transfer and Adjustment Payments Under the Terms of the Federal-Provincial Fiscal Arrangements Act, 1967, Fiscal Years 1967-68, 1968-69, and 1969-70

Fiscal Year and Province	Estimated Total Eligible Post-Secondary Operating Expenditures[1]	Estimated Population April 1, 1967	50% of Eligible Post-Secondary Operating Expenditures	Per Capita Alternative[2]	Estimated Value of Transfer of Fiscal Resources (Greater of 3 or 4)	Estimated Value of Fiscal Transfer Portion (tax abatements and equalization)[3]	Estimated Value of Cash Adjustment Payments Portion (5 minus 6)
	1	2	3	4	5	6	7
	($000)	($000)	($000)	($000)	($000)	($000)	($000)
1967-68							
Newfoundland	6,742[4]	500	3,371	7,500	7,500	5,521	1,979
Prince Edward Island	2,123	109	1,062	1,635	1,635	427	1,208
Nova Scotia	31,397	756	15,699	11,340	15,669	8,465	7,204
New Brunswick	16,234[4]	619	8,117	9,285	9,285	6,941	2,344
Quebec	212,800	5,854	106,400	87,810	106,400	62,639	43,761
Ontario	304,414	7,115	152,207	106,725	152,207	97,343	54,864
Manitoba	35,826	961	17,913	14,415	17,913	10,704	7,209
Saskatchewan	36,540	955	18,270	14,325	18,270	7,370	10,900
Alberta	75,604	1,483	37,802	22,245	37,802	15,846	21,956
British Columbia	67,803	1,938	33,902	29,070	33,902	24,881	9,021
TOTAL	789,483	20,290	394,743	304,350	400,583	240,137	160,446[5]
1968-69							
Newfoundland	8,090[4]	—	4,045	9,398	9,398	6,185	3,213
Prince Edward Island	3,077	—	1,539	2,049	2,049	995	1,054
Nova Scotia	39,346	—	19,673	—	19,673	9,363	10,310
New Brunswick	19,480[4]	—	9,740	11,634	11,634	7,678	3,956
Quebec	266,100	—	133,050	—	133,050	73,129	59,921
Ontario	391,400	—	195,700	—	195,700	113,789	81,911
Manitoba	43,905	—	21,953	—	21,953	11,953	10,000
Saskatchewan	42,708	—	21,354	—	21,354	8,426	12,928
Alberta	91,967	—	45,984	—	45,984	17,476	28,508
British Columbia	82,931	—	41,466	—	41,466	28,943	12,523
TOTAL	989,004	—	494,504	—	502,261	277,937	224,324

TABLE I (Continued)

Estimates of Post-Secondary Education Basic Fiscal Transfer and Adjustment Payments Under the Terms of the Federal-Provincial Fiscal Arrangements Act, 1967, Fiscal Years 1967-68, 1968-69, and 1969-70 (concluded)

Fiscal Year and Province	Estimated Total Eligible Post-Secondary Operating Expenditures[1]	Estimated Population April 1, 1967	50% of Eligible Post-Secondary Operating Expenditures	Per Capita Alternative[2]	Estimated Value of Transfer of Fiscal Resources (Greater of 3 or 4)	Estimated Value of Fiscal Transfer Portion (tax abatements and equalization)[3]	Estimated Value of Cash Adjustment Payments Portion (5 minus 6)
	1	2	3	4	5	6	7
	($000)	($000)	($000)	($000)	($000)	($000)	($000)
1969-70							
Newfoundland	10,113	—	5,057	11,748	11,748	6,759	4,989
Prince Edward Island	3,846	—	1,923	2,561	2,561	1,456	1,105
Nova Scotia	49,183	—	24,592	—	24,592	10,082	14,510
New Brunswick	24,350	—	12,175	15,543	14,543	8,286	6,257
Quebec	332,625	—	166,313	—	166,313	78,677	87,636
Ontario	489,250	—	244,625	—	244,625	122,569	122,056
Manitoba	54,881	—	27,441	—	27,441	12,888	14,553
Saskatchewan	53,385	—	26,693	—	26,693	9,074	17,619
Alberta	114,959	—	57,480	—	57,480	18,855	38,625
British Columbia	103,664	—	51,832	—	51,832	31,174	20,658
TOTAL	1,236,256	—	613,131	●	627,828	299,820	328,008

[1] Eligible post-secondary education operating expenditure estimates for 1967-68 and 1968-69 were submitted by most provinces in 1968. For the initial 1969-70 estimates shown, which will be revised shortly when more precise provincial estimates are available, the 1968-69 figures were increased by 25 per cent.

[2] For 1967-68: $15 multiplied by 1967 population. For 1968-69, the total transfer for each of the three original $15 per capita provinces was increased in proportion to the national increase in estimated expenditures from 1967-68 to 1968-69 (i.e. by just over 25 per cent). For the 1969-70 estimates, a 25 per cent increase over 1968-69 was used.

[3] The figures for 1967-68 include final Department of Finance estimates of the tax abatements (made in March 1969) and preliminary estimates of equalization payments (made in July 1967). The 1968-69 values shown are March 1969 preliminary estimates made by the Department of Finance. The 1969-70 preliminary estimates were made by the Department of Finance in December 1968.

[4] These are not provincially-submitted estimates.

[5] $108 million was paid during the 1967-68 fiscal year. An estimate of the balance required for 1967-68 is included in the 1968-69 Estimates and is expected to be paid before the end of the 1968-69 fiscal year.

Source: House of Commons Debates, Daily Edition, March 26, 1969, 7137-38.

9. The Support of University Research

Today universities have become so central to solving the problems of modern society that they have been referred to as "the knowledge industry". Gone are the days when a scholar could freely choose and pursue his own line of investigation without reference to anyone else. University research has become part of "Big Science", and its support is now a very large item in the budgets of governments. The growing importance and cost of research is now raising a number of serious questions regarding research policy, the allocation of government support to university research, and the proper roles of the provincial and federal governments in the support of research.

A. PROBLEMS OF RESEARCH POLICY

a) THE PROBLEM OF RESEARCH PRIORITIES

The allocation of large sums of money to the support of research inevitably poses the problem of priorities in the allocation of these sums among the various sectors, fields and kinds of research. For instance, how much research should be done by government itself, how much by industry and how much by the universities ? What is the proper division among the broad fields of knowledge: the natural and biological sciences, the social sciences and the humanities ? Or between basic and broadly oriented research on the one hand, and applied research and development on the other ? To further complicate matters, it is difficult to draw a line between the various fields of knowledge and kinds of research.

Another complicating factor is that the cost of research varies between fields and kinds of research. Most research in the natural sciences and much applied research in the social sciences is very costly. The small amount of money spent on scholarly work in the humanities may be no measure of the importance of this work to society. Similarly, a small additional allocation to research in the social sciences may produce much more beneficial results than the same amount of money added to research in "Big Science".

The process of allocating funds for research support requires decisions to be made about all of these difficult problems. But under the present system of research support in Canada, these decisions are not made in a conscious, organized and co-ordinated manner, after thorough study and discussion. Also, although the broad allocation of public funds must remain a government responsibility, the way in which they are allocated influences the objectives and freedom of university research. For this reason, representatives of the academic community should be intimately involved in this decision-making process.

b)   THE TOTAL AND BALANCE OF UNIVERSITY RESEARCH

A related question about which there has been very little thought or discussion has been raised by the recent tremendous growth in the size of universities. There has been a multiplication of the number of academics wishing to do research, and a corresponding automatic growth in the demand for financial support by governments. The absence in English-speaking Canada of a distinction between universities and undergraduate colleges has accentuated this demand. Nearly all institutions of higher learning in Canada are called universities, and either have or aspire to have large programs of graduate teaching and research. The importance to academics of the prestige attached to offering graduate courses and doing research can hardly be overestimated. The almost exclusive attention given to research and publication as factors in promotion has greatly exaggerated this prestige. The result is that nearly all university teachers wish to engage in research, and to receive generous financial support for their projects. There is also a strong pressure upon them to engage in *visible* research activities, involving travel, research assistants, costly equipment, and, in the social sciences, preferably a social survey. This is of course much more expensive than the traditional kind of scholarly study and writing. The question is whether there is a direct relation between the rapidly growing total amount of research that scholars do and the needs of society for the results of that research. In other words, is their research worth the cost ?

The answer is closely related to the problem of the most desirable balance among the different kinds and fields of research. For instance, what is Canada's total need for fundamental research as opposed to applied research and development ? Many writers on science policy look at this question purely in terms of economic benefit. Some claim that the best policy for a small country is to reduce expenditure on basic research to the minimum necessary for training people capable of "parasitizing" the results of research done elsewhere. Others, on the other hand, argue that basic and applied research need each other for the advance of both, and that both are needed for economic growth. [1] Whichever side is right, both sides tend to assume that fundamental research means research in the natural sciences and that applied research means research to improve technology. This neglects the important functions of university research to analyze and criticize society and to help solve social problems.

Governments should consider whether an over-emphasis on research in the natural sciences does not accelerate technological change to such a degree that this in itself becomes a source of serious social problems. Because governments now control the lion's share of support for research, they may actually be able to control the speed of technological change, and thus the magnitude of the social problems created, as well as the resources devoted to their solution, through shifting the general balance of research support from the natural sciences to the social sciences and humanities. Although the impact of American technological innovation upon Canada may make it difficult for Canadian governments to do this, the prospect of even some success is worthy of serious examination. [2]

[1] For an exposition of these arguments, see Joseph BEN-DAVID, *Fundamental Research and the Universities : Some Comments on International Differences,* a report prepared for the third ministerial meeting on science of OECD countries (Paris, 1968), 57-61.

[2] Commissioner Rowat adds that we should not allow a naive faith in science to give us a simplistic approach to the solution of social problems. He feels that the Science Council, for example, borders on a technocratic view of the world in its recent policy report. Thus it has extended its mandate from the narrow one of a policy for science to one called "science policy", which apparently consists in applying all human knowledge to the solution of all human problems. This has resulted in the Council gobbling up, with hardly a trace of indigestion, most of the big problems of public policy not already consumed by the Economic Council. Its attitude seems to be that, given enough money, all one has to

Perhaps it is utopian to think that we can alter the evolution of technology, especially in this age when communications have made every point in the globe accessible. But certainly we court disaster if we do not devote more energy and imagination to the solution of the human problems resulting from technological change, for we risk confusing the means with the ends. [3]

c) THE FEDERAL AND PROVINCIAL ROLES

A basic problem regarding the respective federal and provincial roles in supporting university research is the impossibility of dividing basic research, and the difficulty of dividing applied research, according to the constitutional division of powers. Yet the results of this research are crucial to solving both federal and provincial problems, and both levels of government are interested in its support.

For most of this century the federal government has been involved in the support of basic and applied research at univer-

do is assemble interdisciplinary teams on various vaguely-defined social problems such as "urban development", apply "the scientific method" to these problems, and they will be easily solved. For instance, regarding problems which "reflect on the quality of life within urban society", it says that "the fragmented efforts of the past to alleviate our basic environmental problems have not been successful, *simply because* the complex nature of the total human ecology requires a co-ordinated approach to the solution of its problems" (italics added). It therefore recommends "a systems approach" to community planning and human environment. Other examples are its proposals to apply "the scientific method" to studies of the current system of providing education, and to apply "systems science and other techniques to the process of education, to increase its productivity". SCIENCE COUNCIL OF CANADA, *Towards a National Science Policy for Canada,* report no. 4 (Ottawa, 1968), 41 and 15.

As most social scientists and humanists know, many social problems, such as those involving group power struggles or man's irrational inhumanity to man, are so complex and intractable that they cannot be solved simply by applying "the scientific method" to their study, no matter how interdisciplinary the team nor how many scientists are assigned to the task. Nor can science provide the answers to the moral questions involved. If the social sciences and humanities had been represented on the Science Council, perhaps it would not have taken such a simplistic "scientific" view of the social and political world.

[3] Giving evidence before the Senate's special committee on science policy, Mr. Jean Boucher, Director of the Canada Council, said: "It is mainly for the social sciences and humanities to provide adequate interpretations of the new forces at play and to propose a realistic range of options for man and society in a world where all traditional patterns are being challenged." *Proceedings of the Special Committee on Science Policy: Phase I* (Ottawa, 1968), 3.

sities. It also has large research establishments of its own, and promotes and supports industrial research. Although historically provincial support has been much smaller, the provinces have an equal interest in basic research, and a growing interest in applied research to solve provincial problems. In recent years their general support of university research has grown rapidly, and their assistance to universities for specific projects has increased even faster than that of the federal government. [4]

The problem caused by the differing interests and priorities of the federal and provincial governments, then, is how to co-ordinate their decisions regarding the allocation of support among the different sectors, fields and kinds of research.

d) THE NEED FOR PLANNING AND CO-ORDINATING MACHINERY

The complexity of all of the above problems indicates a need for some kind of machinery to study them in relation to one another, to make recommendations regarding their solution, and to co-ordinate the decisions that must be made with respect to them. Because these are decisions involving public policy and the allocation of the tax-payer's dollar, they must ultimately become political decisions. But our feeling is that they will be much more rational and satisfactory if they have been made after thorough study and discussion by representatives of the main elements involved: the federal and provincial governments, the universities, and other research establishments. We have in mind the creation of a special body representing all these elements, and we submit alternative proposals on this subject in Sections E and F.

B. PROBLEMS OF RESEARCH SUPPORT

a) THE DANGERS OF IMBALANCE

As explained in Chapter 4, university research should be mainly free or broadly oriented basic research rather than

---

[4] From 1961-62 to 1966-67, while federal grants for assisted research increased by a little over three times (from $16.7 million to $52.1 million), provincial grants increased by more than ten times (from $1.1 million to $11.8 million). John B. Macdonald and others, *The Role of the Federal Government in the Support of Research in Canadian Universities*, prepared for the Science Council of Canada and the Canada Council (Ottawa, 1969), Table 3:1; hereafter cited as *Macdonald Report*.

narrowly defined applied research or applied studies and development work. Yet the growing need by government and industry for research to solve specific problems puts increasing pressure on the universities to do narrowly defined research. The tremendous proportion of university research now supported by governments has tempted them to ask universities to do more and more research of this kind. There is therefore a danger that it will become too large a proportion of total university research. [5]

It is difficult to say how much applied research is now being done at universities because of the difficulties of definition and the inadequacies of accounting. A vague indication is given by the amount spent for research in the academic community by federal departments and agencies other than the three research councils. In 1967-68 their share of the federal total was about 27 per cent, not including large sums spent by royal commissions, while the research councils spent the remaining 73 per cent. [6] However, some of the research supported by the departments and other agencies is broadly oriented, while much of the research supported by the research councils is applied research. One calculation indicates that nearly one-third of university research is now applied research. [7]

[5]   The Science Council, for example, stated in its policy report that "more emphasis in future must be placed on development and innovation — on using science and technology to produce new or improved goods and services — and more research and development must be done close to the point where innovation will be initiated. This argument leads the Science Council to expect that *an increasing share of* Canadian R & D will be performed outside government laboratories, *by the universities* and by all levels of Canadian industry . . ." (Italics ours; *op. cit.*, 1.) In its *First Annual Report* the Council made this remarkable statement: "If our industry becomes unprofitable there will be no money for any kind of research. *Therefore,* where the results of research are not expected to be tangible or immediate, the advisability of investing in it will have to be scrutinized with greater care." (Italics ours.) The Council was so pleased with this reasoning that it reprinted the statement in its policy report (*ibid.*, 5).

[6]   Education Support Branch, Department of the Secretary of State, *Federal Expenditures on Research in the Academic Community, 1966-67, 1967-68* (Ottawa, 1968), Appendix A, pie chart.

[7]   SCIENCE COUNCIL, report no. 4, *op. cit.*, Table 2. This calculation also indicates that universities do about 60 per cent of all basic research, about 30 per cent of all research, but only about 20 per cent of all research and development. Totalled for all sectors, the ratio of basic to applied research seems to be about the same in Canada and the U.S. (roughly 1:2), but expenditures on development are relatively much higher in the U.S. (*ibid.*, Table 2 and p. 22).

Since most support for research is in the fields of natural and biological science and engineering, there is also a serious danger that this research will serve the needs of technology and industry at the expense of social needs, and will overbalance research and scholarly work in the social sciences and humanities. Although there are no completely objective criteria for judging how much research should be done in each field, there is good evidence to demonstrate that this has already happened. Returns from a group of six representative universities show that in 1966-67 science and engineering received 48.5 per cent of all outside direct support to research, while the health sciences received 40 per cent. The social sciences and humanities, on the other hand, got only 7.4 per cent. [8] The universities themselves allocate their own small research funds in quite different proportions, with about 40 per cent going to the social sciences and humanities. [9]

In our view, if a large share of the total allocation for university research were to be given in the form of general unconditional grants to universities, this would help to prevent the serious sorts of imbalance that we have just discussed, by giving universities and their scholars a greater influence in deciding on the balance among the kinds and fields of research.

b) THE DANGERS OF DIRECTED RESEARCH

An even greater threat to the universities — because it affects academic freedom and their function as a critic of society — is that government-supported research will direct scholars away from fundamental research and the exploration of new ideas and problems of their own choosing, into areas

----

[8] It is true that there are great differences in the cost of research, but these percentages do not have even the remotest connection with the distribution of scholars in these fields. In 1967-68 the total number of full-time faculty in science-engineering was about 5,400, and in the health sciences was only about 1,600, while the number in the humanities and social sciences was nearly 9,200. In the nine years from 1958 to 1967 the number of full-time faculty in the humanities grew by more than three times and in the social sciences by more than four times, while in science-engineering the increase was considerably less than three times. The above figures and the percentages given in the text were all derived from the *Macdonald Report*, Tables 3:5 and 3:12.

[9] *Ibid.*, Table 3:7.

and subjects chosen by government. For instance, a considerable amount of scientific research activity has been directed into the area of defence research through support given by the Defence Research Board. Where the objective of the research is narrowly defined by government, there is a danger that this objective may virtually dictate the general nature of the conclusions. A more insidious danger is that, though the results may not already have been dictated by the objective, the scholar will have a feeling of dependence upon his benefactors and will try to read their minds for the conclusions that they would like.

Since often the findings and conclusions of research in the social sciences and humanities are not as objective as in the natural sciences, these dangers are likely to become greater if recent proposals are adopted to increase support for "mission-oriented" and contract research in these fields. The federal government is already playing a large role in supporting government-defined research projects. If in future the provinces, too, should shift their support more and more toward government-defined projects in their anxiety to solve specific provincial problems, the dangers will increase.

Those who preach the virtues of "mission-oriented" research for universities usually fail to distinguish between broad fields of research supported by agencies with an objective or "mission" (e.g. a government department) and research whose objective or "mission" is narrowly defined by these agencies. Some "mission" agencies sponsor research in a field which is only very generally defined, and specific proposals for research are made by scholars in that field according to their own choice and interests. In other words, the role of the agency amounts to little more than governmentally expressing a social need for research in its field by making funds available. The federal "mission" agencies in Canada that support university research, in contrast with those in the U.S., distribute much of their support in this way.

In many cases, however, the research is more narrowly defined and is often done under contract. Thus the policy of Atomic Energy of Canada is to support only university research of direct value to its research and development program and to have all of this research done under contract. In other cases the "research" may be simply a report on a specified subject written by a professor at the request of an outside agency. For instance, an industrial firm, a municipality or an agency of a higher government may offer to pay him for a report or brief defending a certain proposal or point of view. Often the agency will keep the report and its findings secret. There is therefore a very broad spectrum of what is commonly called mission-oriented research, ranging all the way from the mere specification of a general field to specific projects for which the conclusions of the so-called research are already laid down.

Both the Science Council and the Macdonald Committee have failed to stress this important distinction between support by outside agencies for research in fields which are very generally defined and within which projects are proposed by scholars, and support for specific research projects which have been proposed by government agencies and which are usually done under contract. We have therefore devised the term *directed research* to describe this latter type of support. Directed research is particularly inappropriate for universities because it focuses the attention of scholars on short-term problems of direct interest to outside bodies and limits the freedom of scholars to investigate problems of their own choice.

Another source of confusion is the frequent assumption (in the Macdonald Report, for example) that if more mission-oriented social research is to be done at universities it must be sponsored by mission-oriented agencies. Yet nearly all social research done at universities is mission-oriented in the sense that it is designed to serve humanity and solve a defined problem. Though proposed by the scholars themselves, much of it is aimed at solving specific social, economic and political problems, some of which are quite narrowly defined. Indeed, many, if not most, of the research projects proposed to the Canada Council are "mission-oriented" or applied research projects of this kind. Hence an increase in the general support for undirected research in the social sciences would automatically increase the amount of applied social research, as well as more basic social inquiry, which the university is especially equipped to do because of its independence.

c)　PROPOSALS TO PROTECT INDEPENDENCE

Since directed research erodes the independence of the university and seriously limits its function as a critic of society, governments should withdraw from support in the form of directed research. Instead they should channel nearly all of their support through the bodies created for the general support of undirected research. Also, universities should receive large unconditional research grants to finance short-term projects of individual scholars and to support scholars who engage in research of their own choosing during the summer. To protect the independence of universities, these grants should not be allocated directly by governments but instead by intermediary bodies which include representatives of the academic community. Proposals for research which cannot be financed out of a university's general research funds should be submitted to these bodies for approval, and expensive projects should be recommended by them to their parent governments for approval and support.

In order to clarify how much of the various types of research is being done at universities and to make it possible to distinguish between directed research and the general support of research, we also propose that universities and government agencies should report their expenditures on university research in various categories, such as free basic, oriented basic, applied and directed research, and should try to agree on a uniform classification. Directed research should be reported under applied research as a sub-category, which might be called "directed studies", and which would include contract research, consulting work and the preparing of reports or briefs for outside agencies.

C.　THE PROVINCIAL ROLE

a)　PRESENT FINANCIAL SUPPORT

The magnitude of the provinces' present financial support to university research is not generally realized. University accounting statements show separately only the income from special or ear-marked contributions for research. This gives the impression that the provinces' share is small. Thus their share of direct grants to universities for assisted, sponsored and contract research in 1966-67 was only about 15 per cent. [10] But their main contribution to research is through their general university grants, which support graduate schools and the heavy overhead costs of research, including academic salaries (i.e. the proportion of the salary which goes to pay the scholar for his time spent on research). Several of the provinces also make grants to graduate students for study and research. For instance, Quebec has a well-developed program of student aid which includes graduate students, and Ontario has a generous program of graduate fellowships, mainly in the humanities and social sciences since these are fields not adequately covered by the federal research councils.

With the recent rapid growth in the size of universities and of their graduate schools, in the total number of staff doing research, and in provincial grants to universities, the provincial share of the total cost of university research has become large, but unfortunately is impossible to calculate with any exactitude. Recent cost studies done by universities under the auspices of the AUCC indicate that the average faculty member — if there is such a creature — spends about 20 per cent of his time on direct research and about 30 per cent of his time on research plus supervision of graduate theses. Since academic salaries are the largest item in university budgets, this gives some indication of the large amount of provincial money being allocated to the support of research. Added to this are the other high capital and operating costs of unassisted research. In addition, the provinces must pay the heavy indirect costs of research on assisted projects, for which the direct costs are paid by the federal government or by industry, foundations and other private organizations. Thus, although the federal government helps to pay for the general and indirect operating costs of research through the 1966 agreement, the provinces are no

[10]   *Macdonald Report*, Table 3:1.

doubt paying for a very large share of the total cost of university research.

b) PRESENT PROVINCIAL MECHANISMS

Because most provincial support has been indirect, and because historically the federal government has played the main role in the support of specific projects, most provinces have taken very little interest in the subject of university research. Few of them have any special machinery for allocating research support to universities, and in the legal instruments which have created the provincial university commissions, research is rarely mentioned as one of the subjects of the commission's concern.

Although historically the provinces have not considered it their role to support university research directly, for many years they have taken an interest in supporting applied research to promote industry and the exploitation of provincial resources. They have done this through the establishment of a provincial research council or foundation with representatives from government, industry and in some cases the universities, using somewhat the same pattern as the National Research Council. These bodies operate research laboratories which do research for the government and also for industry through paid contracts. In some cases they support applied research at universities through grants to staff and awards to graduate students for research on provincial problems. Often their laboratories are located on or near a university campus, but their connection with the university is rather tenuous.

Such research bodies now exist (or are being organized) in all provinces except Newfoundland and Prince Edward Island. Some of them are quite old, such as those in Alberta and Ontario, which date from 1921 and 1928 respectively. The others have all been organized since the Second World War, the most recent being the one in Manitoba. The extent to which they are supported by contract research from industries varies considerably. Some of them, such as the New Brunswick Research and Productivity Council and the Alberta Research Council, are supported largely by government funds, while those which have been organized in co-operation with industry as independent foundations, such as the Ontario Research Foundation and the British Columbia Research Council, derive more than half of their income from contract research, a considerable proportion of which originates outside the province. All of these research establishments are relatively small, the largest one being that of Ontario, with about 250 employees.

c) THE NEED FOR A GREATER ROLE

Although the provinces are indirectly paying a large share of the cost of university research, their role in science and research policy, the planning of research priorities, and the direct support of industrial and university research has not been great. The attitude of most provincial governments seems to have been that their role is only to fill minor gaps left by federal research policies and activities. Yet the provinces have an equal interest in promoting applied research in fields for which they are constitutionally responsible. Also, because of their responsibility for institutions of higher education, they have an obligation to promote independent research in the universities. [11]

So far, Ontario and Quebec seem to be the only provinces that have taken seriously their obligations in this field. Between 1962 and 1965 the Ontario government made special grants totalling $6.5 million to eight universities in order to enable them to expand graduate study and research. In 1966 it transferred the administration of its research grants from the Ontario Research Foundation to the Department of University Affairs, and in 1967 increased their amount to $600,000 a year. [12]

[11]   As was observed in a recent report by a group of foreign experts: "Obviously some long-term solution must be found for the financing of research work in the universities — not only as a necessary condition for the development of satisfactory graduate schools, but as an investment in an important resource. Such a resource is as much a provincial asset as a national one, and reluctant provincial legislators will, no doubt, come round to the view that the support of research is a legitimate item in the normal university budget for which funds must be regularly provided." ORGANIZATION FOR ECONOMIC CO-OPERATION AND DEVELOPMENT, *Training of and Demand for High-level Scientific and Technical Personnel in Canada* (Paris, 1966), 95-6.

[12]   As recommended by a study committee of scientists set up by the Committee on University Affairs, most of these grants are awarded in the natural sciences with first priority given to junior faculty who

The government of Quebec has produced a draft Bill for a provincial research council, which would not only operate a large research establishment but also advise the government on research policies and priorities. In its legislation of 1968 creating the Council of Universities, it also provided for a University Research Commission as an advisory body to the Council. Its members are appointed by the government on the recommendation of the Council, and its function is to advise the Council on any matter relating to university research.

d) PROPOSED MECHANISMS AND METHODS OF SUPPORT

Because of the need to devote more research effort to provincial and regional problems, and because the provinces are already paying such a large share of the cost of university research, we have come to the conclusion that they should play a much greater role in determining research priorities and the nature of financial support for university research. We therefore recommend that the provinces should greatly expand their existing research establishments to serve provincial and regional needs, and should either create an Advisory Council on Research Policy or add this advisory function to their existing provincial research council. The Advisory Council would advise the provincial government on the priorities, balance and co-ordination of research among the government, industry and the universities, and on policies for stimulating industrial research within the province. We also recommend that the provinces should create, as a committee of the proposed University Co-ordinating Commission, a Committee on University Research, with representation from the Advisory Council on Research Policy. One of the main functions of this committee would be to advise the UCC and the government on the priorities and co-ordination of university research and on the balance among

cannot rely on other sources of support, and second priority to applied research by senior faculty if their project seems to be of direct interest to the province. The grants are made on the advice of a General Awards Committee, composed of deans and professors of science and engineering, under the chairmanship of the research director of the Ontario Research Foundation. See *Report of the Committee on University Affairs 1967*, 26-29, and *Report of the Minister of University Affairs of Ontario 1967*, 25-26.

fields and kinds of university research. [13] Both the Advisory Council and the Research Committee should have members from the academic community, and the Research Committee, because it would be so intimately involved with university research, should have a majority of academic members.

Since the federal research councils already have highly developed systems for making grants to individuals and to teams of researchers within universities, and since large federal grants directly to universities are not desirable, we feel that a special role of the provinces should be that of making research grants to universities as institutions. In order to strengthen the independence of universities, large unconditional grants should be allocated to them by the University Co-ordinating Commission on the advice of its Research Committee. As with the general grants to universities, a large proportion of these grants should be allocated among the universities on the basis of an automatic formula, such as so many dollars per full-time faculty member, and the remainder on the basis of considerations such as the age and size of the university, or the need to develop its research capacity.

Because the money would come from the provincial governments, the universities would be influenced to do more applied research in fields of provincial interest. Where teams of researchers proposed expensive research projects of this kind, a university should not be expected to pay the cost from its unconditional research grant. Some of these projects might even be proposed by inter-university teams. We therefore recommend that proposals for provincially-oriented research above a specified cost should go to the Research Committee for approval, and that very expensive projects should be recommended by the Committee to the UCC and the provincial government for approval and support.

Among the fields of provincially-oriented research, there is a pressing need for research on problems of higher education. For instance, the largest educational research establishment in

[13] For proposals similar to those made here, see the brief to our Commission from the Université de Montréal, *Universités, Recherches et Gouvernements*, 28-31.

Canada, the Ontario Institute for Studies in Education, with a staff of about 450 and annual revenues, mainly from the province, of about $8.5 million, devotes relatively little attention to higher education. There is also a need for broadly trained administrators in universities, and in provincial departments and commissions concerned with higher education. We therefore recommend that the provincial authorities concerned should expand their own programs of research on higher education and should encourage some of the universities to create or expand existing graduate programs of research and teaching in this field.

D.   THE FEDERAL ROLE

a)   The Nature and Impact of Federal Support

In the past few years federal support for university research has risen very rapidly. At present about forty federal departments and agencies are involved in this support. The most important of these, showing the amount of money spent on research in the academic community in 1967-68, are as follows: [14]

	$ million
National Research Council	45.0
Medical Research Council	20.5
Canada Council	11.3
National Health and Welfare	7.3
National Defence (Defence Research Board)	3.7
Energy, Mines and Resources	3.4
Atomic Energy Control Board	2.5
Atlantic Development Board	1.8
Forestry and Rural Development	1.7
External Aid Office	1.4
Others	7.3
Total	105.9

Support from the three federal research councils accounts for about three-quarters of all federal expenditures, while departments and other agencies account for about one-quarter (not counting large sums spent by royal commissions). About

14   For source, see footnote 6.

two-thirds of the total income of the Canadian universities for sponsored, assisted and contract research comes from the federal government. [15] Federal agencies also make awards and grants direct to individual scholars and graduate students. The impact of federal research support on the universities is therefore obviously great.

Partly because this support has been granted on an unco-ordinated basis by so many different agencies and without any over-all policy or plan, it seems to have had a number of serious distorting effects upon university research and the development of the universities generally. We have already stressed the dangers of directed research. It is also likely that federal support has had an imbalancing effect upon the kinds and fields of research. For instance, the long-standing policy of the National Research Council in favour of basic research probably inhibited the development of applied research of value to industry and technology. This helps to explain why the provinces felt it necessary to create research councils of their own for applied research.

There can be little doubt that a serious imbalance has been created by the federal government's long favouring of research in science and engineering, and more recently in medicine, in relation to the social sciences and humanities. The Macdonald Committee has revealed that, despite the creation of the Canada Council and the increased resources given to it in recent years, federal expenditures for university research in science, engineer-ing and medicine accounted for over 84 per cent of the total in 1967-68, while the social sciences and humanities received only about 16 per cent. [16]

There may also be an imbalance in the support given to established scholars versus young ones. We heard the complaint

---

[15] About 15 per cent comes from the provinces, 17 per cent from foundations and similar sources, and only 3 per cent from business and industry. Directly supported research accounts for about 17 per cent of total university income, and the federal share accounts for about 11 per cent (*Macdonald Report*, Tables 3:1 and 3:9). We have calculated that research done for mission-oriented federal agencies accounts for about 16 per cent of directly supported research done at universities. What proportion of this is directed research as we have defined it is not known.

[16] *Ibid.*, 69.

that because the award committees of the federal research councils are staffed by older, nationally known scholars, they tend to favour researchers with established reputations whom they know rather than take a chance on a younger man with potential. Since the need to encourage a young scholar is likely to be better known locally, we feel that small grants to individual scholars should be awarded by the universities themselves.

Furthermore, federal research support has probably had a distorting effect upon the development of universities in a number of disturbing ways. For instance, the total amount of research support, by fostering graduate versus undergraduate work and research versus teaching, may have been mainly responsible for developing the unwarranted prestige attached to graduate study and research. Another impact upon the development of universities is called the "Matthew effect" — after the biblical quotation from Matthew, "To him who hath shall be given." The Macdonald Report reveals that in 1965-66 five universities in Canada received over 50 per cent of the total funds for assisted research, and ten universities received 82 per cent, while fifteen universities received no research income. [17]

Similarly, anglophone universities may have been favoured in relation to francophone universities, or at least the "Matthew effect" means that they have not been given any special consideration to enable them to catch up with their more fortunate anglophone neighbours. For a number of complex reasons the French-speaking universities, and in particular their graduate schools and research activities, were very late in developing. The brief submitted to our Commission by the Université de Montréal reveals that in 1967-68 Quebec's three francophone universities received only about 12 per cent of the federal research support given by the three research councils, and an even smaller percentage of that given by other departments and agencies. [18] Yet the number of full-time students in these universities is about 21 per cent of the total for Canada.

[17]   *Ibid.*, Table 3:3.
[18]   *Op. cit.*, 46. See also the evidence given by the francophone universities of Quebec to the SENATE SPECIAL COMMITTEE ON SCIENCE POLICY, *Proceedings* (May 28, 1969).

b) The Disregard of Provincial Interests

The difficulty is that federal policies to prevent the above-mentioned types of distortion are likely to involve the federal government too directly in the financing of universities. This was the main theme of Dr. Dugal's minority report of the Macdonald Committee. He objected in particular to the Committee's proposal for federal payment to the universities of large capital grants for research space and facilities.

The federal government is already making sizeable grants direct to universities. Most of the grants by the three federal councils for specific research projects are paid to and administered by the universities. The NRC also pays, as an unconditional grant, a minimum of $25,000 a year to small universities and 7.5 per cent of its research grants to large ones, and it makes large negotiated grants to develop existing research programs at selected universities. The Canada Council also makes grants to universities for special collections of books. The Department of Forestry makes a grant of $40,000 a year to each faculty of forestry in Canada, and the Medical Research Council makes a similar grant of $24,000 to the deans of medical faculties. In some of its research grants, the MRC even provides for the payment of faculty salaries. The Macdonald Committee proposed to make most of these grants less automatic and to give more discretion to the granting bodies regarding their allocation. It also proposed that the MRC's policy of "strategic development grants" for new programs at selected universities be extended to the other research councils. [19] All such payments have a direct impact upon the development of universities as educational institutions. Yet there is no consultation with the provinces on policies with respect to them.

Another illustration of the federal government's disregard of provincial interests is its policy regarding indirect costs. Direct grants for research involve very large indirect costs for staff time, other overhead and capital expenditures. These costs are difficult to calculate and vary according to the definition given to indirect costs. In particular, they vary according to

[19] *Macdonald Report,* 127-8.

whether one counts the value of the time of the researcher himself, since salaries are such a large proportion of total operating costs. The Bladen Commission calculated that indirect costs were about 30 per cent of the direct costs, and therefore proposed that the federal government should pay this proportion as an additional amount along with its direct grants for research. But the Commission's calculation was admittedly only a "guess-timate". By dint of an elaborate calculation, the Macdonald Committee came up with a similar proportion, 35 per cent, while the method of calculation used in AUCC cost studies indicates that it may be about 75 per cent. It should be noted that none of these calculations includes capital costs. Estimates of in-direct costs given during our hearings ranged from 20 per cent to 200 per cent.

In any case, with every federal grant for research received by a provincially-supported university, a province incurs an automatic and uncontrolled indirect cost through its general grants to universities. Even where such grants are based on a formula using cost per student, the indirect cost is included, though the indirect cost to a university of any increase in the *proportion* of its supported research must be squeezed out of the rest of its budget. It is true that the federal government pays a large share of the indirect costs through its general support of higher education under the 1966 agreement, but the provinces still must involuntarily bear the remainder. So far the federal government has ignored the modest recommendation of the Bladen Commission, and has consistently refused to pay the full costs, even though this is the general practice with federal grants for research in the United States.

c) THE SCIENCE COUNCIL AND MACDONALD REPORTS

The Science Council and the Macdonald Committee have shown an even greater disregard for university and provincial interests. Their reports reveal a lack of serious concern with most of the problems of distortion and imbalance discussed above. To be fair, we must note that both bodies have taken a stand in favour of more research support going to the humanities and social sciences. In their enthusiasm for more mission-oriented research at universities, however, both bodies have failed to stress the important distinction between objectives set outside the university and those set by scholars themselves. Further, neither body seems to have been impressed by the fact that constitutionally the provinces are responsible for the welfare and development of universities.

Although the Science Council is a federal body, it has not hesitated to state its views and make recommendations on matters falling within provincial jurisdiction. In its recent report on a national science policy, for example, it stated six national goals as a framework for policy: 1) national prosperity, 2) health, 3) education, 4) freedom, security and unity, 5) leisure and personal development, and 6) world peace. [20] Its discussion of objectives under each of these heads, except possibly "world peace", includes matters falling under provincial jurisdiction, while "education" is clearly a provincial matter.

Since the Science Council is only an advisory body, it is perhaps not illegitimate for it to be making pronouncements on matters of provincial interest. But the fact that it is a federal emanation means that inevitably its point of view is warped in the federal direction and will not take provincial interests sufficiently into account. This is revealed particularly in the nature of the group which it appointed in consultation with the Canada Council to study the federal government's support of research in Canadian universities, the so-called Macdonald Committee. It was perhaps inevitable that such a federally-appointed and supported group, with only two out of seven members from outside Ontario, only one of these from Quebec, and with two from the University of Toronto, should virtually ignore the interests of the provinces, of French-speaking Canada, and of the smaller universities. This is a main reason why Commissioner Rowat feels that nothing short of a fully joint advisory body, with members named by both levels of government, is necessary to deal with problems of research.

The Macdonald Committee revealed an almost complete disregard of political reality in its proposed over-extension of

[20] *Op. cit.*, Section 3.

the federal role. The assumption throughout its report seems
to be not only that university research should be a federal
responsibility, but that the definition of research should be
extended to include the whole of graduate study. Yet of the
four aspects of the university's role in research described in
its Chapter 1, all of them equally fall under the constitutional
jurisdiction of the provinces. These are: 1) generating new
knowledge, 2) undertaking research on behalf of the government,
3) developing manpower to conduct research, and 4) enhancing
the quality of teaching. Indeed, the last two of them, since they
are closely related to education, may be regarded as more
provincial than federal. Similarly, defining research to include
nearly all graduate work stretches the definition too far into the
field of education, and would involve the federal government
too directly in the control over universities as educational institutions. The effects of the Committee's proposals would be to
fragment the universities by further dividing graduate from
undergraduate work, to distort university development generally,
and to create a constitutionally divided and unco-ordinated
control over the universities.

d) PROPOSALS FOR IMPROVING AND RESTRICTING THE FEDERAL ROLE

In view of the Science Council's disregard of provincial
interests, we recommend that it should restrict its scope more
directly to federal matters, and should become more concerned
with the long-term distorting effects of unco-ordinated federal
support to university research. Also, because its reports and
proposals have portentous implications for university research,
its membership should include more representatives from the
federal research councils and from the university community,
especially some from the social sciences and humanities.

In order to co-ordinate the activities of the federal research
councils and other agencies heavily involved in the support of
university research, the federal government should create a
co-ordinating body representing all these agencies. This body
should co-ordinate their policies and practices for supporting
research and should make general recommendations on the

allocation of federal funds among them for this purpose. During our hearings we heard complaints that a number of important academic disciplines were left without support by the federal research councils. We agree with the Macdonald Committee that there seems to be no logical justification for these gaps, and therefore recommend that the policies of the councils be co-ordinated so as to cover all academic disciplines recognized by the universities.

We also approve the Macdonald Committee's recommendations that the federal government should greatly increase its support for research in the social sciences and humanities, and that, because this support involves quite different considerations and techniques from support for the performing arts, the Canada Council should be divided into two separate councils for these purposes. Although this would increase the number of councils, the body proposed above would provide for their co-ordination.

In view of the provincial interest in the nature and indirect cost of large research projects at universities, we also recommend that before giving support to a large project costing more than a specified amount, federal agencies, including the research councils, should obtain the approval of the appropriate provincial Committee on University Research. Furthermore, since federal support for university research involves such heavy indirect operating and capital costs to the universities and the provinces, representatives of the federal and provincial governments and of the universities should agree on a method of calculating and paying for these costs. If the federal government is to pay the full costs it should do so in a way that will not interfere with the development priorities of the universities and the provinces. For example, it should not pay the salaries of academic staff as part of the grant for a specific project.

If the universities receive unconditional research grants from the provinces as recommended in Section B, the federal research councils and other agencies should withdraw from short-term and other small research grants below a specified amount. However, the federal councils should continue making grants for more costly research proposals for which the independent judgment of senior scholars in the same specialty from other universities is necessary in order to judge their value. Where the indirect costs to a university of a project proposed by a scholar are likely to exceed a specified sum, he should submit the project to the university authorities for approval before proposing it to a federal agency for support.

E.   PROPOSAL FOR A JOINT COUNCIL ON RESEARCH

by Commissioner ROWAT

Because of the complexity of the problems having to do with research policy and university research and because of the difficulties caused by the division of jurisdiction between the federal and provincial governments in the field of research, I think that a body should be created which is fully representative of the main parties involved — the federal government, the provinces, the academic community and, to a lesser extent, industry. This body would study and advise on the complex problems that we have discussed and would help to co-ordinate federal and provincial policies designed to solve them. I therefore recommend that the federal and provincial governments should by agreement create a Joint Council on Research. [21]

a)   NATURE AND COMPOSITION

It is proposed that this Council be divided into two parts, which might be called the Joint Advisory Committee and the Joint Governmental Committee. The first committee would be made up of representatives of the federal and provincial research councils and of industrial research establishments, to be appointed by the federal and provincial governments, plus a number of members nominated by organizations in the academic community. The second committee would consist of federal and provincial ministers, who would have power to give direction to the activities of the Council and to follow up its recommendations to their respective governments.

[21] For a recommendation similar to this, see the brief from the Université de Montréal, 32.

The Council should have an expert staff and budget of its own, with costs shared between the federal government and the provinces. The whole Council would meet periodically, while the Joint Advisory Committee would meet much more frequently in order to provide continuity and direction to the research work of the secretariat, and to formulate proposals for approval by the whole Council.

A precedent for such a Council is the Science Council of Western Germany, created by a federal-state agreement in 1957. It is a joint body of thirty-nine members, with a Scientific Committee of twenty-two members and a Governmental Committee of seventeen members. The Scientific Committee consists of six members named jointly by the federal and state governments and sixteen others nominated by various scientific and university organizations. The Governmental Committee consists of six members appointed by the federal government and one by each of the states including Berlin. The Chairman of the Council has traditionally been a scholar rather than an official, and the Council has had a good deal of independence, including a budget of its own and a secretariat of twenty to thirty members. Since its inception, this Council has produced numerous important studies, reports and recommendations, nearly all of which have been adopted in their main lines by the federal and state governments. An almost exactly parallel body, the federal-state Council on Education, was created in 1965.

In Canada a somewhat similar joint federal-provincial body is the Canadian Council of Resource Ministers, which has its own budget and secretariat and is supported by a co-ordinating committee of senior officials. The federal government pays one-third of the costs, and the remaining two-thirds are shared by the provinces on a per capita basis. The chairman changes each year, and the Council meets in the capital city from which the chairman comes. Other examples of such fully joint bodies recently created in Canada are the continuing Constitutional Conference and its full-time secretariat, the Tax Structure Committee of ministers and its supporting committee of senior officials on fiscal and economic matters, and an intergovernmental committee of officials on urban and regional research, which has its own secretariat in Toronto.

It is suggested that the size and composition of the Canadian Joint Council on Research might be similar to that of the West German Science Council, except that each province would name a minister, probably its minister of education, to the Governmental Committee, and also a representative to the Advisory Committee, probably the chairman of either the proposed Council on Research Policy or the Committee on University Research. The university representatives should be nominated by organizations which represent all segments of the university community. [22]

b) Functions

The influence of governmental support to university research, especially that of the federal government, is at present so great that any change in its total or balance is of vital interest to the academic community. One of the main functions of the Joint Council on Research, therefore, would be to study and make recommendations to the federal and provincial governments regarding the total amount of research support and also its desirable allocation among government, industry and the universities, among the fields of knowledge, among types of universities (e.g. large and small, old and new, anglophone and francophone), among kinds of research (e.g. pure and applied, directed and undirected), kinds of researchers (e.g. old and young, individual and team), and kinds of research equipment (e.g. computers and libraries).

The Council would also make recommendations on the most desirable division between the federal and provincial governments of the amount and the nature of their support for research, including university research, and on the nature of the machinery required for granting this support. Because the indirect costs of federal-supported research are so difficult to determine to everyone's satisfaction, the Council should also try

[22] The Council might be a body of 40 members, with the Governmental Committee composed of, say, 3 federal and 10 provincial ministers, and the Advisory Committee composed of, say, 5 named by the federal government to represent federal research bodies, 5 by the federal government ofter consultation with industry, 10 by the provinces and 7 by university organizations.

to work out an agreed method of calculating and paying these costs to the universities or the provinces. The Council would issue published studies and reports for public discussion, of course, just as the Science and Economic Councils have done.

F. A COMMITTEE OF THE COUNCIL OF MINISTERS OF EDUCATION: A COUNTER-PROPOSAL

by Commissioner HURTUBISE

I have great difficulty in being convinced by Professor Rowat's proposal for the creation of a Joint Council on Research. In the first place, the addition of this new body to the structure we have proposed in Chapter 10 for the Council of Ministers of Education might be unwieldy. Modelled on the Science Council of the German Federal Republic, this Council on Research would mean an entirely new mechanism, and I have not sufficiently analyzed the concrete implications of its organization or method of operation. I must also add that this proposal evidently lies beyond the scope of our terms of reference. I cannot deny the need for a national planning and co-ordinating body to supervise all research done by the various federal councils and ministeries: the Lamontagne committee (the special Senate committee on research policy) will very likely make recommendations to this effect, for a federal body parallel with similar bodies at the provincial level. But this is global planning. Our terms of reference, as I interpret them, limit us to research in universities. Personally, I would rather respect this limit even if it means a reduced mandate because, as previously indicated in Chapter 4, I hold the opinion that universities should not engage in all kinds of research indiscriminately. One must be logically consistent to the end.

Moreover, Professor Rowat's suggestion appears to me incomplete in that nowhere does it spell out the necessary functional relations between this Joint Council on Research and the various university commissions (or their equivalent) at the provincial level. He gives this Council almost identical — at least overlapping — powers with those of the university commissions, which is unacceptable.

We have previously considered in Chapters 6, 7 and 9, the nature of the university commissions and their committee on university research. As a result, we have proposed viable mechanisms: we have described their nature, analyzed the limits of and the areas within their jurisdiction, and formulated recommendations. We must therefore respect the dynamism of these provincial bodies; otherwise we would be contradicting ourselves. How can this dynamism be preserved, how can these bodies fulfil their role of planning and co-ordinating advanced studies and research if federal assistance is not subjected to some control ? Wouldn't planning then be nothing but a fiction ? We know that each research dollar coming from sources other than provincial, demands a substantial contribution from the province (though it is impossible to say precisely how much). This contribution must cover, for instance, the indirect cost of a research project, or the added cost of advanced education at the master's or doctorate level. The risk is quite evident, for a research project is often linked with advanced studies, and the provincial minister of education often has to be called upon, after the fact, to pay the extra cost. The end result is the virtual impossibility of devising a rational plan for flexible development. Graduate education is largely left to improvisation because it escapes the primary responsibility of a provincial university commission and its committee on research.

How can we achieve our goal ? I would propose a joint committee attached to the Council of Ministers of Education. Thus the approach is more rational: we would not be creating a completely distinct body absolutely unrelated to the body which — within the limits specified in Chapter 10 — is concerned with higher education across Canada.

This committee would be composed of representatives of either the university commissions (or their equivalent) or their committee on research, representatives of the federal bodies dealing with the financing of university research, and possibly a certain number of academic researchers. They would attempt to establish common priorities; in principle this would not be impossible in so far as federal interests are compatible with and coincide with provincial priorities. It should be possible, then, to arrive at an agreement, which would be revised periodically, and to provide some minimal planning within the terms of this agreement. The main lines of development would then be known. Reciprocity would be more easily secured in the sense that there would be an implicit agreement that the provinces would contribute their share. The global approach of the university commissions would be more fully respected and the cancerous growths within universities due to subsidies from federal bodies would be reduced. This type of agreement would also be more adaptable because it could take into consideration the different needs of the regions and provinces of the country. I should like to add a note of warning: the members of the committee would have to reserve part of the total sum and make it available for free fundamental research, which is difficult to plan. [23]

I could not resist the desire to make this proposal. I am very conscious of the fact that, while it follows a certain logic, neither the reality of events nor the ambitions of the different universities necessarily conform to logic. But the alternative is the multiversity, the liberal hodge-podge, the unjustified multiplication of costs. At least my proposal would not encourage the birth of two parallel strata of universities: one operating at the undergraduate and master's level, but headless, and financed mainly by provincial subsidies; the other, concentrating only on research and doctoral-level teaching, and supported almost exclusively by federal grants, as the Macdonald Report partly suggests. This idea our own report has consistently rejected.

[23] Dr. Hans Selye declared before the Senate's special (Lamontagne) committee (op. cit., 193): "The greatest discoveries are made by accident, but you have to prepare a man so that he can profit from the accident. Such non-planned research is therefore the most original, and since the resulting discoveries cannot be calculated, the computer has very little place in it."

10. Interprovincial Co-ordination

As the foregoing pages have made abundantly clear, Canada has now moved from the era of the university as an isolated unit to the era of universities as a *network* or *system*. Though the degree of interdependence among universities varies from region to region, this inter-relationship is a fundamental characteristics of modern Canadian institutions of higher learning. It has manifested itself at two levels. At the level of university-provincial relations, most provinces have created intermediary bodies to mediate and co-ordinate relations among the universities and with the provincial government. [1] At the level of inter-university relations, horizontal relationships have grown up not only among university presidents and other administrators, but also in the form of associations of students and professors. [2]

The regional need for university co-ordination mainly coincides with provincial boundaries in the case of the larger provinces — Ontario, Quebec and British Columbia. These provinces can therefore meet the need reasonably well. [3] This need is not met, however, in the less-populated provinces, which individually do not constitute mega-regions. In their case, the need for regional co-ordination and co-operation transcends provincial boundaries. This does not mean that in the case of the three first-mentioned provinces there is no need for interprovincial co-operation in certain problem areas. Despite the relatively larger populations in these provinces, their systems of higher education are not capable of an independent existence.

[1]   See our critical evaluation of these bodies in Chapter 6.
[2]   Examples of province-wide student organizations are Action in New Brunswick, the Alberta Association of Students, the British Columbia Assembly of Students, the Manitoba Association of Students, the Saskatchewan Federation of Students, and the Union générale des étudiants du Québec (to the extent that it still exists); similar associations of professors are the Fédération des Associations de professeurs des universités du Québec, the Nova Scotia Council of University Faculty Associations, and the Ontario Confederation of University Faculty Associations.
[3]   Though it should be noted that in British Columbia, Notre Dame University in Nelson has been completely isolated from the three other universities.

On the contrary, even these provinces must co-operate in areas such as cultural relations. This was highlighted by the June 1969 cultural agreement between Ontario and Quebec. Because of its simplicity and flexibility, this technique of co-operation and co-ordination could well serve as an example for the other provinces.

A.   REGIONAL INTERPROVINCIAL CO-OPERATION

Regional interprovincial co-operation here means co-operation among several smaller provinces grouped into regional units, specifically the Atlantic Maritimes and the Prairies. The provinces in each of these regions have a certain degree of cultural similarity, common interests and, except for Alberta, considerable economic problems. In view of their unenviable economic situation, these provinces must co-ordinate the use of their limited material and human resources in order to avoid over-lapping programs.

a)   THE MARITIMES

In the Maritimes some regional agreements involving both the provincial governments and the universities already exist. For example, there are interprovincial agreements on the amounts the institutions are to be paid for students who come from other provinces to the Dalhousie University Medical School, the Nova Scotia Technical College, and Mount Allison University in New Brunswick. Also, there are regional organizations which are centered on the universities: the Association of Atlantic Universities (AAU), and the Atlantic Provinces Inter-University Committee on the Sciences (APICS), which was organized as a committee of AAU in 1964. These organizations merit further attention.

1)   *The Association of Atlantic Universities*

Established in 1964, AAU comprises representatives from universities in the Maritime provinces, as well as from universities in the West Indies that are members of the Commonwealth Association of Universities. Associate member status has also been accorded to certain colleges.

The AAU Charter of June 24, 1966, outlines the organization's functions:

(a) To assist the co-ordination of higher education in the Atlantic provinces;

(b) To ensure high academic standards in a period of rising costs of academic personnel, laboratories, libraries, etc.;

(c) To avoid unnecessary duplication of faculties and courses of study.

Through its various committees, which co-ordinate library development, publication, teaching qualifications, etc., the Association expands areas of co-operation and co-ordination.

2) *The Atlantic Provinces Inter-University Committee on the Sciences*

Mainly concerned with co-ordinating scientific studies in AAU member institutions, APICS formulates comprehensive policies and programs regarding both educational matters and research. The organization's subcommittees, such as those concerned with biology, chemistry, geology, mathematics, physics and computers, act as catalyzers and co-ordinators for studies in the natural sciences.

Since both AAU and APICS operate in a region with severe economic problems, overstressing their weakness is obviously fruitless and unfair. Professor Hubert W. Kitchen made an analysis of the situation and avanced a number of constructive proposals in 1968. [4] In a more cynical mood, one of the professors at our hearing in Halifax told us that a good starting point for co-operation and co-ordination among the various institutions of higher learning in Halifax would be for them to begin by communicating with each other.

3) *A special case: l'Université de Moncton*

Before turning to the problems of the Prairies, a brief digression must be made regarding the special position of

[4] In a study sponsored by the Atlantic Development Board entitled, *University Education in the Atlantic Provinces : The Next Decade.*

l'Université de Moncton. This French-language university in the heart of a predominantly English-speaking mega-region not only shares the same economic problems as its English-speaking counterparts, but also is confronted with the problem of cultural isolation.

We believe that the New Brunswick Higher Education Commission should give special attention to this cultural problem which is peculiar to the region, and take the concrete measures that such attention requires. We also think that, in order to overcome the cultural isolation of their university, the professors, administrators and students of l'Université de Moncton should establish closer relations with their counterparts in Quebec, for instance by obtaining the status of observers in Quebec's Federation of Associations of Professors and in the Conference of Rectors and Principals.

b) THE PRAIRIES

The Inter-Provincial Committee on University Rationalization (IPCUR) is the Prairie region's organ for co-ordination and co-operation. [5] The Economic Council of the Prairie Provinces created IPCUR as one of its committees in October 1966. IPCUR is composed of the provincial ministers responsible for higher education, the chairmen of the provincial university commissions (or their equivalent), the deputy ministers of education, and the presidents of all of the universities in the three participating provinces, i.e. Manitoba, Saskatchewan and Alberta. [6] In 1968 representatives of British Columbia's three publicly-supported universities were invited to attend IPCUR's meetings for the first time. The Committee's main task is to co-ordinate the development of regional higher education in terms of existing resources; it makes recommendations in this respect to the provincial governments. It attempts to solve such problems as the co-ordination of library automation, new graduate studies, and new

[5] In a special field there is also an organization whose initials spell TRIUMF. It is composed of forty-two physicists and chemists from the University of British Columbia, Simon Fraser University, the University of Victoria and the University of Alberta.
[6] Plus the principals of the two campuses of the University of Saskatchewan.

programs in such fields as mining engineering, architecture and veterinary medicine. In principle, provincial universities must submit proposals for new programs to the Committee for its approval.

Despite its wide-ranging functions, IPCUR has elicited mixed reactions from both university and provincial spokesmen. The universities have generally reacted more favourably to the activities of the Committee, while the provincial governments have often been less impressed. Provincial politicians see little or no concrete results from the efforts of IPCUR. One minister asserted that provincial authorities lost interest in the Committee when they found that it was dominated by the universities.

We should also mention the existence of the Conference of Faculty Associations of the Western Provinces, which, as the name implies, is essentially concerned with professional matters. To cap the efforts made during the last three or four years to set it up as a continuing organization, the Conference may soon be endowed with an official charter.

c) CONCLUSION

Certain findings stand out in this brief overview of regional co-operation and co-ordination among Canada's universities:

i) Each of the mega-regions discussed above has organizations for assuring at least some co-ordination among its universities;

ii) Though these organizations have produced varied results, their very existence reflects a real need to deal regionally with such problems as library co-ordination, educational planning, research, student mobility and the exchange of professors, to name only a few;

iii) Every effort should be made to develop and ensure the viability of such organizations, for they constitute an important foundation upon which to build a governmental structure for interprovincial co-ordination that encompasses the whole of Canada.

B.   CANADIAN INTERPROVINCIAL CO-ORDINATION

For the sake of clarity, a distinction should be made between regional co-ordination and Canadian interprovincial co-ordination; the latter phrase is used to encompass all of the provinces and mega-regions. In this respect, an organization that requires particular emphasis is the Council of Ministers of Education, and a brief historical analysis of its operations follows. The Canadian Education Association should also be mentioned. Though it has no decision-making authority, it performs a liaison role regarding problems of common interest to provincial ministers of education.

a)   THE COUNCIL OF MINISTERS OF EDUCATION

The origin of the Council goes back to a decision on September 21, 1966, to establish, on the advice of the executive committee of the Canadian Education Association, an ad hoc committee of the provincial ministers of education to promote co-operation among the provinces in educational affairs. At their request, the executive secretary of the Association, Dr. F. K. Stewart, prepared a brief study entitled, "Report to the Ministers of Education on a Secretariat for a Council of the Ministers of Education", which he submitted to them on March 22, 1967, after having gone to Bonn, in the company of three deputy ministers, to meet officials of the secretariat for the Conference of the Ministers of Cultural Affairs of the West German laender, or states. In June 1967 the ministers agreed on the need for establishing a Council supported, at Dr. Stewart's suggestion, by a secretariat of some forty persons. [7] Then on September 26 the ministers, with the approval of their respective governments, agreed on the constitution of the Council. The founding document stated that the Council's aims were "to enable the ministers to consult on such matters as are of common interest, and to provide a means for the fullest possible co-operation among provincial governments in areas of mutual interest and concern in education".

[7]   See pp. 12-13 of his Report: "Additional proposal (d), Secretariat with secretary of the Council and secretary of the C.E.A., the latter serving also as associate secretary of the Council."

Referring to the concept of ministerial responsibility, section 5 specified that no Council resolution would bind the ministers and their governments except decisions on questions concerning the internal functioning of the Council. This important point should be noted. For by December 1967 it appeared that the Council, making a virtue of prudence, had back-tracked to some extent concerning its expansion and the size of its secretariat. Though the reasons for this re-orientation are not officially known, presumably they were politically motivated. Nevertheless, the Council, then under the chairmanship of the Hon. Wm. G. Davis, decided to create committees to study education techniques (particularly audio-visual aids), post-secondary education, and vocational education. It also considered a report by the Ontario Minister of University Affairs on the formula financing of university operating budgets. The Council later pursued its activities under the chairmanship of the Hon. Jean-Guy Cardinal, who succeeded Mr. Davis in September 1968.

In concluding this historical account we feel obliged to state that the effectiveness of the Council has been minimal. The reasons are difficult to specify. One reason may be that, because of political change, the participation by the ministers in the activities of the Council is short-lived. To bridge the gaps imposed by electoral politics, a sizable secretariat is needed. However, a more fundamental reason for the reduced effectiveness of the Council may be the attitude of some of the ministers: they doubt the value of such a council. Thus political restraints are involved, and such barriers are hard to overcome.

b)   RECOMMENDATIONS

In our view, as shown in the preceding chapters, university teaching cannot be isolated from other levels of education, and all should form part of one interdependent system. The problem of defining and developing workable relations between the various sectors — secondary, college and university — is so difficult that the provinces must co-operate in order to solve this problem, as well as other problems facing higher education. For this reason, the Council of Ministers of Education must take a new lease on life and must greatly strengthen its activities.

We therefore recommend that the Council should create the necessary instrument for its work: a permanent secretariat similar to that built up by the West German Conference of the Ministers of Cultural Affairs. Such a secretariat could easily be staffed in large part with personnel from the Canadian Education Association.

Under this arrangement, university education would be only one of the concerns of the Council, and similarly in the secretariat it would be the concern of only one of several sections. Therefore, due to the profound importance and special nature of university education, we further recommend the creation of a Commission on Higher Education, whose members would maintain close contact with the Council and its secretariat. This Commission would also ensure liaison with that portion of the public particularly interested in university affairs.

We wish to emphasize here that in making our recommendations we have had to concentrate on the problems of higher education in order to remain within our terms of reference. It should also be noted that our proposed superstructure would be added to the co-ordinating mechanisms already existing in the mega-regions. Because of the virtues of decentralization, these mechanisms must not be ignored.

1) *The Functions of the Council*

The Council's activities regarding higher education should of course be oriented almost exclusively toward political and administrative problems rather than purely academic ones. Yet there is a whole host of such problems with which it could deal. The following are some examples of valuable functions that it could perform.

i) In co-operation with provincial and federal statistical agencies, the Council could create a bank of information, statistics and forecasts of trends in education.

ii) It could approve joint studies, whenever these would save money by avoiding duplication, or would be superior because of the greater abundance of data that could be made available. These research activities would be especially useful regarding problems which are common to all mega-regions or go beyond their borders. By way of example, we give the following sketch-list of problems.

— *The financing of universities:* Should there be a financial formula ? Should there be one for both operating and capital expenditures ?

— *The construction of buildings:* What criteria should be used ? What are the implications of new teaching methods and techniques ? How long should one expect buildings to be used (15, 25 or 100 years) ?

— *Television and computers:* What is their impact on university life, on teaching and research, and on construction ? What are the benefits of co-operation and exchange in these fields ?

— *The labour market:* What are the trends and forecasts of future needs for university graduates ? Are there two different labour markets in Canada, one English-speaking and the other French-speaking ? What of regional employment opportunities and the geographic mobility of university graduates ? These questions would of course be investigated in close collaboration with the governmental authorities concerned, and only in so far as the graduates of the educational system are involved.

— *The financing of students:* What is the best system of student scholarships and loans ?

iii) The Council could also foster interprovincial agreements on specific matters, such as: students from other regions or abroad, including admission policies, equivalent levels of education, etc.; exchanges of professors; joint research or teaching projects; or a network of libraries. [8]

This outline of activities is far from complete. At the same time, it is subject to two limitations. The first is that the Council should avoid activities that are best undertaken at the regional level. The second is that the Council must not create a pseudo-ministry of university affairs for the whole of Canada. That would contradict the Canadian reality.

[8] See the brief from the Canadian Library Association.

2) *The Members of the Council*

The present Council includes all of the ministers of education. [9] This is desirable because their presence is necessary when the time comes to conclude agreements of a political nature. However, the new powers of the Council ought to rest on a basic *Agreement*, to which all provincial governments would have given their official assent. Moreover, because of the many other duties of these ministers, the little time they have available, and their frequently short tenure in office, they cannot be expected to provide continuity or to supervise the daily operation of the organization. To be explicit, since such ministers are mainly motivated and confronted by changing political considerations, they must be served by a continuing organization. They should therefore transfer part of their responsibilities to the proposed Commission and to the secretariat.

3) *The Commission on Higher Education*

As an intermediate organ, the Commission on Higher Education would be interposed between the Council and its secretariat, and between these bodies and the public at large. It would be composed of the ten deputy-ministers of education or their representatives, the ten chairmen of the University Co-ordinating Commissions (or their equivalents) and one university representative from each of Canada's five mega-regions, for a total of twenty-five members. At this point our earlier recommendation for a larger representation from the university community on the University Commissions should be noted. In accordance with this recommendation, we assume that their chairmen will fully appreciate the academic point of view or, better still, will be academics themselves.

The Commission would serve in an advisory capacity to the ministers, and would submit recommendations either on its own initiative or at their request. It would not have any political authority, of course, and its responsibilities would be delegated to it by the ministers. Its operations would depend on the

[9] Assisted, if necessary, by any other minister designated by a provincial government, such as a minister of university affairs, or culture, or finance.

services provided by the secretariat, and by the various departments of education and University Commissions. Through them it would be able to initiate a wide range of studies and research, as well as to carry on its program of activities.

In order to stimulate the public discussion of university problems, the Commission should directly invite representatives of all interested groups to meet with it periodically and thus make their views publicly known. To accomplish this end, the Commission should travel around, much as the Superior Council of Education does in Quebec.

The twenty-five members should meet at least every two months. Otherwise, they will never get beyond the stage of good intentions. At the outset, moreover, the Commission's sphere of competence should not be set forth too rigidly. Rather, its functions and its relationship to the secretariat should be periodically redefined in concrete terms on the basis of experience.

4) *The Secretariat*

We cannot stress too strongly the need for a secretariat to ensure continuity in the operations of both the Council and the Commission between their meetings. The secretariat would pursue necessary studies, accumulate information, and play the role of co-ordinator and catalyzer of the work of the various committees. On this point we fully support Dr. Stewart's suggestion that a staff of about forty, including eighteen professionals, would be required. This would be for all of the activities of the Council, not just matters related to university affairs. The work of the secretariat should be directed by the secretary general, as in the case — for example — of the Canadian Council of Resource Ministers.

5) *The Committees*

Part of the work of the Council and its Commission could be done by the secretariat, and part by the various departments of education, but committees would also be necessary in order to be able to call upon the services of experts in various fields, especially from the academic community or the civil services. The activities of the committees may be inferred fairly easily from our proposals regarding the functions of the Council. To the committees in certain areas, such as research, manpower requirements, health sciences, educational statistics and student aid, it would of course be desirable to invite representatives of the federal government.

Concluding Reflections

Conscious of the particular limitations affecting this document, we bring it to a close. These limitations have included such material factors as time, money, and the number of personnel available; they involve also the greatness of the challenge, the shifting nature of the ideas which are dealt with, the inherent dynamism of the concepts university and society, and the inevitability of the conclusions as dictated by our assumptions. From the beginning, and more now than ever, we have approached this task with humility, diffidence and enthusiasm. Here is the result: a working document which we hope will aid your reflections, stimulate your critical sense and arouse your creative powers.

We know it to be an imperfect work, the product of two cultures which have lived side by side and have made a serious effort to understand each other. It is, nevertheless, with a certain nostalgia that we add these few final reflections. They are thoughts delivered in bulk, like grain into a bin, destined either to settle and grow mouldy, or to be carried far and wide.

I. — The university, a many-sided reality in time and space, should be envisaged as making a constant effort to reach an equilibrium between the poles of socialization and critical research.

To this end, while recognizing that structures do not constitute a cure-all and that they must at all times remain flexible, we must institutionalize and indeed incarnate the principle of "a university of participation" so as to profit from the creative tension, which is indispensable as a catalyst and motive force.

II. — It is necessary to reach a basic consensus on the functions and responsibilities appropriate to a university with respect to: other levels of teaching; [1] centres and agencies of

---

[1] In particular, the problem of teaching at the college level is critical in all parts of the country: will it parallel teaching at the university level ? To what extent is it an element of democratization within the educational system ? Is it necessary to open a college in every important region of a province so as to decentralize institutions and reduce costs ?

research; and the obligations which are incumbent on other social institutions.

This is all the more necessary because the speed of growth which the universities have known during the last few years could not be continued without danger to their very existence as rational entities. Pressures are coming from all directions: governments, industry, professional associations, etc. The field of research (in all of its aspects) is also provoking unforeseen developments. The university is losing its spirit of synthesis : it risks becoming a conglomeration, a fragmentation of interests so varied that, paradoxically, its success — understood in the sense of ultra-rapid growth — threatens its very *raison d'être*. [2]

III. — The university of the future will tend to democratize itself. It will do this, first, from the point of view of recruitment from various social classes. It will guarantee, as a long term goal, a place for all who have the required intellectual ability and motivation, and it will remove present glaring inequalities by offering an equal chance to all candidates regardless of origin. This will necessitate a re-thinking of existing concepts of admission, teaching and examination, which have been applied in the context of a favoured group. It will undoubtedly even be necessary to reform, in depth, the system of public education, right from kindergarten. [3] This approach implies, moreover, a conscious choice between orientation and selection, [4] and a disavowal of the idea that the university is reserved for the upper and middle classes.

Secondly, the university will also be democratized from the point of view of relations between professors and students. This is a matter over which it has full jurisdiction. In accordance with the first point, the aim of the university must be not only to open its doors equally to all candidates but also to

[2] Cf. James A. PERKINS, "The Dynamics of University Growth", in *Higher Education in the Revolutionary Decades*, edited by Lewis B. MAYHEW, 113; Eric ASHBY, "The Future of the 19th Century Idea of a University", *Minerva*, vol. VI, no. 1: "Today, universities everywhere face a common peril: the peril of success", 8.

[3] On this point see, amongst others, the briefs submitted by the Saskatchewan Federation of Labor and the Alberta Federation of Labor.

[4] See the study prepared for our Commission by M. Richard Joly.

promote the successful completion of their studies. In other words, it must assure that students who come from less favoured social classes will not be eliminated along the way for various reasons attributable to the flaws, omissions or faults of the institution or its members, nor of the system or techniques used. [5]

IV. — The university of the future will be permanent. This involves putting an end to the idea of "catching up" for those who during their youth were not able to complete university studies, and eliminating the notion that studies constitute an accumulation which is stored up during a fixed period. In breaking with this concept, it will be necessary to insert into the curricula courses which can be completed at any time of life. [6]

V. — The university will be creative. This complements the ideas developed in the preceding sections.

It will be creative because it will be able to shake off the weight imposed by its present structures, ties and interests. [7] Consequently, it will accept the positive contributions offered to it by those primarily interested (professors and students) and by members of the community that it serves most directly (spokesmen for the government, for other levels of the educational system, and for socio-economic bodies).

It will not be a slave to any particular science but will attempt to realize a synthesis for the benefit of man. As a philosopher has expressed it, the university must triumph over

[5] In a complementary field, see the study by Allison and David Black, "The University, the Student and Rules".

[6] See the brief from Professor Eric Beecroft, and *La promotion des adultes : défis nouveaux pour l'université* (Association canadienne de l'éducation des adultes des universités de langue française, 1967).

[7] Thus breaking with the reputation of extreme conservatism which has been gratuitously attributed to it: e.g., Clark KERR in *Métamorphose de l'Université* (Paris, 1967), 104: "In all these periods of revolution, intellectual or social, the university as an institution was, at the beginning, a 'bastion of reaction' rather than a revolutionary force, even though the ideas of its members, taken individually, were often incitements to transform the world." In *Un projet de réforme pour l'Université Laval* (Quebec, 1968), 11-12, the authors speak of the university "in retreat", "incapable of anticipating necessary re-organization", whose "initiative has diminished", etc.

the crisis "of contemporary intelligence, its disarray, its dispersal before the infinite multiplication of avenues of learning, and the need for unity, which it attempts to satisfy by mystifying successively each of these avenues". He added, not surprisingly, "This is why the contribution of philosophy seems to me more necessary than ever, provided that philosophy does not itself turn to mythology." [8]

As an intellectual power, the university will be able to advance knowledge, and to re-establish the equilibrium which has been lost between the pure sciences and the health sciences on the one hand, and the humanities and social sciences on the other, rejecting the confusion between the means and the end, between science for the sake of science and the human being.

It will no longer be satisfied with preserving culture by the transmission of acquired knowledge and the establishment of conservatories and museums, but will participate in the creation of culture both within its own core and by establishing productive relations with the innovating elements in its environment. [9]

Finally, it will be able to make an intelligent appeal not only to the intellect but also to the other creative forces : imagination, sensibility and intuition, which are intrinsic and inalienable attributes of the human being. [10]

VI. — The future university will be critical, as we have frequently pointed out. The public must understand that this is an essential part of the role of the university. This function is as necessary to a state which calls itself democratic as are the basic public liberties and the parliamentary system, particularly at a time when monopolies of the media of information are rapidly developing. [11] A fundamental reason for the critical

----

[8] Professor Guy Godin, paper presented in November 1967 to l'A.C.F.A.S., and quoted in *Les Éditions de Sainte-Marie*, no. 11, 1968, 66.

[9] See again: *Un projet de réforme pour l'Université Laval, op. cit.*, 11.

[10] It was the biologist Jean Rostand who stated recently, "We live by instinct much more than by reason." *Le sel de la semaine* (Montréal, Les Editions de l'Homme, 1969), 84. See also the *Rapport sur l'enseignement des arts au Québec*, called the *Rapport Rioux* (Québec, 1968).

[11] This is why the constitution of certain countries or states, e.g. the Federal Republic of Germany and some member states of the United States, guarantee academic freedom or the freedom of research.

function is, to quote Professor Guy Michaud, that "existing truth is only relative, that is in relation to a moment of research".

Once this aspect of the responsibilities of the university has been properly identified and understood, one can then insist on the objectives appropriate to a system of education, in particular university education. When programs of teaching and research are being planned, this approach helps one to recall that, parallel with the technical demand for education, based on the needs of the labour market, there also exists a social demand, which has its origin in the hopes and aspirations of men. The two do not coincide, and the first cannot exclusively claim the right to dictate the objectives for education. [12] This reaffirms, in other terms, the need for independence by the universities, and the indispensable character of academic freedom.

VII. — The university will look to the future. Far from impaling itself upon the present state of science, it will force the gates of time and attempt to learn what the morrow will be for the world, society, science and the environment.

The world will live in an era of planets and outer space which is already opening dimensions that, until now, have been in the realm of dream and imagination. This world may serve as a vast field of exploration for the benefit of man or it might revive aspirations that are purely imperialistic and militaristic. It will be the duty of academics to explain this world of infinite magnitude in order to rationalize its exploitation.

Society and science will be closely identified because the former cannot remain indifferent to the progress of the latter. Society will see a second renaissance or experience a second industrial revolution. Just as printing made possible the free

[12] See J. B. GALBRAITH, *The New Industrial State* (Signet Books, 1968), ch. XXV, "The Educational and Scientific Estate"; ch. XXXIII, "Education and Emancipation", in particular page 379, where the author writes: "The industrial system has induced an enormous expansion in education. This can only be welcomed. But unless its tendencies are clearly foreseen and strongly resisted, it will place a preclusive emphasis on education that *most serves the needs*, but *least questions the goals, of that system.*" See also G. ANTOINE and J. C. PASSERON, *La Réforme de l'université* (Paris, Calmann-Levy, 1966), in particular p. 171 and following.

circulation of ideas and brought about a new concept of man some five hundred years ago, so today electronics opens virtually unlimited dimensions to science, research, knowledge and the re-definition of the individual and society. [13] There will be a crisis of reason, which one of our collaborators described as a tension and a rapid change in the "intermediate means", referring here to the connection between a society's body of aims and ideals, and its body of presuppositions and implicit values, and the means used to pass from presuppositions to aims. The university will have to be sufficiently sensitized to this problem. It must assume its responsibilities fully in the communities of today and tomorrow, in order that post-industrial society will not crown the all-powerful computer, which may function for the profit of a small, privileged group with information and the power of decision concentrated in their hands. [14]

The environment will confront the university with those problems inherent in conglomerations of populations in great urban centres. The era of the university's indifference to its immediate urban environment will come to an end; gone will be the era of the small university in a pastoral setting. The university will be an emanation of the urban milieu, involved in all the problems of transportation, housing, unemployment, pollution, leisure and the development of culture. [15] In this new environment and in society as a whole, will new social values, new virtues or norms be forged ? Will a new edition of the social contract be written ? Will there be a preaching of specific new civic obligations which will be synchronized with changes in the society of tomorrow ? Will there be an evolution

[13] Is the university conscious of this new age ? Professor Hugh Lawford has serious doubts. Here is the first paragraph of the introduction to his study on computers for our Commission: "By the time the universities learn how a computer can be used, it probably will be too late. Others outside the universities will have been more perceptive and more aggressive and they will have established the systems and laid down the rules which will condemn the universities to a secondary role. Others will conduct the research. Others will decide what the universities may know, and hence, what those in the universities may think."

[14] See the study done by M. Claude Lagadec.

[15] See the briefs from: la Corporation des enseignants du Québec, ch. IV; le Département de l'éducation permanente, Université Laval; the Faculty Association of Queen's University; and the General Faculty Council, University of Calgary.

in the terms of authority, in hierarchical ties, in known behaviour ? And what of morality ? What of the right of property ? Will public liberties be enriched with new social, economic and cultural rights ?

The university of the future will reflect, will analyze, will foresee and, utilizing the almost inexhaustible resources of present-day science, will be in a position to influence greatly, if not to determine, the future.

Appendix

1. Briefs Received by the Commission

(*means brief not presented at a public hearing)

1. Dr. Walter Johns, President, University of Alberta.
2. Faculté des Arts, Université de Sherbrooke.
3. National Research Council. *
4. Senate, University of Manitoba.
5. Mr. P. Quittner, Toronto. *
6. Division of Health Sciences, University of Toronto.
7. L'Université Laval:
    (i)   La Faculté de Théologie;
    (ii) Département de l'Éducation permanente;
    (iii) L'Administration.
8. Students' Union, University of Manitoba.
9. Board of Governors, University of Manitoba.
10. University Council, Notre Dame University of Nelson.
11. Committee of Presidents of Ontario. *
12. Liberal Party in Manitoba.
13. President's Council, McMaster University. *
14. Senate, Carleton University.
15. University of Lethbridge Faculty Association.
16. Canadian Nurses' Association.
17. Canadian Home Economics Association.
18. University of Manitoba Faculty Association.
19. Canadian Association of Graduate Schools.
20. Mr. Tim Reid, Member, Ontario Legislative Assembly.
21. Royal College of Physicians and Surgeons of Canada. *
22. Queen's University Faculty Association.
23. Carleton University Students' Council.
24. Faculty Association, Carleton University.
25. Saskatchewan Federation of Labour.
26. St. Dunstan's University Faculty Association. *
27. Administration of St. Francis Xavier University. *
28. Canadian Dental Association. *
29. Dr. Howard Clark, Dept. of Chemistry, University of Western Ontario.
30. Dr. Eric Beecroft, Dept. of Political Science, University of Western Ontario.
31. Dr. S. J. Noel, Dept. of Political Science, University of Western Ontario.
32. Canadian Library Association.
33. Committee on Medical Technologists and Paramedical Personnel, Ontario Medical Association.
34. University of Guelph, Department of Agriculture.

35. University of Guelph, Dept. of Veterinary Bacteriology, Ontario Veterinary College.
36. Trent University Faculty Association.
37. University of Guelph Students' Union.
38. Lakehead University Faculty Association. *
39. Senate-Council, Dalhousie University.
40. University of Saskatchewan, Joint Committee of Councils, Senate and Board.
41. Dr. Edward B. Champagne, Montreal.
42. Canadian Institute of Chartered Accountants.
43. Association des Professeurs, Université Laval.
44. Ontario Council of Graduate Studies. *
45. Ontario Society of Medical Technologists.
46. Association des Professeurs et des Étudiants de l'École Polytechnique, Montréal.
47. University of Toronto Faculty of Medicine.
48. Dr. Edward Sheffield, Professor of Higher Education, University of Toronto.
49. University of Calgary General Faculty Council.
50. Dr. Willard Allen, Dept. of Chemistry, University of Alberta.
51. Students' Union, University of Saskatchewan, Saskatoon.
52. Alberta Teachers' Association.
53. Universities Grants Commission of Manitoba.
54. Alberta Universities Commission.
55. Dr. R. C. Pratt, International Studies Programme, University of Toronto. *
56. President's Advisory Committee, University of British Columbia.
57. Canadian Medical Association.
58. Saint Mary's University Senate.
59. St. Francis Xavier Association of University Teachers.
60. Faculty Association of St. John's College, Winnipeg. *
61. Liberal Party in Ontario.
62. Canadian Guidance and Counselling Association.
63. University of Saskatchewan Faculty Association, Saskatoon.
64. Alberta Federation of Labour.
65. Miss Marilyn Pilkington, student, University of Alberta.
66. Association of Canadian Teachers of English.
67. Dalhousie Student Union.
68. Students' Union, Memorial University.
69. Professor Joseph Gold, Dept. of English, University of Manitoba.
70. Professor Stéphane Sarkany, Département de Sociologie, Université de Moncton.
71. Dr. Henry Hicks, President, Dalhousie University.
72. Blake Frisby and Brian Sharples, graduate students, Dept. of Education Administration, University of Alberta. *
73. Mount Allison University Senate.

74. Dr. H. A. Buckmaster, Dept. of Physics, University of Calgary.
75. Professors Robin Mathews and James Steele, Department of English, Carleton University.
76. Dr. Victor Ross, Doyen de la Faculté des sciences, Université de Moncton.
77. New Democratic Party of Ontario.
78. Canadian Federation of University Women (Ontario Committee on Education).
79. L'Association des professeurs de l'Université de Moncton et la Fédération des étudiants de l'Université de Moncton.
80. Ontario Confederation of University Faculty Associations.
81. Corporation des Enseignants du Québec.
82. C. D. Crenna, graduate student, University of Western Ontario.
83. Canadian Association for Adult Education (Saskatchewan Division).
84. Dr. V. M. Adamkievicz, Département de Physiologie, Université de Montréal.
85. Memorial University Faculty Association.
86. Association of Universities and Colleges of Canada. *
87. Anna Girouard, Université de Moncton.
88. Students' Union, University of Saskatchewan (Regina Campus).
89. Le Syndicat des professeurs de l'Université de Montréal.
90. Ontario Conference of University Schools of Nursing. *
91. General Faculty Council (Committee on University-Government Relations), University of Winnipeg. *
92. L'Université de Montréal. *
93. Miss Janet Amy, Ottawa.

2. Studies Prepared for the Commission

1. Community Objectives for Higher Education: A Framework for Analysis, by Albert J. Robinson, Department of Economics, York University, 42 pp.
2. The Academy and its Clients, by Hall T. Wilson, Faculty of Administrative Studies, York University, 46 pp.
3. Three Cultures and the Student Revolution, by R. S. Ratner and Ronald J. Silvers, Department of Anthropology and Sociology, University of British Columbia, 24 pp.
4. L'Université et les Finalités des Sociétés, par Michel Brûlé, Département de Sociologie, Université de Montréal, 34 pp.
5. De la Fin de l'Université conçue comme Entreprise de Fabrication de Science objective et de la Naissance de l'École permanente conçue comme Entreprise politique et comme Œuvre d'Art, par Claude Lagadec, Département de Philosophie, Université de Montréal, 46 pp.
6. L'Orientation professionnelle: Le Passé — l'Avenir: Dynamismes d'évolution, par Richard Joly, Faculté des Sciences de l'éducation, Université de Sherbrooke, 41 pp.
7. L'Université bidimensionnelle, par Luc Martin, Département de Sociologie, Université de Montréal, 34 pp.
8. Universities and Newspapers — Press Releases and Coverage, by Bruce Yemen and Paul Williamson, graduate students, School of Journalism, Carleton University, 55 pp.
9. Discriminatory Requirements on University Admission Forms, by Edward D. Maher, Department of Business Administration, University of New Brunswick, 17 pp. and appendix.
10. The University, the Student and the Rules, by Alison and David Black, graduate students, 56 pp. and appendices.
11. Universities and Governments — a Preliminary Political Analysis, by Henry B. Mayo, Department of Political Science, Carleton University, 32 pp.
12. Efficiency in the University, by H. M. Good, Department of Biology, Queen's University, 40 pp.
13. The Functional Spending Priorities of Canadian Governments, by the Institute of Intergovernmental Relations, Queen's University, 88 pp.
14. Structures and Procedures for the Determination of Grants to the Universities of the Province of Quebec, by J. P. Pétolas, Director of Planning, Physical Facilities, Sir George Williams University, 28 pp.
15. The Place of the Universities in Supporting Scientific Research in Canada, by J. W. Grove, Department of Political Studies, Queen's University, 42 pp.

3. Provincial Intermediary Bodies

A. BASIC INFORMATION

1. NEWFOUNDLAND

Name of Body (and Size)

Board of Regents (19).

Creating Instrument (and Date)

Memorial University Act (1949, as revised to 1969).

Composition

Fifteen members are appointed by the Lieutenant-Governor-in-Council. The chancellor and president of the university are also members and are appointed by the Lieutenant-Governor-in-Council. One of the fifteen members is appointed to be chairman of the Board, but the Board elects its own vice-chairman. Two members of the Board are elected by Convocation. Members hold office for three years, and may be re-appointed or re-elected, but the elected members may hold office for only six consecutive years.

Scope of Jurisdiction

Memorial University. There is only one university, and there is no other intermediary body between the university and the government.

Powers

Section 35: "The management, administration and control of the property revenue, business and affairs of the University." Sec. 36 (2) of the original Act made the most important powers of the Board "subject to the approval of the Minister of Education", but this provision was removed in 1954.

Operating and Capital Grants

The budget of the university is carried in several departmental budgets: a block grant is received from the Department of Education to cover major current expenditures; the Medical School and the School of Nursing are carried in the budget of the Department of Public Health; capital expenditures are shown in the budgets of both the Department of Education and the Department of Public Works, but the latter actually makes the expenditures. Including the Ministry of Finance, the university deals with four Ministers and Deputy Ministers apart from the Premier himself. It has been the Board's custom to submit an annual budget for discussion with the Premier and the Ministers concerned, in which it can make its views known. The Act (Sec. 37) forbids the Board to incur any liability beyond the grant approved by the Legislature of Newfoundland. The accounts must be audited either by the Auditor General of the Province or by "some person" appointed by the Lieutenant-Governor-in-Council (Sec. 39). The requirement for an annual report stipulates that it "shall be set forth in detail".

2.   PRINCE EDWARD ISLAND

Name of Body (and Size)

Commission on Post-Secondary Education (3).

Creating Instrument (and Date)

An Act to Establish a Commission on Post-Secondary Education (1968; proclaimed 1969).

The Commission took office in October 1969.

Composition

The Commission consists of three members appointed by the Lieutenant-Governor-in-Council. According to the Act, one is to be a full-time Executive Director, and two are to be part-time Directors appointed for a term of two years, at least one of whom "shall have sufficient academic experience or background so as to be considered a representative of the interests of the academic community". In fact, however, all are part-time members. The chairman is Dr. E. F. Sheffield, Professor of Higher Education at the University of Toronto.

Scope of Jurisdiction

The University of Prince Edward Island, the College of Applied Arts and Technology (Holland College), and grants to institutions outside P.E.I. The Island now has only one university; Prince of Wales College and St. Dunstan's University were merged into the University of P.E.I. in 1969. The new university has a governing board of eighteen members, nine of whom are appointed by the government, and the chairman is elected from these; the other members are: the president and the chancellor, the president of Holland College, two members elected by and from the Senate, two elected by and from the teaching staff, and two elected by and from the student body.

Powers

The Commission has both advisory and executive powers, but so far has used only its advisory powers. Its main functions are to advise the Executive Council on financial requirements and spending priorities and to "take full responsibility for the Province's allocation of financial assistance to post-secondary training", including "provision for special programs of student assistance". It is also to "prescribe a Master Plan for the long-term development of post-secondary education to the Executive Council and supervise the implementation of such Plan after approval by the Executive Council", and to advise the Executive Council on matters of interprovincial or regional co-operation and on participation in federal programs "deemed to be of assistance to the development of training at the post-secondary level".

Operating and Capital Grants

The Commission is to receive all requests for financial assistance, establish the priority of grants to meet these requests, and assess the expenditure of these grants "to insure efficiencies and economies as far as is possible without unduly interfering with academic standards".

Other Relations with the Government

The Commission must submit an annual report to the Executive Council. The Provincial Auditor or his agent must annually audit the Commission's accounts and make a report on them to the Executive Council and the Commission.

3.   Nova Scotia

Name of Body (and Size)

University Grants Committee (7).

Creating Instrument (and Date)

Universities' Assistance Act (1963, revised 1965).

Composition

Sec. 3 (1): "The Governor-in-Council may appoint a University Grants Committee of such number of persons as he considers advisable and may appoint one of the members to be chairman of the Committee."

Scope of Jurisdiction

Post-secondary institutions: thirteen universities and colleges, including the Nova Scotia Technical and Agricultural Colleges.

Powers

Advises the government on its financing of universities and colleges, on their courses of study and standards, and on duplication of services.

Operating Grants

Early in the year 1968, the Committee recommended to the government operating grants to institutions of $1,150 per student, with weightings as follows: students in the faculties of Medicine and Dentistry, 5; candidates for the degree of Doctor of Philosophy, 5; candidates for the degree of M.A., 3; students in the Faculty of Law, 2; students in the Faculty of Music at Acadia University, 3; candidates for the degree of Master of Social Work, 2; others, 1. A special grant of $35,000 was recommended for the Extension Dept. of St. Francis Xavier University and a special grant of $100,000 for computer services to Dalhousie University. The total grants recommended for the provincial fiscal year 1968-69 were $19 million (an increase of 32 per cent over the previous year). These recommendations were accepted by the government.

Capital Grants

Recommendations by the UGC are made once a year to the government for capital assistance loans to institutions.

Consultation with Institutions

Visits to institutions are carried out during the year, and in the autumn the whole Committee visits them to discuss problems of higher education generally and of specific institutions. In 1968 there were two meetings (June and September) under the chairmanship of Dr. Murphy, chairman of the UGC, on co-operation and co-ordination of effort in the Halifax area. The institutions were represented by their presidents. A co-ordinating committee was set up, representative of the institutions concerned, and chaired by the chairman of the UGC. Under this group, sub-committees were formed. Dalhousie, acting as the focal point, named half of each sub-committee to meet the other half, which was appointed by each of the other institutions. These committees are to work out the details of their respective affiliations and co-operative efforts.

Other Contacts

The UGC has some relations with institutions in other provinces of the Atlantic area, mainly through the Association of Atlantic Universities, and has participated in plans for an Atlantic Institute of Education.

4. NEW BRUNSWICK

Name of Body (and Size)

New Brunswick Higher Education Commission (9).

Creating Instrument (and Date)

Post-Secondary Education Act (1967, revised 1968).

Composition

The chairman is appointed by the Lieutenant-Governor-in-Council for a period of seven years. He may be removed from office by a resolution of the Legislative Assembly.

Other Members: Three are appointed by the Lieutenant-Governor-in-Council upon the recommendation of a committee consisting of: the presidents of the universities and the heads of organizations of university teachers recognized by the universities for purposes of negotiations with respect to employment and conditions of professional service. For the first appointments, the nominating committee submitted the names of six persons to the Lieutenant-Governor-in-Council, which appointed three of them to be members of the Commission. Section 5 of the Act specifies that no more than one of these members may be from the same educational institution. The other five members are selected by the Lieutenant-Governor-in-Council from among senior public officials concerned with non-university post-secondary education, leading businessmen, and representatives of organized labour. At least one member must be appointed from each of these categories. Other than the chairman, the members of the Commission hold office for three years (except that, of those first appointed, two are appointed for two years, three for three years, and three for four years). When there is a vacancy among the three members drawn from the university community, the nominating committee submits the names of two candidates, one of whom is appointed.

Scope of Jurisdiction

Universities, colleges, teachers' colleges and post-secondary technical schools (Sec. 10).

Powers

Advisory powers: to advise on the needs and the pattern of future development of all forms of post-secondary education in New Brunswick, including the amounts of financial aid required. The Commission also has the power to consider the needs for student aid, and to recommend programs of student aid to the government (Sec. 10, para. d). Executive powers: to pay to post-secondary institutions, within and outside the province, grants as approved by the Lieutenant-Governor-in-Council; and "to publish such reports and studies as it sees fit" (Sec. 10, paras. f and e).

Operating and Capital Grants

The Commission has assumed administrative responsibility for the payment of operating and capital grants to the universities and colleges. Most of the payments made in 1967-68 were based on the program of assistance recommended by the Deutsch Committee. The program comprised total payments of $41.8 million for 1967-68 and 1968-69, of which some $21 million was for operating purposes and $20.8 million for capital aid. A special operating grant of $307,312 was paid to compensate for the withdrawal of the federal grants in 1966-67. At the government's request, the Commission has made operating and capital grants to Shippagan's Collège Jésus-Marie, which is affiliated with the University of Moncton. All operating grants are provided out of funds allotted for this purpose by the Legislative Assembly.

In order to finance its capital aid, the Commission has issued bonds totalling $20 million (in American funds). Dated April 15, 1968, these bonds will be due on April 15, 1993. In accordance with the Post-Secondary Education Act, the province must pay the principal, interest and, if applicable, the premium on this borrowing.

Consultation with Institutions

A number of institutions and groups have submitted briefs to the government and to the Commission regarding the level of subsidies. According to Section 10 (b): The Commission must "plan, in consultation with the institutions concerned, the future organization and co-ordinated development of the various forms of post-secondary education . . ." Section 13 provides that "the Commission may establish such advisory committees as it deems necessary".

Relations with the Government

According to Section 12 (4), "The staff of the Commission shall be paid such salaries and expenses as are fixed by the Commission with the approval of the Treasury Board." Section 12 (5): "With the approval of the Treasury Board, the Commission may engage specialized or technical personnel or advisors on a temporary basis, or enter into contracts for the conduct of such special studies as the Commission requires for its purposes."

5. QUEBEC

Name of Body (and Size)

Council of the Universities of Quebec (17).

Creating Instrument (and Date)

Council of Universities Act (1968).

Composition

Members are appointed by the Lieutenant-Governor-in-Council on the recommendation of the Minister of Education. The chairman is appointed for five years. Nine members from the academic community are appointed for a four-year term after consultation with the administration, faculty and students of the universities, and their appointments can be renewed only once; four persons are appointed after consultation with organizations representing the business world and labour, for a four year term, renewable only once. There are two civil servants from the government. The Council appoints a Commission on University Research, but its chairman is appointed for three years by the Lieutenant-Governor-in-Council, after consultation with the Council, and he remains a member of Council as long as he fulfils that function.

Scope of Jurisdiction

The new Université du Québec and the six other universities.

Powers

The principal function of the Council is to advise the Minister of Education on the needs of higher education and university research (sec. 2). The Department of Education has organized a separate branch to administer higher education, and the Council has no executive powers. However, the Minister is obliged to submit to the Council for its opinion the principal steps he proposes to take regarding the universities. Thus he must submit any program of development, the annual operating and investment budgets of the universities, the proposed apportionment among them, steps for co-ordination, and rules for standardized accounting (Scc. 4).

Operating Grants

To date, operating grants have been based on the principle of deficit financing, whereas capital grants have been assigned on a priority basis. According to the method of deficit financing, the government provides sufficient funds to meet budgetary deficits of each university after taking into account approved expenditures and all other sources of revenues. The government and the universities have been attempting to establish a formula for operating grants on a per-capita basis capable of respecting the great differences among Quebec's universities.

Capital Grants

University capital grants are not based on a formula; they depend on the ability of each institution to present a convincing case that must fit into the overall policies of the provincial government. Each institution is encouraged to draw up a long-range plan expressed in terms of dollars projected over a period of five years, reviewed every year. The government does not pay the entire costs of capital programs of the universities; each institution is requested to launch a public fund campaign to pay about 15 to 20 per cent of the cost of each project.

According to the University Investment Act (1968), Sec. 2, the Minister of Education is authorized to prepare each year, after requesting the necessary information from the universities, investment plans for the five ensuing years, divided into annual portions. Sec. 3: In order to benefit by the Act, the universities must forward to the Minister each year, before a date that he specifies, their quinquennial investment plans. Sec. 4: Any plan prepared under Section 2 must indicate in detail the purpose and amount of the investments for the first year, and contain a statement of the investments estimated for subsequent years; such a plan must be submitted to the Lieutenant-Governor-in-Council for approval and a copy of it must be laid before the Legislative Assembly forthwith.

Consultation with Institutions

Before the creation of the Council of Universities, the government had established an Ad Hoc Committee reporting jointly to the Minister of Education and the Minister of Finance. The two ministers served as co-chairmen and representatives from the universities formed the body of the Committee. There were two sub-committees, one for operating grants and the other for capital grants, with some members named by each institution and others by the government. The government chose the chairman of each and appointed to them a number of its own officials, plus one representative from industry and one from labour on the sub-committee for operating grants. The new Council of Universities also has representatives from the universities and the outside community.

Commission of Higher Education

The Superior Council of Education, which was created in 1964, is a large body appointed by the government to advise it on all aspects of education. It has appointed a number of standing commissions on various subjects, with usually only the chairman being a member of the Council. Among these is the Commission of Higher Education, which has fourteen members, all except the chairman being from the various universities. It advises the Superior Council, and through it the government, on various aspects of higher education. Its activities are summarized in the published annual reports of the Superior Council.

6.   ONTARIO

Name of Body (and Size)

Committee on University Affairs (12).

Creating Instrument (and Date)

Order-in-Council no. OC-4157/64 (1964).

Composition

Sec. 3 (3) of the Department of University Affairs Act, 1964: "The Lieutenant-Governor-in-Council may appoint such advisory committees or other consulting bodies as are deemed necessary from time to time." Twelve members including the chairman are appointed by the Lieutenant-

Governor-in-Council on the recommendation of the Minister of University Affairs. Six constitute a quorum. The members of the Committee serve under annual, renewable appointments made by order-in-council. The chairman serves full time. The Deputy Minister of University Affairs is secretary of the Committee.

Scope of Jurisdiction

The CUA is concerned with the fourteen provincially-assisted universities, and also with Scarborough and Erindale Colleges of the University of Toronto, Algoma and Nipissing Colleges of Laurentian University, the Ontario College of Art, the Art Gallery of Ontario, the Royal Ontario Museum and the Royal Botanical Gardens.

Powers

Advisory to the Minister of University Affairs. The Department of University Affairs provides the secretariat for the Committee on University Affairs and its sub-committees. Hence it has only a small permanent office staff.

Operating Grants and Formula Financing

In 1965 the CUA appointed a special sub-committee which worked together with a corresponding sub-committee appointed by the Committee of Presidents under the chairmanship of D. T. Wright, later chairman of the CUA, to develop a policy for formula financing, a method of distributing provincial operating grants to provincially-assisted universities. This method was adopted, and operating grants are now paid by the Department of University Affairs according to: (i) enrolments in various categories, (ii) weighting numbers reflecting average costs, faculty by faculty and (iii) a dollar multiplier, or unit value, which, once fixed, determines all grants and expenditures. The unit value for 1967-68 was established as $1,320. In its 1967 Report, the CUA recommended that the value of the basic income unit for 1968-69 be fixed at $1,450 (an increase of 10 per cent). There are some extra-formula grants, such as for bilingual operation at Laurentian University and the University of Ottawa (a 7 per cent premium over ordinary formula income), for new universities, and for major new programs (e.g. medicine at McMaster University).

Capital Grants

Since July 1, 1964, capital support has been provided through the Ontario Universities Capital Aid Corporation on a project-by-project basis under a cost-sharing program. The provincial government assumed responsibility for financing 85 per cent of the approved cost of academic buildings and essential services, 50 per cent of the approved cost of facilities for student unions, cafeterias and gymnasia, and 100 per cent of the approved cost of health science projects. In 1967 the CUA recommended an interim policy covering the years 1964-69 through which the government would provide 85 per cent of the first ten million and 95 per cent subsequently for approved capital projects. This policy was instituted early in 1968. The CUA, in co-operation with the Committee of Presidents, has recently developed a formula for allocating capital grants, and it has been adopted by the government.

Consultation with Institutions

The CUA meets approximately twenty days a year, and in 1967 inaugurated the practice of holding regular meetings at university campuses, with meetings in Toronto, London, Ottawa, Peterborough, St. Catharines, Sudbury and Waterloo. In addition to its meetings with representatives of individual universities, the CUA has met once or twice each year with the chairmen of the boards of governors and presidents of the universities, and on several occasions with representatives of the Committee of Presidents of Universities of Ontario. The CUA recognizes the CPUO as representing the Ontario universities collectively. Communications with this group are well established, and the chairman of the CUA regularly joins the meetings of the CPUO for informal discussions.

Activities re Student Aid

The CUA is represented on the Minister's Advisory Committee on Student Awards.

7.   MANITOBA

Name of Body (and Size)

Universities Grants Commission (9).

Creating Instrument (and Date)

Universities Grants Commission Act (1967).

Composition

The members are appointed by the Lieutenant-Governor-in-Council, who also appoints the chairman and vice-chairman. Each member of the Commission is appointed for a term of three years, and may be reappointed for a further term. Terms are staggered, so that three are appointed each year. The Deputy Minister of Education is a member, and the chairman is also a government official and former Deputy Minister of Education.

Scope of Jurisdiction

The three universities (Brandon, Manitoba, and Winnipeg) and their affiliated colleges.

Powers

Advisory : To study the financial requirements and budgetary forecasts of the universities, and to make recommendations to the Minister; to study the needs and development of higher education. Executive: To distribute grants and to approve or veto university action in certain instances which might involve duplication of services, facilities or programs of studies (see Secs. 12, 13, 15, 16).

Operating Grants and Formula Financing

The Commission has adopted a graded grant formula which provides eleven categories of teaching programs, each category being assigned a weight. The weight assigned to a category is broadly related to the operating costs for its student population. These operating costs are estimates based on such information as is available to the Commission. The grant formula, as constructed, supplies an index of basic units derived from these related operating costs and estimated student enrolment. There are three broad classifications of per-student costs: general education, education for the professions, and graduate studies. Per-student costs for general education were found to be low, while those for the professions were either at the top or close to it, exceeding in some cases the costs at the graduate level.

Capital Grants

Secs. 11-13, 15: The Provincial Treasurer, with the approval of the Lieutenant-Governor-in-Council, may make grants or advances to the UGC (including the payment of interest). Grants for capital expenditure are distributed to the universities by the UGC. After the Commission has studied the requirements of the universities, and before the beginning of each fiscal year, it submits to the Minister a proposed program, including a budget for capital purposes.

Relations with the Government

Sec. 6 (1): "There may be appointed as provided in the Civil Service Act such officers and employees as are necessary to carry out the business of the Commission." Sec. 6 (2): "The Commission may obtain the advice and services of such professional, technical and expert persons as it deems necessary to carry out the business of the Commission and it may, with the approval of the Lieutenant-Governor-in-Council, fix the remuneration for such advice and services." Sec. 18: The UGC is audited by the Comptroller General.

8.   SASKATCHEWAN

Name of Body (and Size)

Board of Governors (18).

Creating Instrument (and Date)

University of Saskatchewan Act (1907, revised 1968).

Composition

The Board consists of: the president and the chancellor of the university; the Deputy Provincial Treasurer and the Deputy Minister of Education; the principals of the two campuses; seven members appointed by the Lieutenant-Governor-in-Council and five members elected by the Senate. The Board appoints a chairman and a vice-chairman from among its members. The members appointed by the Lieutenant-Governor-in-Council and those elected by the Senate hold office for a term of three years, and they are eligible to serve for a second term. A member who has served for two terms is eligible for further appointment after one year has elapsed.

Scope of Jurisdiction

University of Saskatchewan (Saskatoon and Regina campuses).

Powers

"The management, administration and control of the property, revenues, business and affairs of the University."

Operating Grants

The university's operating budget goes before the legislature as a total sum. The money granted is then distributed internally by the Board between the two campuses and among specific university programs, departments and colleges.

Capital Grants

The university submits its capital budget in the same manner as its operating budget, and the amounts are approved in two separate sub-votes. Sec. 66: "The Board shall not incur any liability or make any expenditure exceeding $50,000 for the purchase of lands or the erection of buildings without the prior approval of the Lieutenant-Governor-in-Council, and all plans, specifications and other data pertaining to building projects exceeding $50,000 shall be subject to the approval of the Minister of Works, who shall be responsible for calling for tenders and the awarding of contracts for such buildings."

Other Relations with the Government

The Provincial Auditor each year audits the accounts and the university's financial report must be transmitted to the Provincial Treasurer and laid before the Legislative Assembly within the first ten days of the next session.

9. ALBERTA

Name of Body (and Size)

The Alberta Universities Commission (9).

Creating Instrument (and Date)

The Universities Act (1966).

Composition

The Commission consists of a chairman appointed by the Lieutenant-Governor-in-Council, the Deputy Minister of Education, the Deputy Provincial Treasurer and six other persons appointed by the Lieutenant-Governor-in-Council. The members of the Commission may elect one of their own number to be acting chairman in the absence of the chairman. A person has to be a Canadian citizen or British subject and a resident of the province to be eligible for appointment. The chairman holds office during pleasure unless otherwise stated in his appointment, whereas the other members hold office for a term of three years and are eligible for re-appointment for two further terms of three years. Where the Universities Commission advises the Lieutenant-Governor-in-Council that a member is no longer capable of acting, the Lieutenant-Governor-in-Council may terminate the appointment.

Scope of Jurisdiction

The three universities — Alberta, Calgary and Lethbridge.

Powers

Advisory and executive: The commission must not only examine university operating and capital financial requirements and advise the government on grant allocation, but also allocate to the institutions, funds voted by the Legislature. It is authorized to approve the establishment of any new faculties or schools and, by regulation, of other academic programs and facilities, in order to minimize unnecessary and undesirable duplication. Acting in its intermediary role as set forth in the Act, it also gathers and communicates information to the universities and the government.

Operating Grants and Formula Financing

The extent of governmental support of the operating budgets of the universities, collectively, is determined by the provisions of the Universities Act. Regulations provide that the amount available in any fiscal year is to be calculated on the basis of the number of full-time students enrolled in the universities as of December 1 that year. The amount per student is stipulated by an order-in-council, which provided for a figure of $2,440 per full-time student in 1968-69. A major task facing the Commission early in 1967 was the development of a formula for operating grants. In the formula adopted for 1967-68, special arrangements were made for the University of Lethbridge, which is a new university.

Capital Grants

In 1967 the government advised the Commission that it intended to make available to the three universities over the ensuing five-year period the sum of $175 million for all capital purposes. It placed upon the Commission the responsibility of apportioning it among the universities. The Commission may borrow money, with a provincial guarantee, subject to the approval of the Lieutenant-Governor-in-Council, for the purposes of the universities.

Other Relations with the Government

The Provincial Auditor audits the Commission's accounts.

10. BRITISH COLUMBIA

Names of Bodies (and Size)

Advisory Board on Finance (7), and
Academic Board (9).

Creating Instrument (and Date)

The Universities Act (1963).

Composition

Advisory Board. Sec. 75: The Minister of Education *may* appoint an Advisory Board to make recommendations to him respecting the dividing of government grants among the universities. It consists of a chairman appointed by the Minister of Education, members in equal number nominated by each of the three public universities (British Columbia, Simon Fraser and Victoria), and an additional number appointed by the Minister of Education equal to the total number nominated by the universities. Three have been appointed by the Minister, and three have been nominated by and from the universities' boards of governors.

Academic Board. Two members are appointed by the Senate of each of the three public universities, and three by the Lieutenant-Governor-in-Council. The Academic Board elects its own chairman. The members hold office for three years and are eligible for re-appointment. They may be paid reasonable expenses incurred by them in the course of their duties. The expenses incurred by the Academic Board must be borne by the universities in proportion to their respective enrolments.

Scope of Jurisdiction

The Advisory Board deals only with university affairs, while the Academic Board is concerned with the whole of post-secondary education and, in practice, has concentrated its attention on the new regional colleges.

Powers

The Advisory Board was created at the discretion of the Minister and only advises him on the allocation of operating grants, while the Academic Board is statutory and has the advisory power "to acquire, analyse and provide information regarding academic standards and to advise appropriate authorities on academic development" (Sec. 81). The latter has become, in practice, an accrediting board for new regional colleges.

Operating Grants

There is no overall formula for grants. Budget estimates are prepared by the several academic departments by the end of the summer semester, incorporated after review into the estimates of the universities, and submitted to the government by November. Under the present practice, the government incorporates a lump sum operating grant for the three public universities in its annual budget estimates.

Capital Grants

The government decides how much it will allow the universities for buildings and leaves it to the universities to acquire any funds they can muster from other sources. The Advisory Board is not consulted. Both the total contribution to the universities for capital purposes and its division among them are probably determined by the Premier, who is also the Minister of Finance. There is a Universities Real Estate Development Corporation, of which the Minister of Finance is the fiscal agent.

B. COMPARATIVE CHART

PROVINCE	CREATING INSTRUMENT AND DATE	SCOPE (Number of Univs. & Colleges)	NAME OF BODY	TYPE OF POWER	SIZE OF BODY	COMPOSITION		CHAIRMAN APPOINTED BY
						OFFICIALS	REPRESENTATIVES SPECIFIED	
Newfoundland	Act of 1949 (Revised 1969)	1	Board of Regents	Governing	19	None specified	Two by Convocation	Government
Prince Edward Island	Act of 1968	2	Commission on Post-Sec. Education	Advisory & Executive	3	None specified	"At least one shall have... academic experience."	Government
Nova Scotia	Act of 1963 (Revised 1965)	13	Univ. Grants Committee	Advisory	7	Deputy Min. of Finance	None	Government
New Brunswick	Act of 1967 (Revised 1968)	7	Higher Education Commission	Advisory & Executive	9	At least 1: "concerned with non-university post-secondary education".	3 proposed by a university committee. At least one each from business & labour.	Government
Quebec	Act of 1968	7*	Council of Universities	Advisory	17	Two specified	Nine from univs. after consultation. Four after consultation with business and labour	Government on recommendation of Min. of Education
Ontario	Order-in-Council of 1964	14**	Committee on Univ. Affairs	Advisory	12	Deputy Min. of Univ. Affairs is Secy.	None	Government on recommendation of Min. of U.A.
Manitoba	Act of 1967	3	Universities Grants Commission	Advisory & Executive	9	Deputy Min. of Education; chairman was D.M. of Ed.	None	Government
Saskatchewan	Act of 1907 (Revised 1968)	1 (2 campuses)	Board of Governors	Governing	18	Deputy Treasurer; D.M. of Ed.	Five by Senate	Board
Alberta	Act of 1966	3	Universities Commission	Advisory & Executive	9	Deputy Treasurer; D.M. of Ed.	None	Government
British Columbia	Minister of Education (under Act of 1963)	3	Advisory Board on Finance	Advisory	7	Three at present	Three: one by each Board of Governors	Minister of Education
	Act of 1963	3**	Academic Board	Advisory	9	None specified	Six: two by each Senate	Board

* Includes the new University of Quebec, which has three campuses: Montreal, Trois-Rivières and Chicoutimi.
** Shows the number of universities only.

4. Selected Bibliography

A. CANADA

1. Books

ADLEMAN, H., and D. LEE, *The University Game* (Toronto: House of Anansi, 1968), 178 pp.

ASSOCIATION DES DIPLÔMÉS DE L'UNIVERSITÉ DE MONTRÉAL, *Les Investissements universitaires; Planification et Co-ordination* (Montréal: Éditions du Jour, 1968).

BERTRAM, Gordon W., *The Contribution of Education to Economic Growth* (Ottawa: Queen's Printer, 1965), 150 pp.

BISSELL, C. T., *The Strength of the University; a Selection From the Addresses of Claude T. Bissell* (Toronto: University of Toronto Press, 1968), 261 pp.

BOWDEN, Lord, *et al, Science and the University,* the Frank Gerstein Lectures, York University (Toronto: Macmillan of Canada, 1967), 104 pp.

BRONOWSKI, J., *et al, Imagination and the University,* the Frank Gerstein Lectures, York University (Toronto: University of Toronto Press, 1964), 103 pp.

BRUCHÉSI, J., *L'Université* (Québec: Les Presses de l'Université Laval, 1953), 117 pp.

COOPER, W. M., *et al, Governments and the University,* the Frank Gerstein Lectures, York University (Toronto: Macmillan of Canada, 1966), 92 pp.

DADSON, D. F. (ed.), *On Higher Education : Four Lectures* (Toronto: University of Toronto Press, 1966), 149 pp.

DUNTON, A. D., and D. PATTERSON, *Canada's Universities in a New Age* (Ottawa: Le Droit, 1962), 166 pp.

L'Éducation dans un Québec en Évolution (Québec: Les Presses de l'Université Laval, 1966), 247 pp.

FIRESTONE, O. J., *Industry and Education* (Ottawa: University of Ottawa Press, 1969).

GANGUE, P. *L'Enquête sur la Recherche en Sciences sociales au Canada* (Montréal: Faculté des Sciences sociales, Université de Montréal), 1967.

HARE, Kenneth, *On University Freedom in the Canadian Context,* lectures at Carleton University (Toronto: University of Toronto Press, 1968), 80 pp.

HARRIS, Robin Sutton, and Arthur TREMBLAY, *A Bibliography of Higher Education in Canada* (Toronto: University of Toronto Press, 1960).

— *A Supplement to the Bibliography of Higher Education in Canada* (Toronto: University of Toronto Press, 1965).

HARRIS, Robin Sutton (ed.), *Changing Patterns of Higher Education in Canada* (Toronto: University of Toronto Press, 1966), 106 pp.

— *Quiet Evolution; a Study of the Educational System of Ontario* (Toronto: University of Toronto Press, 1967), 168 pp.

HODGETTS, J. E. (ed.), *Higher Education in a Changing Canada* (Toronto: University of Toronto Press, 1966).

KIDD, J. R., *Adult Education in the Canadian University* (Toronto: Canadian Association for Adult Education, 1956), 137 pp.

KIRKCONNELL, W., *A Slice of Canada: Memoirs* (Toronto: University of Toronto Press, 1967).

KRUGER, Arthur, and Noah M. MELTZ (eds.), *The Canadian Labour Market: Readings in Manpower Economics* (Toronto: Centre for Industrial Relations, 1968), 312 pp.

LAIDLAW, Alexander F., *The Campus and the Community: The Global Impact of the Antigonish Movement* (Montreal: Harvest House, 1961), 173 pp.

LLOYD, Trevor Owen, *Agenda 1970: Proposals For a Creative Politics* (Toronto: University of Toronto Press, 1968), chapter by H. E. Hodgetts.

LLOYD, W. S., *The Role of Government in Canadian Education* (Toronto: Gage, 1959).

MACKINNON, Frank, *The Politics of Education* (Toronto: University of Toronto Press, 1960), 184 pp.

— *Relevance and Responsibility in Education* (Scarborough: Gage, 1968), 92 pp.

MARSH, L., *A Regional College for Vancouver Island* (Vancouver: Best Printer, 1966).

PORTER, John, *The Vertical Mosaic* (Toronto: University of Toronto Press, 1965).

ROSS, Murray G. (ed.), *New Universities in the Modern World* (London: Macmillan; New York: St. Martin's Press, 1966), 190 pp.

ROSS, Murray G., *The New University* (Toronto: University of Toronto Press, 1961), 110 pp.

SHEARER, Ron (ed.), *Exploiting Our Economic Potential* (Toronto: Holt, 1968), chapter by G. Neil Perry.

SISSONS, C. B., *Church and State in Canadian Education: An Historical Study* (Toronto: Ryerson, 1959), 414 pp.

SPINKS, J. W. T., *A Decade of Change* (Saskatoon: University of Saskatchewan, 1965).

STANLEY, G. F. B., and G. SYLVESTRE (eds.), *Canadian Universities Today*, symposium presented to the Royal Society of Canada, 1961 (Toronto: University of Toronto Press, 1961).

STEWART, F. K., *Interprovincial Co-operation in Education* (Toronto, 1957).

SYLVESTRE, Guy (éd.), *Structures sociales du Canada français*, études des membres de la section I de la Société royale du Canada (Toronto: University of Toronto Press ; Québec : Les Presses de l'Université Laval, 1966).

THISTLE, Mel, *The Inner Ring : The Early History of the National Research Council* (Toronto: University of Toronto Press, 1966), 435 pp.

VACHON, Louis-Albert, *Progrès de l'Université et Consentement populaire* (Québec: Presses de l'Université Laval, 1964).

WHALLEY, George (ed.), *A Place of Liberty : Essays on the Government of Canadian Universities* (Toronto: Clarke, Irwin, 1964).

WOODSIDE, C. W., *The University Question : Who Should Go ? Who Should Pay ?* (Toronto: Ryerson Press, 1958).

2. ARTICLES

ANDREW, G. C., "A Centennial View of the Role of Universities and Colleges in the Development of Canada", excerpts from an address, 9 *University Affairs* (October 1967), pp. 4-5.

— "Higher Education", centennial papers, pt. 1 of 10 pt. series, 4 *School Administration* (February 1967), pp. 11-20.

— "The Politics and Economics of National Unity in Post-Secondary Education", in *National Conference on the Economics of Unity* (Banff: School of Advanced Management, 1967).

BROWN, Malcolm G., "M.R.C.: Growing Program Opens Many Paths But Basic Problems Remain", I *Science Forum* (April 1968), pp. 9-13.

BRUNET, Michel, "Quebec's French-Speaking Universities and the Law of Double Imbalance", LXXV *Queen's Quarterly* (Winter 1968).

CANADIAN ASSOCIATION OF UNIVERSITY TEACHERS, "Brief to the Minister of Finance on the Financing of Universities", *CAUT Bulletin* (April 1964), pp. 25-35.

— "National Security and the Universities", a brief submitted by the CAUT to the Royal Commission on Security, September 25, 1967, 16 *CAUT Bulletin* (December 1967), pp. 4-32.

— "Policy Statement on Academic Appointments and Tenure", *CAUT Bulletin* (February 1968), pp. 4-20.

— "The Public Financing of Universities", *CAUT Bulletin* (February 1966), p. 24.

— "Statement on University Grants Commissions", *CAUT Bulletin* (February 1967), pp. 82-83.

CARDINAL, J.-G., "Ce que la Société attend de l'Université", 9 *University Affairs* (December 1967), pp. 4-6.

CORRY, J. A., "Higher Education in Federal-Provincial Relations", 8 *University Affairs* (December 1966), pp. 1-4.

— "University and the Canadian Community", 73 *Queen's Quarterly* (Autumn 1966), pp. 301-10.

— "Universities, Government and the Public", 75 *Queen's Quarterly* (Autumn 1968).

COURTNEY, J. C., "The Government-University Controversy in Saskatchewan, 1967-68", 17 *CAUT Bulletin* (December 1968).

CUNNINGHAM, W. B., "Within or Without: The Location of the Faculty Association", 16 *CAUT Bulletin* (December 1968), pp. 34-46.

DRUMMOND, Ian, "Some Economic Issues in Educational Expansion", in A. ROTSTEIN (ed.), *The Prospect of Change* (Toronto: McGraw-Hill, 1965).

FELLMAN, D., "Academic Freedom", *CAUT Bulletin* (October 1965), pp. 34-43.

GARIGUE, Philippe, "La Recherche au Québec et le Problème constitutionnel", 2 *Science Forum* (April 1962).

GAUTHIER, G., "Les Relations entre l'Université et l'État", allocution, 4 *Hebdo-Éducation* (10 novembre 1967).

GÉRIN-LAJOIE, P., "Co-ordination of Relations between the State, the University, and Society", 2 *Education Weekly* (March 1966), pp. 299-301.

"Government and University : The Cambridge Discussion", IV *Minerva* (No. I, 1965).

HARRIS, R. S., "Higher Education in Canada", CLII *Dalhousie Review* (1963), pp. 423-36.

HURTUBISE, R., "La Commission Rowat-Hurtubise", 17 *Bulletin de l'ACPU* (février 1969), pp. 6-9.

— "La Confessionnalité de notre Système scolaire et les Garanties constitutionnelles", *Revue du Notariat* (1962), p. 165.

— "D'une Évolution nécessaire: les Collèges classiques et leur Intégration", *Cité libre* (avril 1963), p. 20.

— "La Stabilité d'Emploi des Professeurs d'Universités de la Province de Québec", 14 *Bulletin de l'ACPU* (février 1966), p. 4. (Texte anglais, *ibid.*, p. 13.)

LAPOINTE, M., "Subventions du Conseil national de Recherches 1964-65, 1965-66, 1966-67", *Bulletin de l'ACPU* (avril 1968), pp. 39-69.

MACKENZIE, N. A. M., and D. C. ROWAT, "The Federal Government and Higher Education in Canada", XVI *Canadian Journal of Economics and Political Science* (November 1950), pp. 353-70.

MACKINNON, F., "The University: Community or Utility ?", *CAUT Bulletin* (December 1961), pp. 4-11.

MACKINNON, F., *et al*, "The University as a Public Institution", *Canadian Public Administration* (March 1961).

MACPHERSON, C. B., "Forces Relating University and Community", 17 *CAUT Bulletin* (February 1969), pp. 2-5.

MAYO, H. B., "University Government — Trends and a New Model", *CAUT Bulletin* (May 1965), pp. 10-24.

MILNER, J. B., "Academic Freedom and Tenure in the Young University", *CAUT Bulletin* (December 1967), pp. 54-57.

Mitchener, R. D., "The Pattern of University Government Relationships in Canada", 16 *CAUT Bulletin* (December 1968), pp. 12-19.

Monahan, Edward J., "Consultation and Participation: A Report on the Ontario College of Art", 16 *CAUT Bulletin* (December 1968), pp. 46-54.

— "Parliament and the Control of University Expenditure", *CAUT Bulletin* (October 1967), pp. 96-101.

Neher, P. A., and K. A. S. Hay, "Education and Capital Misallocation in A Growing Economy", 1 *Canadian Journal of Economics/Revue canadienne d'Économique* (August/août 1968).

Ontario Council of University Faculty Associations, "University Education in Ontario. A Brief prepared for Presentation to the Prime Minister of Ontario", XII *CAUT Bulletin* (February 1964), pp. 10-41.

Pike, R. M., "Public Financial Aid to Undergraduates in Canadian Universities for the year 1969-70", 10 *University Affairs* (Supplement, 1969), pp. 1-6.

Porter, John, "The Class Bias of Canadian Education", *University of British Columbia Alumni Chronicle* (Summer 1968).

Robinson, Albert J., "Canadian Colleges in an Affluent Society", *College and University Journal* (Summer 1966).

Rowat, Donald C., "Democracy in the University Community", 14 *CAUT Bulletin* (April 1966), pp. 36-42.

— "The Duff-Berdahl Report", 14 *CAUT Bulletin* (April 1966), pp. 23-30.

— "The Government of Canadian Universities", *Culture* (September and December 1956), pp. 268-83 and 364-78.

— "The Uniqueness of University Administration", 10 *CAUT Bulletin* (April 1962), pp. 22-27.

Schneider, W. G., "NRC: Emphasis Needed in Applied Science and in Industrial Research", I *Science Forum* (April 1968), p. 6-8.

Sirluck, Ernest, "The Future Development of Graduate Programmes in Ontario", LXXV *Queen's Quarterly* (Summer 1968).

Smith, J. P., "Questions Old and New", *CAUT Bulletin* (April 1967), pp. 9-14.

— "The University and Society", *CAUT Bulletin* (April 1963), pp. 4-26.

— "University-Government Relations: A Case in Point", *CAUT Bulletin* (April 1968), pp. 78-81.

Solandt, O. M., "The Science Council: the Search for a National Science Policy", I *Science Forum* (April 1968), pp. 4-6.

Stanbury, R., "Federal Role in Education", 74 *Queen's Quarterly* (Autumn 1967), pp. 363-79.

Stewart, D. A., "Aims of a University Education", XXX *Dalhousie Review*, pp. 81-89.

Stewart, F. K., "Intergovernmental Co-operation in Education", 5 *Education* (No. 4), p. 44.

Trudeau, P.-E., "Les Octrois fédéraux aux Universités", XVI *Cité libre* (1957), pp. 9-31.

UNDERHILL, F. H., "The University and Politics", LXVI *Queen's Quarterly* (1959), pp. 217-25.

University Affairs (bulletin of the Association of Universities and Colleges of Canada), "Federal Provincial Conference" (December 1966), p. 5.

— "Federal Support for Research" (December 1966), p. 10.

— "Le financement des Universités au Québec" (October 1966), pp. 7-8.

— "Le financement des Universités: Question de Participation" (February 1968), pp. 4-5.

— "The Freedom and Autonomy of Universities" (February 1968), pp. 9-10.

— "A Guide to Grants Committees — and to Sharing of Resources" (September 1968), p. 8.

— "Is University a Government Spending Department ?" (December 1967), p. 2.

— "Quebec Completes Structure for Universal Post-secondary Education" (April 1969), pp. 1-2.

— "Quelles doivent être les Relations Universités-État ?" (February 1968), p. 8.

— "Remarks on Research Policies" (October 1967), pp. 10-11.

— "Les Universités du Québec favorisent la Co-ordination des Efforts" (September 1968), pp. 1-3.

— "Universities have Obligations to Society" (April 1968), p. 17.

— "Universities Seek New Definition of the Nature of the University" (October 1968), p. 1.

— "The Universities, Strongholds of the Two Cultures" (February 1965), pp. 5-8.

— "We See the University a Servant of Industry and Government" (October 1968), p. 11.

WRIGHT, D. T., "Remarks on Research Policies" 9 *University Affairs* (October 1967), pp. 10-11.

3. DOCUMENTS AND PAMPHLETS

1) *General*

ASSOCIATION OF ATLANTIC UNIVERSITIES, *Education in the Atlantic Provinces*, a report submitted to the Commission on the Financing of Higher Education (Halifax: Association of Atlantic Universities, 1965), 77 pp.

ASSOCIATION OF UNIVERSITIES AND COLLEGES OF CANADA, *Proceedings of the Annual Conference* (Ottawa: AUCC).

CANADIAN ASSOCIATION OF UNIVERSITY TEACHERS, COMMITTEE ON UNIVERSITY GOVERNMENT, "The Reform of University Government", 8 *CAUT Bulletin* (October 1960).

CANADIAN UNIVERSITIES FOUNDATION, *Brief to the Prime Minister of Canada Presented May 1963* (Ottawa: The Foundation, 1963).

COMMISSION TO THE ASSOCIATION OF UNIVERSITIES AND COLLEGES OF CANADA, *Financing Higher Education in Canada* (Toronto: University of Toronto Press; Québec: Les Presses de l'Université Laval, 1968), 94 pp. (Bladen Report).

COMMISSION SPONSORED BY THE CANADIAN ASSOCIATION OF UNIVERSITY TEACHERS AND THE ASSOCIATION OF UNIVERSITIES AND COLLEGES OF CANADA, *University Government in Canada* (Toronto: University of Toronto Press; Québec: Les Presses de l'Université Laval, 1966), 97 pp. (Duff-Berdahl Report).

DOWNS, Robert Bingham, *Resources of Canadian Academic and Research Libraries* (Ottawa: AUCC, 1968), 301 pp.

FALCONER, Sir Robert, "American Influences on Higher Education in Canada", *Transactions of the Royal Society of Canada*, Section II (1930), pp. 29-31.

— "Scottish Influences on Higher Education in Canada", *Transactions of the Royal Society of Canada*, Section II (1927), p. 16.

Federal-Provincial Conference Ottawa, October 24-28, 1966 (Ottawa: Queen's Printer, 1968), esp. "Meetings on Financing Higher Education", pp. 6-60.

LA JEUNESSE ÉTUDIANTE CATHOLIQUE, *Le pouvoir étudiant* (Montréal, 1968).

KITCHEN, Hubert W., *A Preliminary Study of Demographic and Socio-Economic Factors in the Atlantic Provinces and Their Relationships to Measures of Educational Output* (The Atlantic Development Board, 1968), 58 pp.

— *University Education in the Atlantic Provinces : The Next Decade* (The Atlantic Development Board, 1968), 49 pp.

LEBEL, M., *Quelques Considérations sur le Rôle de l'Université au XXᵉ Siècle* (Québec: Les Presses de l'Université Laval, 1961), 30 pp.

MEDICAL RESEARCH COUNCIL, *Canadian Medical Research : Survey and Outlook*, report No. 2 (Ottawa: Queen's Printer, 1968), 416 pp.

MURRAY, W. C., "State Support and Control of Universities in Canada", *Transactions of the Royal Society of Canada*, Section II (1925), pp. 19-32.

NATIONAL CONFERENCE OF CANADIAN UNIVERSITIES, *Year Round Operation of the University* (Ottawa: Canadian Universities Foundation, 1964), 181 pp.

ORGANIZATION FOR ECONOMIC CO-OPERATION AND DEVELOPMENT, COUNTRY REPORTS ON THE ORGANIZATION OF SCIENTIFIC RESEARCH: *Canada* (Paris, 1963), 46 pp.

RABINOVITCH, Robert, *An Analysis of the Canadian Post-Secondary Student Population : Part I-A Report on Canadian Undergraduate Students* (Ottawa: Canadian Union of Students, 1966), 101 pp.

SMILEY, D. N., *Conditional Grants and Canadian Federalism; a Study on Constitutional Adaptation* (Toronto: Canadian Tax Foundation, 1963), 72 pp.

THOMPSON, W. P., *Graduate Education in the Sciences in Canadian Universities* (Toronto: University of Toronto Press; Québec: Les Presses de l'Université Laval, 1963), 112 pp.

VACHON, M.-L., *Ressources financières et autonomes de l'Université* (Québec: Université Laval, 1964).

2) Government of Canada

A *Bibliographical Guide to Canadian Education*, 2nd ed. (Ottawa: Dominion Bureau of Statistics, 1964).

COMMISSION ROYALE D'ENQUÊTE SUR LE BILINGUISME ET LE BICULTURALISME, *Rapport*, livre II: *L'Éducation* (Ottawa: Imprimeur de la Reine, 1968), 350 pp.

DOMINION BUREAU OF STATISTICS, *Canada Year Book 1968* (Ottawa: Queen's Printer, 1968).

DOMINION BUREAU OF STATISTICS, EDUCATION DIVISION, HIGHER EDUCATION SECTION, *Survey of Higher Education, Part II: Degrees, Staff and Summary, 1965-66, 1966-67* (Ottawa: Queen's Printer, 1969), 61 pp.

ECONOMIC COUNCIL OF CANADA, *Towards Sustained and Balanced Economic Growth*, second annual review (Ottawa: Queen's Printer, 1965), 204 pp.

Federal-Provincial Fiscal Arrangements Act, 1967, Post-Secondary Education Adjustment Payments Regulations (Ottawa: Queen's Printer, 1968).

LEVINE, Oscar H., *Graduate Students and Faculty Resources at Canadian Universities and Colleges* (Ottawa: National Research Council, 1967).

— *Profiles and Characteristics of Graduate Students Enrolled for the Doctorate in Science and Engineering in Canadian Universities* (Ottawa: NRC, 1968).

MACDONALD, John B., *et al, The Role of the Federal Government in Support of Research in Canadian Universities* (Ottawa: Queen's Printer, 1968), 550 pp.

MACDONALD, John B., *et al, Le Gouvernement fédéral et l'Aide à la Recherche dans les Universités canadiennes* (Ottawa: Imprimeur de la Reine, 1968).

MANPOWER AND IMMIGRATION DEPARTMENT, MANPOWER INFORMATION AND ANALYSIS BRANCH, PROGRAM DEVELOPMENT SERVICE, *Career Outlook University Graduates 1968-1969* (Ottawa: Queen's Printer, 1968), 65 pp.

— *Directory of Employers Offering Employment to New University Graduates 1968-1969* (Ottawa: Queen's Printer, 1968), 124 pp.

— *Directory of Canadian Employers Offering Employment to Canadians Studying at Foreign Universities*, Operation Retrieval 1968-1969 (Ottawa: Queen's Printer, 1968), 132 pp.

— *Guide, Graduations, Enrolments, Salaries, Universities, Colleges and Technological Institutes* (Ottawa: Queen's Printer, 1968), 45 pp.

MINISTÈRE DE LA MAIN-D'ŒUVRE ET DE L'IMMIGRATION, *Rapport intermédiaire sur la Demande et Taux de Salaires pour les Diplômés d'Universités en 1968*, français et anglais (Ottawa: Imprimeur de la Reine, 1968).

MUNROE, David C., *Statistical Services in Education for Canada*, A Report to the Dominion Statistician on the Statistics Program in Education (Ottawa: Dominion Bureau of Statistics, 1968).

NATIONAL RESEARCH COUNCIL AND MEDICAL RESEARCH COUNCIL, *Annual Report on University Support* (Ottawa, National Research Council).

PARLIAMENT, *An Act to Authorize the Making of Certain Fiscal Payments to Provinces, to Authorize the Entry into Tax Collection Agreements With Provinces, and to Amend the Established Program* (Ottawa: Queen's Printer, 1967).

ROYAL COMMISSION ON BILINGUALISM AND BICULTURALISM, *Report*, Book II, *Education* (Ottawa: Queen's Printer, 1968), 350 pp.

ROYAL COMMISSION ON HEALTH SERVICES, *Report*, vols. I and II (Ottawa: Queen's Printer, 1964 and 1965), 914 pp.

ROYAL COMMISSION ON INDUSTRIAL TRAINING AND TECHNICAL EDUCATION, *Report, Part I — II* (Ottawa: Printer of the King's Most Excellent Majesty, 1913), 437 pp.

ROYAL COMMISSION ON NATIONAL DEVELOPMENT IN THE ARTS, LETTERS AND SCIENCES, *Report* (Ottawa: King's Printer, 1951).

ROYAL COMMISSION ON TAXATION, *Report*, 7 vols. (Ottawa: Queen's Printer, 1966), vol. 3 on exemptions for students and parents, pp. 229-32.

ROYAL COMMISSION ON UNIVERSITY FINANCES, *Report*, 2 vols. (Ottawa: King's Printer, 1921).

SCIENCE COUNCIL OF CANADA, *Towards a National Science Policy for Canada*, report No. 4 (Ottawa: Queen's Printer, 1968), 56 pp.

SECRÉTARIAT D'ÉTAT, DIRECTION DE L'AIDE À L'ÉDUCATION, *Dépenses affectées aux Recherches dans la Collectivité universitaire, 1966-1967 et 1967-1968* (Ottawa: Imprimeur de la Reine, 1968).

— *Dépenses fédérales pour l'Enseignement post-secondaire, 1966-1967 et 1967-1968* (Ottawa: Imprimeur de la Reine, 1969).

SECRETARIAT OF THE CONSTITUTIONAL CONFERENCE, *Report of the Conclusions of the Meeting*, Constitutional Conference, First Working Session, June 11-12 (Ottawa, 1969), 5 pp.

SECRETARY OF STATE DEPARTMENT, EDUCATION SUPPORT BRANCH, *Federal Expenditures on Post-Secondary Education 1966-67 and 1967-68* (Ottawa: Queen's Printer, 1969), 34 pp.

— *Federal Expenditures on Research in the Academic Community, 1966-67 and 1967-68* (Ottawa: Queen's Printer, 1968), 113 pp.

SENATE, SPECIAL COMMITTEE ON SCIENCE POLICY, *Proceedings* (October 1968 - June 1969).

WILKINSON, B. W., *Studies in the Economics of Education,* Occasional
Paper No. 4, Economics and Research Branch, Department of Labour
(Ottawa: Queen's Printer, 1966), 148 pp.

3) *Newfoundland*

An Act Respecting the Memorial University of Newfoundland, Chapter
108, the Revised Statutes of Newfoundland, 1952, as amended to 1967
(St. John's: Queen's Printer, 1967).
*The Government and Administration of Memorial University of Newfound-
land,* report of a committee (1967), 127 pp.
ROYAL COMMISSION ON EDUCATION AND YOUTH, *Report* (St. John's: Queen's
Printer) vol. I, 1967, 217 pp.; vol. II, 1968, 229 pp.

4) *Prince Edward Island*

CAMPBELL, Premier Alex, *Policy Statement on Post-Secondary Education,*
delivered to the Legislative Assembly of Prince Edward Island,
April 2, 1968.
LEGISLATIVE ASSEMBLY, *An Act to Establish a Commission on Post-
Secondary Education* (1968), and *An Act to Establish the University
of Prince Edward Island* (April 1969).
ROYAL COMMISSION ON HIGHER EDUCATION, *Report* (Charlottetown: Govern-
ment Printer, 1965), 46 pp.
UNIVERSITY AND COLLEGE PLANNING COMMITTEES FOR PRINCE EDWARD
ISLAND, *Second and Third Joint Reports to the Minister of Education*
(October 1968).

5) *Nova Scotia*

UNIVERSITY GRANTS COMMITTEE, *Higher Education in Nova Scotia,*
Annual Reports (Halifax: University Grants Committee, 1964-1968).

6) *New Brunswick*

COMMISSION DE L'ENSEIGNEMENT SUPÉRIEUR DU NOUVEAU-BRUNSWICK,
*Niveau des Subventions de Fonctionnement accordées en 1968-1969
aux Universités du Nouveau-Brunswick* (Frédéricton, avril 1968),
3 pp.
— *Niveau courant d'assistance gouvernementale aux universités, col-
lèges et étudiants* (Frédéricton, mars 1968), 21 pp.
— *Premier Rapport annuel 1967-68* (juin 1968), 22 pp.
— *Un Regard vers l'Avenir,* un programme d'aide du gouvernement aux
écoles techniques et à leurs étudiants (janvier 1969), 72 pp.
COMMITTEE ON THE FINANCING OF HIGHER EDUCATION IN NEW BRUNS-
WICK, *Report* (Fredericton: Queen's Printer, 1967), 72 pp.

Conseil des Gouverneurs de l'Université de Moncton, *Les besoins de l'Université de Moncton et de ses Étudiants*, mémoire (1967).

Higher Education Commission, *First Annual Report 1967-8* (June 1968), 20 pp.

— *Investing in the Future*, A programme for government assistance to universities, technical schools and their students (January 1969), 70 pp.

— *Level of Operating Grants for N.B. Universities in 1968-9* (Fredericton, April 1968), 3 pp.

Post-Secondary Education Act, office consolidation, Chapter 19, Statutes of New Brunswick, 1967, as amended by Chapter 47, 1968 (Fredericton: Queen's Printer, 1968).

Post-Secondary Education Commission, *Current Level of Government Assistance for Universities, Colleges and Students* (Fredericton, March 1968), 23 pp.

Royal Commission on Higher Education in New Brunswick, *Report* (Fredericton: Queen's Printer, 1962), 118 pp. (Deutsch Report.)

Université de Moncton, *Brief to the New Brunswick Higher Education Commission*, projections covering the years 1969-70 to 1973-74 (Moncton, 1968), 72 pp.

7) Québec

Assemblée législative de Québec, *Loi du Conseil des Universités* (Québec: L'Imprimeur de la Reine, 1968).

— *Loi de l'Université du Québec* (Québec: L'Imprimeur de la Reine, 1968).

Brunet, Michel, *Le Financement de l'Enseignement universitaire au Québec* (Montréal: Académie canadienne-française, 1963), 31 pp.

Commission d'Enquête sur l'Enseignement des Arts au Québec, *Rapport* (Québec, 1968). (Rapport Rioux.)

Commission royale d'Enquête sur l'Enseignement dans la Province de Québec, *Rapport*, première partie: *Les Structures supérieures du Système scolaire* (Québec: L'Imprimeur du Gouvernement, 1963). (Rapport Parent.)

Commission royale d'Enquête sur les Problèmes constitutionnels, *Rapport* (Québec, 1956). (Rapport Tremblay.)

Comité d'Étude des Relations entre l'Université Laval, la Faculté de Médecine et les Hôpitaux d'Enseignement, *Rapport* (Québec: Les Presses de l'Université Laval, 1967). (Rapport Bonneau.)

Comité d'Étude sur l'Enseignement technique et professionnel, *Rapport* (Québec, 1962).

Conseil supérieur de l'Éducation, *Le Développement de l'Enseignement supérieur.*

— *Rapport annuel, 1966-1967.*

GROUPE "RECHERCHE ET DÉVELOPPEMENT", *L'Organisation de l'Enseignement et de la Recherche dans L'Université du Québec*, 2ᵉ rapport du groupe au ministre de l'Éducation (3 juin 1968).

HURTUBISE, René, *Le Système scolaire de la Province de Québec*, étude préparée pour la Commission royale d'Enquête sur le Bilinguisme et le Biculturalisme (Montréal, 1966).

MINISTÈRE DE L'ÉDUCATION, *L'Enseignement collégial et les Collèges d'Enseignement général et professionnel*, documents d'éducation, 3 (octobre 1967).

— *Rapport 1966-67.*

ROYAL COMMISSION OF INQUIRY ON EDUCATION IN THE PROVINCE OF QUEBEC, *Report, Part One : The Structure of the Educational System at the Provincial Level* (Quebec: Government Printer, 1963).

SUPERIOR COUNCIL OF EDUCATION, *The Teacher Faces Social and Educational Change : Report 1965/66, 1966/67* (Quebec: Quebec Official Printer, 1968), 365 pp.

UNIVERSITÉ LAVAL, COMITÉ DE DÉVELOPPEMENT ET DE PLANIFICATION DE L'ENSEIGNEMENT ET DE LA RECHERCHE, *Un Projet de Réforme pour l'Université Laval*, rapport préparé pour le Conseil de l'Université (Québec: Les Presses de l'Université Laval, 1968). (Rapport Roy.)

L'Université, son Rôle, le Rôle de ses Composantes, les Relations entre ses Composantes (Montréal: Les Presses de l'Université de Montréal, 1969).

8) *Ontario*

COMITÉ PROVINCIAL SUR LES BUTS ET OBJECTIFS DE L'ÉDUCATION DANS LES ÉCOLES DE L'ONTARIO, *Vivre et s'instruire*, édition abrégée (Toronto: Department of Education, 1968), 82 pp.

COMMISSION TO STUDY THE DEVELOPMENT OF GRADUATE PROGRAMMES IN ONTARIO UNIVERSITIES, *Report*, to the Committee on University Affairs and the Committee of Presidents of Provincially Assisted Universities (Toronto, 1966), 110 pp. (Spinks Report.)

COMMITTEE OF PRESIDENTS OF PROVINCIALLY ASSISTED UNIVERSITIES AND COLLEGES OF ONTARIO, *The City College* (Toronto: University of Toronto Press, 1965), 115 pp.

— *Collective Autonomy*, second annual review 1967-68 (Toronto: University of Toronto Press, 1968), 68 pp.

— *From the Sixties to the Seventies*, an appraisal of higher education in Ontario by the Presidents' Research Committee for the Committee of Presidents of Universities of Ontario (Toronto: University of Toronto Press, 1967), 101 pp.

— *The Health Sciences in Ontario Universities*, recent experience and prospects for the next decade, Report of the Presidents' Research Committee to the Committee of Presidents of Universities of Ontario (Toronto: University of Toronto Press, 1966), 26 pp.

— *Ontario Universities' Applications Centre,* a proposal for the establishment of a central clearing house for applications for admission to the Universities of Ontario (revised March 1965), 37 pp.

— *Post-Secondary Education in Ontario, 1962-1970,* report of the Presidents of the Universities of Ontario to the Advisory Committee on University Affairs, May 1962, revised January 1963 (Toronto: University of Toronto Press, 1963), 44 pp.

— *The Structure of Post-Secondary Education in Ontario,* supplementary report No. 1, June 1963 (Toronto: University of Toronto Press, 1963), 30 pp.

— *Student Participation in University Government* (Toronto: University of Toronto Press, 1968), 21 pp.

— *System Emerging,* first annual review 1966-67 (Toronto: University of Toronto Press, 1967), 59 pp.

— *University Television,* supplementary report No. 3 (Toronto: University of Toronto Press, 1965), 28 pp.

COMMITTEE ON UNIVERSITY AFFAIRS, *Extra-Formula Costs for "Emerging" Universities* (January 10, 1968).

— *Operating Support for Emerging Universities in Ontario, Fiscal Year 1968-69,* special study subcommittee study and report (1968).

— *Report 1967* (Toronto: Queen's Printer, 1968).

— *Study of Capital Assistance to Provincially Assisted Universities in Ontario since 1955-56.*

EDUCATION DEPARTMENT, *Colleges of Applied Arts and Technology : Basic Documents* (June 1967), 40 pp.

PROVINCIAL COMMITTEE ON AIMS AND OBJECTIVES OF EDUCATION IN THE SCHOOLS OF ONTARIO, *Living and Learning* (Toronto: Department of Education, 1968), 222 pp., esp. "Organizing for Learning", pp. 145-68.

Statutes Governing the Provincially Assisted Universities of Ontario, office consolidation (Toronto: Government Printer, 1965).

UNIVERSITY AFFAIRS DEPARTMENT, *Address to the Spring Convocation, McMaster University,* by the Honourable William G. Davis, Minister of University Affairs (May 31, 1968).

— *A Formula for Operating Grants to Provincially Assisted Universities in Ontario* (January 1968).

— *Higher Education in Ontario,* statement by the Honourable William G. Davis, Minister of University Affairs to the Legislative Assembly (Toronto, 1967), 10 pp.

UNIVERSITY OF TORONTO, PRESIDENTIAL ADVISORY COMMITTEE ON UNDERGRADUATE INSTRUCTION IN THE FACULTY OF ARTS AND SCIENCE, *Report* (Toronto: University of Toronto Press, 1967), 149 pp.

— PRESIDENT'S COMMITTEE ON THE SCHOOL OF GRADUATE STUDIES, *Report* (Toronto: University of Toronto Press, 1965), 143 pp.

— *Toward Community in the University,* report of the Commission on University Government (Toronto: University of Toronto Press, 1969).

UNIVERSITY OF WESTERN ONTARIO, PRESIDENT'S COMMITTEE OF INQUIRY INTO SOCIAL BEHAVIOUR, *Report* (London: University of Western Ontario, March 1968), 55 pp.

WRIGHT, Douglas T., *Report on the Organizational Structure and Administration of the Ontario College of Art* (Toronto, Government Printer, 1968).

9) *Manitoba*

ASSOCIATION OF THE ACADEMIC STAFF OF THE UNIVERSITY OF MANITOBA, *Brief Presented to Law Amendments Committee, Manitoba Legislature, Concerning Proposed University Grants Commission Act* (April 29, 1967).

LEGISLATIVE ASSEMBLY, *Universities Grants Commission Act* (1967).

UNIVERSITIES GRANTS COMMISSION, PROVINCE OF MANITOBA, *Estimates of Operating Income and Expenditures* (1968), 8 pp.

— *Grant Formula 1968-69* (December 1967), 6 pp.

UNIVERSITY OF MANITOBA, *Report of the Senate Committee on the Universities Grants Commission* (1968), 5 pp.

10) *Saskatchewan*

COURTNEY, John C., "The Government-University Controversy in Saskatchewan, 1967-68", *CAUT Bulletin* (February 1969).

JOINT COMMITTEE ON HIGHER EDUCATION, *Second Interim Report*, vols. I and II (Saskatoon: 1967 and 1968).

LEGISLATIVE ASSEMBLY, *An Act Respecting the University of Saskatchewan* (1968).

REA, K. J., *Community Colleges*, a report prepared for the Faculty Association Committee on Higher Education (University of Saskatchewan, 1966).

11) *Alberta*

"The New Universities Act in Alberta", *CAUT Bulletin* (October 1967).

UNIVERSITIES COMMISSION, PROVINCE OF ALBERTA, *Annual Report 1966-67*.

12) *British Columbia*

MACDONALD, John B., *Higher Education in British Columbia and a Plan for the Future* (Vancouver: University of British Columbia, 1962).

NICOL, E. P. (ed.), *Guideposts to Innovation : Report of a President's Committee on Academic Goals* (Vancouver: University of British Columbia, 1964), 67 pp.

SIMON FRASER UNIVERSITY, SENATE, COMMITTEE TO STUDY THE CONSTITUTION AND FUNCTIONS OF GOVERNING BODIES OF THE UNIVERSITY, *Report* (October 10, 1968).

B. OTHER COUNTRIES

1. Books

ADAM, D. (ed.), *Educational Planning* (Syracuse: Syracuse University Press, 1964).

ANTOINE, G., et J.-C. PASSERON, *La Réforme de l'Université* (Paris: Calmann-Lévy, 1966).

ASHBY, (Sir) Eric, *Universities : British, Indian, American*, a study in the ecology of higher education (London: Weidenfeld and Nicolson, 1966), 558 pp.

BAADE, Hans W., and R. O. EVERETT (eds.), *Academic Freedom : The Scholar's Place in Modern Society* (Dobbs Ferry, New York: Oceana Publications, 1964), 241 pp.

BARZUN, Jacques, *The American University* (New York: Harper and Row, 1968).

BERDAHL, Robert O., *British Universities and the State* (Berkeley: University of California Press), 1959, 229 pp.

— *Statewide Systems of Higher Education*, a study for the American Council on Education (not yet published).

BRITISH COUNCIL AND ASSOCIATION OF UNIVERSITIES OF THE BRITISH COMMONWEALTH, *Higher Education in the United Kingdom* (London: Longmans, Green, 1962), 244 pp.

BROOK, G. L., *The Modern University* (London: Deutsch, 1965), 192 pp.

BRUBACHER, J. S., *Bases for Policy in Higher Education* (New York: McGraw-Hill, 1965), 121 pp.

CAFFREY, John, and C. J. MOSMANN, *Computers on Campus* (Washington: American Council on Education, 1967), 207 pp.

CARMICHAEL, O. C., *Graduate Education : A Critique and A Program* (New York: Harper Brothers, 1962), 208 pp.

— *Universities : Commonwealth and American, A Comparative Study* (New York: Harper Brothers, 1954).

LE CENTRE DE REGROUPEMENT DES INFORMATIONS UNIVERSITAIRES, *Quelle Université ? Quelle Société ?* (Paris: Éditions du Seuil, 1968).

CHAMBERS, M. M., *Freedom and Repression in Higher Education* (Bloomington, Indiana: The Bloomcraft Press, 1965), 126 pp.

DRUCKER, Peter F., *The Age of Discontinuity; Guidelines to Our Changing Society* (New York: Harper and Row, 1969), 394 pp.

DUPRAT, François, *Les Journées de Mai 68, les dessous d'une révolution* (Paris: Nouvelles Éditions latines, 1968), 232 pp.

FLETCHER, Basil, *Universities in the Modern World* (Oxford: Pergamon Press, 1968), 170 pp.

FLEXNER, A., *Universities : American, English, German* (New York: Oxford University Press, 1968; first edition, 1930).

GALLIE, W. B., *A New University : A. D. Lindsay and the Keele Experiment* (London: Chetto and Winders, 1960), 152 pp.

GLENNY, Lyman A., *Autonomy of Public Colleges, The Challenge of Co-ordination* (New York: McGraw-Hill, 1959).

GOODMAN, Paul, *The Community of Scholars* (New York: Random House, 1963), 175 pp.

— *Compulsory Mis-education and the Community of Scholars* (New York: Vintage Books, 1964), 339 pp.

GOROVITZ, Samuel (ed.), *Freedom and Order in the University* (Cleveland: Press of Western Reserve University, 1967), 218 pp.

GRANT, Nigel, *Soviet Education* (Middlesex, England: Penguin Books, 1964), 189 pp.

HARTSBORNE, E. Y., *The German University and National Socialism* (Cambridge: Harvard University Press, 1937).

HOFFMAN, Nicholas von, *The Multiversity* (New York: Holt Rinehart, 1966), 201 pp.

HOFSTADTER, Richard, and W. P. METZGER, *The Development of Academic Freedom in the United States* (New York: Columbia University Press, 1955).

HOWES, Raymond (ed.), *Vision and Purpose in Higher Education* (Washington: American Council on Education, 1962), 223 pp.

JENCKS, Christopher, and David RIESMAN, *The Academic Revolution* (Garden City: Doubleday, 1968), 580 pp.

JOUGHIN, Louis (ed.), *Academic Freedom and Tenure*, a handbook of the American Association of University Professors (Wisconsin: University of Wisconsin Press, 1967), 343 pp.

KERR, A., *Universities of Europe* (London: Bowes and Bowes, 1962).

KERR, Clark, *Métamorphose de l'Université* (Paris, 1967).

— *The University and Utopia* (Cambridge: Harvard University Press, 1967).

— *The Uses of the University* (New York: Harper and Row, 1966), 140 pp.

KERR, Clark, *et al, The University in America* (New York: Fund for the Republic, 1967).

LAUWE, Paul-Henry Chombart de, *Pour l'Université* (Paris, 1968).

MACIVER, Robert M., *Academic Freedom in Our Time* (New York: Columbia University Press, 1955), 329 pp.

MAYHEW, Lewis B. (ed.), *Higher Education in the Revolutionary Decades* (Berkeley: McCutchan, 1967), 466 pp.

McGRATH, Earl J. (ed.), *Universal Higher Education :* (New York: McGraw-Hill, 1966), 247 pp.

MINTER, W. J. (ed.), *Campus and Capitol : Higher Education and the State* (Boulder, Colorado: Western Interstate Commission for Higher Education, 1966).

MOOS, Malcolm, and Francis E. ROURKE, *The Campus and the State* (Baltimore: The Johns Hopkins Press, 1959), 414 pp.

MOUNTFORD, (Sir) James, *British Universities* (London: Oxford University Press, 1966).

NEVINS, A., *The State Universities and Democracy* (Urbana, Illinois: University of Illinois Press, 1962).

ORLANS, Harold, *The Effects of Federal Programs on Higher Education : a Study of 36 Universities and Colleges* (Washington: Brookings Institution, 1962), 361 pp.

PERKINS, James A., *The University in Transition* (Princeton, New Jersey: Princeton University Press, 1966).

PROST, Antoine, *L'Enseignement en France : 1800-1967* (Paris: A. Colin, 1968).

PUSEY, Nathan N., *The Age of the Scholar : Observations On Education in a Troubled Decade* (New York: Harper and Row, 1964), 210 pp.

RIDGEWAY, James, *The Closed Corporation : American Universities in Crisis* (New York: Random House, 1968).

ROURKE, F. E., and G. E. BROOKS, *The Managerial Revolution in Higher Education* (Toronto: Copp Clarke, 1966), 185 pp.

SAUVAGEOT, S., A. GEISMAR, D. COHN-BENDIT, and J. P. DUTEUIL, *La Révolte étudiante, les Animateurs parlent* (Paris: Éditions du Seuil, 1968), 128 pp.

SCHULTZ, T. W., *The Economic Value of Education* (New York : Columbia University Press, 1963).

STROUP, Thomas Bradley (ed.), *The University in the American Future* (Lexington: University of Kentucky Press, 1965).

TIEDT, S. W., *The Role of the Federal Government in Education* (New York: Oxford University Press, 1966), 243 pp.

TOURAINE, Alain, *Ce n'est qu'un Début* (Paris: Philippe Labro et l'Équipe d'Édition spéciale, 1968).

— *Le Mouvement de Mai ou le Communisme utopique* (Paris: Éditions du Seuil, 1968), 297 pp.

TRUSCOT, Bruce, *Red Brick University* (London: Faber and Faber, 1943).

VAISEY, J., *Education in the Modern World* (Toronto: McGraw-Hill, 1967), 254 pp.

VEBLEN, Thorstein, *The Higher Learning in America : A Memorandum on the Conduct of Universities by Business Men* (Stanford: Stanford University Press, 1954), 286 pp.

VUILLEMIN, Jules, *Rebâtir l'Université* (Paris: Fayard, 1968), 82 pp.

WILSON, L. (ed.), *Emerging Patterns in American Higher Education* (Washington: American Council on Education, 1965).

2. ARTICLES

"Academic Freedom", special issue, XXVIII *Law and Contemporary Problems* (Summer 1963).

A.U.T. Bulletin, four items on the accountability of British universities and the role of the Public Accounts Committee (March 1967), pp. 4-22.

BELOFF, Max, "British Universities and the Public Purse", V *Minerva* (Summer 1967), pp. 520-32.

BOUCHARD, Marcel, "The Universities in France: Freedom and Autonomy", 19 *Science and Freedom* (June 1961), pp. 15-21.

BOWDEN, Lord, "The Universities, the Government and the Public Accounts Committee", VI *Minerva* (Autumn 1967), pp. 28-43.

COMMAGER, H. S., "The University and Freedom", 34 *Journal of Higher Education* (1963), p. 361.

DETWILER, Donald S., "The State and the University: The West German System", 18 *Science and Freedom* (March 1961), pp. 16-24, and a reply by Werner BURMEISTER, pp. 24-27.

LIPSET, S. M., "Students and Politics in Comparative Perspective", *Daedalus* (Winter 1968), pp. 1-20.

MASSART, Lucien, "The Belgian Universities: A Note on Their Problems and Prospects", 19 *Science and Freedom* (June 1961), pp. 21-26.

OETTINGER, Anthony, "The Myths of Educational Technology", *Saturday Review* (May 18, 1968), pp. 76-77, 99.

"Probing the UGC", special section of four articles on the British University Grants Committee, 23 *Universities Quarterly* (Spring 1969), pp. 127-171.

RIDGEWAY, James, "Universities and Big Business", 237 *Harper's Magazine* (September 1968), pp. 29-36.

3.   DOCUMENTS AND PAMPHLETS

1) *General*

BEN-DAVID, J., *Fundamental Research and the Universities* (Paris: Organization for Economic Co-operation and Development, 1968).

Commonwealth Universities Yearbook 1968 (London: Association of Universities of the British Commonwealth, 1968).

CONFÉRENCE DES MINISTRES DE L'ÉDUCATION DES ÉTATS D'EUROPE MEMBRES DE L'UNESCO SUR L'ACCÈS À L'ENSEIGNEMENT SUPÉRIEUR, *Accès à l'Enseignement supérieur en Europe, études et documents comparatifs et rapport de la conférence* (Paris: UNESCO, 1967).

CONFERENCE OF MINISTERS OF EDUCATION OF EUROPEAN MEMBER STATES OF UNESCO, *Access to Higher Education in Europe* (Paris, 1967).

INTERNATIONAL ASSOCIATION OF UNIVERSITIES, *University Autonomy: Its Meaning Today*, Papers — 7 (Paris: International Association of Universities, 1965), 139 pp.

ORGANIZATION FOR ECONOMIC CO-OPERATION AND DEVELOPMENT, *Economic Aspects of Higher Education* (Paris: OECD Publications, 1964), 256 pp.

— *Social Objectives in Educational Planning*, Study Group in the Economics of Education (Paris: OECD Publications, 1967), 312 pp.

Round Table on the Nature and Role of Higher Education in Contemporary Society, Paris, 17-20 September 1968, *Final Report* (Paris: UNESCO, 1968).

UNESCO and the International Association of Universities, *Access to Higher Education*, the international study of university admissions, I, by Frank Bowle; and II, National Studies (Paris: UNESCO and the International Association of Universities, 1963 and 1965), 860 pp.

World Survey of Education, vol. IV: *Higher Education* (Paris: UNESCO, 1966).

World Year Book of Education 1967, *Educational Planning* (Paris: UNESCO, 1967).

2) *Specific Countries*

Association of American Universities, *The Federal Financing of Higher Education* (Washington, AAU, 1968), 31 pp.

Australia, *An Act to Establish the Australian Universities Commission* (1959).

Australia, Committee on the Future of Tertiary Education in Australia, *Tertiary Education in Australia*, report to the Australian Universities Commission (Canberra, AUC, 1964-65), 3 vols.

Australia, Commonwealth Government, *Universities (Financial Assistance) Acts* (1963-67).

Australian Universities Commission, Third Report: *Australian Universities, 1964-69* (Canberra: Commonwealth Printer, 1966).

Bowen, Howard L., *The Finance of Higher Education* (Berkeley: Carnegie Commission on Higher Education, 1968).

Bowen, W. G., *The Economics of the Major Private Universities* (Berkeley: Carnegie Commission on Higher Education, 1968).

California University, Berkeley, *Education at Berkeley*, Report of the Select Committee on Education (Berkeley: University of California, 1966), 250 pp.

Carnegie Commission on Higher Education, *Quality and Equality: New Levels of Federal Responsibility for Higher Education* (Berkeley, 1968).

Committee on Government and Higher Education, *The Efficiency of Freedom* (Baltimore: Johns Hopkins Press, 1959), 44 pp.

Cox Commission, *Report: Crisis at Columbia* (New York: Vintage Edition, 1968).

Crawford, Sir John, "The Accountability of Universities", a speech by Sir John Crawford, Vice Chancellor of the Australian National University (May 11, 1968).

France, Gouvernement, *Loi d'orientation de l'enseignement supérieur* (7 novembre 1968).

"Godesberg Rectorial Declaration of January 6, 1968, Regarding University Reform", *Westdeutsche Rektorenkonferenz*, pp. 7-18.

GREAT BRITAIN, COMMITTEE ON HIGHER EDUCATION, *Higher Education*, Report of the committee appointed by the Prime Minister under the chairmanship of Lord Robbins 1961-63 (London, HMSO, 1963), 5 vols.

GREAT BRITAIN, COMMITTEE OF PUBLIC ACCOUNTS, *Parliament and Control of University Expenditure*, Special report from the Committee (London, HMSO, 1967).

HARVARD COMMITTEE, *Report : General Education in a Free Society* (Cambridge: Harvard University Press, 1948).

INDIA, EDUCATION COMMISSION, *Report, 1964-66 : Education and National Development* (Delhi: Government of India Press, 1966), 692 pp., esp. Chs. XI-XIII.

INDIA, MINISTRY OF EDUCATION, *Report of the Committee of Members of Parliament on Higher Education* (1964).

PAKISTAN, MINISTRY OF EDUCATION, COMMISSION ON NATIONAL EDUCATION, *Report* (Karachi: Government of Pakistan Press, 1961), 370 pp.

PAKISTAN, MINISTRY OF EDUCATION, COMMISSION ON STUDENT PROBLEMS AND WELFARE, *Report* (Karachi: Government of Pakistan Press, 1966), 234 pp.

SECRETARIAT OF THE STANDING CONFERENCE OF MINISTERS OF EDUCATION (KMK), WITH THE COOPERATION OF THE SECRETARIAT OF THE WEST GERMAN RECTORS' CONFERENCE, *Higher Education in the Federal Republic of Germany, Problems and Trends* (Bonn: German Academic Exchange Service, 1965), 61 pp.

UNITED STATES, ADVISORY COMMITTEE ON HIGHER EDUCATION, *The Federal Government and Higher Education*, report to the Secretary of Health, Education and Welfare, July 1, 1968 (Washington: USGPO, 1968).

UNITED STATES, HEALTH EDUCATION AND WELFARE DEPARTMENT, *Toward a Long-Range Plan for Federal Financial Support for Higher Education*, a report to the President, January 1969 (Washington: USGPO, 1969).

UNIVERSITÉ DE GENÈVE, *Projet de Réforme des Structures universitaires* (octobre 1968), 19 pp.

WESTRATE, J. Lee, *The Administration of Government Supported Research at Universities* (Washington: United States Bureau of the Budget, 1966).

PB-4428-31-SB
75-29T
B-T

Printed by

LE DROIT LTÉE

Ottawa, Canada

FCIL CSN 89